Hunting Book

David McWhir,
Hilton Catt,
Patricia Scudamore,
Mo Shapiro and
Alison Straw

KT-583-391

WITHDRAWN

The Teach Yourself series has been trusted around the world for
over 75 years. This book is designed to help people at all levels
and around the world to further their careers. Learn, from one
book, what the experts learn in a lifetime.

David McWhir (Part 1) has been involved in management and training consultancy for over 20 years. He has worked with private, public and not-for-profit organizations across the world, including most of Europe, USA, China, India and the Middle East. With an MA in Psychology and thousands of hours of experience in training and coaching individuals to reach their potential, he is well aware of what employers look for from their new hires. With a practical and humorous approach to the advice he offers, David is particularly interested in helping new generations prepare for the world of work.

Hilton Catt and **Patricia Scudamore** (Parts 2 and 3) have operated in the employment field for many years. They run their own business, the Scudamore Catt Partnership, and have written a number of books on career management. You can visit their website at www.scudamorecatt.com

Mo Shapiro (Part 4), a partner at INFORM T&C, is a Master Practitioner in NLP and Coaching. She has an outstanding record as a communications and presentation skills coach and trainer and an international public speaker. Mo contributes regularly to all broadcast media, has authored *Successful Interviewing* and *Neuro-Linguistic Programming* and co-authored *Tackling Tough Interview Questions*.

Alison Straw (Part 4) is an independent consultant and executive coach. Her career has been devoted to helping individuals, groups and organizations to develop. She is passionate about engaging and inspiring people and has worked with many senior executives, supporting them in developing themselves, their careers and their organizations. She has co-authored *Tackling Tough Interview Questions* and *Networking*.

Teach Yourself®

The Ultimate Job Hunting Book

Write a Killer CV, Discover Hidden Jobs, Succeed at Interview

David McWhir, Hilton Catt,
Patricia Scudamore,
Mo Shapiro and
Alison Straw

First published in Great Britain in 2015 by Hodder & Stoughton. An Hachette UK company.

First published in US in 2015 by The McGraw-Hill Companies, Inc.

This edition published in 2018 by John Murray Learning.

Based on original material from *CVs In A Week*, *Successful Job Hunting In A Week*, *Successful Cover Letters In A Week* and *Succeed At Interviews In A Week*.

Previously published as *Job Hunting in 4 Weeks*

British Library Cataloguing in Publication Data: a catalogue record for this title is available from the British Library.

Library of Congress Catalog Card Number: on file.

Paperback: 978 1 473 68393 8

eBook: 978 1 473 68394 5

Audiobook: 978 1 473 68396 9

1

The publisher has used its best endeavours to ensure that any website addresses referred to in this book are correct and active at the time of going to press. However, the publisher and the author have no responsibility for the websites and can make no guarantee that a site will remain live or that the content will remain relevant, decent or appropriate.

The publisher has made every effort to mark as such all words which it believes to be trademarks. The publisher should also like to make it clear that the presence of a word in the book, whether marked or unmarked, in no way affects its legal status as a trademark.

Every reasonable effort has been made by the publisher to trace the copyright holders of material in this book. Any errors or omissions should be notified in writing to the publisher, who will endeavour to rectify the situation for any reprints and future editions.

Typeset by Cenveo® Publisher Services.

Printed and bound in Great Britain by CPI Group (UK) Ltd, Croydon CR0 4YY.

John Murray Learning policy is to use papers that are natural, renewable and recyclable products and made from wood grown in sustainable forests. The logging and manufacturing processes are expected to conform to the environmental regulations of the country of origin.

Carmelite House
50 Victoria Embankment
London EC4Y 0DZ
www.hodder.co.uk

Contents

PART 1
Your CVs Masterclass

Introduction

Alongside your passport, your CV is one of the most important documents you possess. In many ways, it is as important as your passport, enabling someone at a gateway to decide whether you can pass to the next stage of your career. Unlike a passport, however, a CV is a document that you can strengthen and develop as your career progresses. In fact, the phrase *curriculum vitae,* for which CV is an abbreviation, means 'life path'. Look after your CV and its accurate representation of your career achievements will serve you well as you move to new career challenges.

This Part of the book will help you build, maintain and navigate your way around your own successful CV. Career-wise it remains the single most important means of getting yourself noticed and in you reaching that critical first-stage interview.

Prospective employers vary widely in the degree of sophistication they apply in assessing CVs as the first stage of finding the right job candidate. Increasingly, organizations are turning to professional recruitment agencies to undertake the first stage of assessment. A number of others have started to use software to pick up on key words and phrases in electronically submitted CVs. What is clear is that, in economically challenging times, organizations are necessarily ruthless in reducing the high volumes of CVs they receive down to manageable numbers. In order to stand a realistic chance of passing through this rigorous first stage, your CV must be extremely well constructed, concise and relevant.

CHAPTER 1

Planning a successful CV

In this chapter we will explore what organizations generally look for when assessing the CVs they receive for a particular role. Due to demographics and challenging economic pressures, securing a role, whether it is your first position or a step up in your career, is increasingly competitive. We therefore focus on how to increase the odds of your CV getting you through to the critical first interview stage.

The truth is that no matter how good your interview and interpersonal skills, one small error in your CV could prevent you having the opportunity to demonstrate those skills to a potential employer.

In this chapter we will look at:

● points to consider before you start to write your CV
● how a prospective employer will typically deal with your CV.

The press often carries stories about seemingly industrious and committed individuals who have submitted tens if not hundreds of CVs (or to be more accurate, the same CV tens or hundreds of times) but appear unlucky not to have secured even one interview from their efforts. Is this indeed simply bad luck or is there something significantly amiss in their approach?

One of the problems in mass mailing the same CV to multiple organizations is that to the potential employer that is exactly what it looks like. It says to them that you are looking for any role and will take the first opportunity that comes along. While it is perfectly understandable for someone to adopt this approach if they are desperate to generate income, it is unlikely, other than in the most fortunate of circumstances, to get you the role that you desire. If you do secure a job using this technique, it is unlikely to be one that you will stay with for long, since the chances of your skills and the job's requirements matching will be slim – leading you or the organization to look for a way out.

Points to consider before creating your CV

You may feel under pressure to get a job, or increase your income by moving role, and be tempted to take the mass numbers approach described above. However, you are more likely to be successful if you take the following key steps.

Step 1

Be absolutely honest with yourself about what you want to do in your life and what types of role you enjoy. Think about which roles you are suited to through your skills, qualifications, experience and personality.

You may not necessarily secure your ideal role immediately but knowing what you are aiming for and being able to articulate your career goals will make you a more plausible candidate, not only from your CV but in the event that you are successful in getting to the interview stage.

Step 2

Seek feedback from family and friends as to what they see as being your strengths as well as areas that you may need to work on. Having, and admitting to, aspects of performance you need to improve is absolutely acceptable. In fact, many organizations are particularly interested in individuals who have recognized areas of development in themselves *and* have done something to address them.

Step 3

Invest time in understanding what a potential employer is looking for when they publicize a job vacancy. If your skills and experience are well below or, indeed, well above the required levels, it is unlikely that your CV will get you through to the interview stage. Although it is tempting to manipulate the description of your skills and experience to those requested, any gaps are likely to be identified by a competent interviewer, or when you actually start in the role.

An active decision not to continue an application based on a ruthless appraisal of the job description for the role in question will be to your advantage in the long term, because you will then be more likely to focus on roles that do fit your career goals.

Step 4

Thoroughly research the employment sectors you are interested in. Most sectors have a range of specialist publications which not only include vacancies in that particular sector but carry articles on issues and trends of relevance to it. An awareness of current issues within the sector of interest to you will place you in a good light with a potential interviewer as well as helping you understand what types of achievement will be of particular interest in a CV.

Spend time getting to know individuals already employed in that sector or role. Find out how they got into their role; what skills and experience their employers find particularly attractive in their employees; what roles are in demand and which organizations appear to be growing stronger (or doing less well, and which you may wish to avoid).

Step 5

It is important that you keep your skills and experience current while you research your next career step. Even if you are already in a role and looking to move internally to a different role, an employer will welcome evidence that you have continued to improve your skills. Recruiters often use phrases such as 'drifted', 'coasted' or 'reached a plateau' to describe an applicant who appears from their CV to lack direction or purpose. It is vitally important that you are seen as proactive in the progression and ownership of your own career.

There are a number of skills that are core to many positions. These can be categorized broadly into:

● interpersonal and communication skills
● IT and computer literacy skills
● time and project management skills
● managing a budget.

Demonstration of increased competence in any of these aspects, together with proficiency in any specialist skills required, are positive aspects to be included in your CV.

How a prospective employer typically deals with your CV

From experience, I believe that there are up to five common stages of CV review that will determine whether you and your CV get to the next stage of the selection process – this normally meaning the first-stage interview.

Not all potential employers will follow all five stages and others may amalgamate or reorder two or more of these. However, if you test your CV against what follows, you will increase your chances in getting through to the next stage of the selection process.

The glance over

This is a very quick scan across the first page for 'look and feel'. It may stagger you to learn that many organizations can reduce the CV pile by up to 90 per cent at this stage, without the reviewer having read a complete sentence in the document. Indeed, some organizations and recruiters are now using software at the first stage in order to identify key words and phrases of interest as well as negative aspects such as spelling mistakes.

Reasons for rejection at this stage include the following:

- **Spelling errors** – even just one. Many CV reviewers can spot a spelling error the second they raise the document to read; it immediately catches their attention. The view runs that this is a document you have had time to craft and check before submitting to an organization as an indicator of you at your best. With resources such as online spell checkers, the traditional dictionary and a family member or friend to check your document, there is no excuse for spelling errors. These are often interpreted by CV reviewers as being from someone who has hurried through the exercise, has poor attention to detail or is indiscriminately churning out CVs by the dozen. Whichever way, these are not impressions that are seen positively by most potential employers.
- **Fonts** that are too small, difficult to read or in different colours. These just take too much effort to read. As such, a CV may be rejected within a few seconds, regardless of the skills or experience of the CV's owner.
- **Opening personal statements** that are not backed up by evidence – and usually exaggerated, often baffling and frequently written in the third person. Such statements are normally ignored but can be cause for immediate rejection if they are particularly clichéd or outrageous in their claims: *'Joe Smith is a dynamic and indomitable individual who is a huge asset to any team. He is simultaneously a team player while striving to lead those around him in surpassing objectives.'*

The read through

Having passed the 'glance over' stage, your CV will then be subject to a more studied and structured examination. Your challenge for this stage is to make the reviewer read your complete CV without finding cause for rejection.

What the reviewer is looking for in particular now is:

● the relevance of your skills and experience to the role, particularly those deemed essential for the job
● evidence/indicators of your ability to perform at the level of the role or, indeed, slightly above it
● indicators of your approach to work and general attitude.

To increase your chances of successfully navigating the 'read through' stage and getting to the interview stage, you may wish to use my **CAREER** acronym:

● **Complete:** Your CV should be up to date and cover your career achievements to date. Unexplained gaps are likely to lead to immediate rejection, so any periods of non-work such as family time or unemployment should be covered – be truthful and give reasons for these particular periods. The majority of organizations understand that such absences from work occur and are accepting of them if reasons are provided. Please do not mistake 'complete' for 'lengthy'. If the prospective employer requires further detail, they will ask for it at the interview stage; your CV needs to be succinct and accurate.

● **Authentic:** The one sure-fire way to get your CV rejected is to include material that is exaggerated or even completely untrue (in other words, a lie). Such an approach is likely to be uncovered at the interview stage when it becomes clear that you cannot back up a statement. Even if inaccuracies are not identified and you do secure the position, it is still possible to be dismissed months, if not years, later if your CV is found to be inaccurate. This will cause problems not only for the current job but for future progression, because your employer may point out this issue to future potential employers seeking references.

● **Relevant:** As the next section explains, most positions are now defined by a job description, providing details of roles and responsibilities. The reviewer will be looking for the relevance and 'fit' of your CV to the job description for the position in question. It is important, therefore, that you invest time in reading and understanding the job description before tailoring and submitting your CV for this particular job.

Think about the roles you have undertaken and what you have achieved. How can you word these achievements to demonstrate how you can apply your successful approach to the requirements of the new role? Organizations continue to rely heavily on the view that previous behaviours are a reliable indicator of your future performance. If you can demonstrate that you are already performing many elements of the role for which you are applying, you will increase your chances of getting to the interview stage.

- **Evidenced:** Be prepared to back up at the interview stage any statements you make within your CV. Test each statement you make with a possible question that an interviewer might ask to 'go deeper' into a particular statement or element of your career to date. Think about how you will answer such questions on the basis of what you included in your CV. Assemble additional material that can be used to support your CV at the interview stage. Unless specifically asked to do so, you should not include such additional material with your CV. Instead, prepare it alongside your CV for use at the next stage.

TIP *View your CV as a series of signposts that highlight different aspects and achievements in your career to date.*

At the interview stage, the interviewer may ask for further evidence to support statements you make in your CV. For example, you may say in your CV: 'I was the top performing sales person at my present organization in the previous year, beating my personal annual target by 25 per cent.' Assuming this statement is relevant to the role in question, such a statement is likely to make a positive impression on the CV reviewer and add support to the decision to ask you to attend an interview. At the interview stage, be prepared to provide documentation that confirms your statement and to answer questions that search behind the statement for evidence of your personal contribution to such an outcome: 'How did you achieve this result?' or 'What planning did you do and what steps did you take?'

- **Emotionally intelligent:** An increasingly important quality considered by potential employers is your ability to interact effectively with people around you. Even if the intended role involves a significant proportion of time working on your own, most employers are looking for individuals who can communicate effectively with customers, colleagues and their manager. Therefore, your CV should include evidence of your ability to interact with other individuals and of self-awareness, a key element of emotional intelligence.

For more information on this topic, I would recommend Daniel Goleman's book *Emotional Intelligence: Why It Can Matter More Than IQ* (Bloomsbury Publishing, 1996). There are also many articles and discussions on the Internet on this important topic.

● **Referenced:** Any elements you include in your CV should be capable of being backed up at the interview stage or via further reference checks by the potential employer. Information contained in your CV should be consistent with information a potential employer may obtain from previous employers and from other sources such as social media.

TIP

To help you plan your CV, try checking it against the CAREER acronym. Your successful CV should be:
Complete
Authentic
Relevant
Evidenced
Emotionally intelligent
Referenced

Validating your CV against role requirements

This stage may be wholly or partly incorporated within the read through described above but is one to consider very carefully when creating your CV. The majority of roles today are normally defined by a 'job description' detailing the roles and responsibilities of the job holder: what is expected of the job holder, to whom they report, how their performance will be measured and so on. The key point here is that the organization already has a very good idea of the type of person they require. It is fundamental to your chances of success that your CV matches the requirements of the role as stated in the job description as closely as possible.

Example job description

Company: Cool Vectors Inc.
Job title: Sales and Marketing Executive
Reporting to: Sales and Marketing Vice Principal, Alphaville
Based at: Cool Vectors Inc., Ivory Towers, Alphaville

Job purpose:
To plan, co-ordinate and execute direct marketing and sales activities, so as to maintain and develop sales of CV Inc.'s Vector Tool range to US major accounts and targets, in accordance with agreed business objectives.

Key responsibilities:
1. Maintain and develop computerized customer and prospect database
2. Plan and carry out direct marketing activities to agreed budgets, sales volumes, values, product mix and timescales
3. Develop sales campaigns and create offers for direct mail and marketing to major accounts by main market sector and CV product range
4. Respond to and follow up sales enquiries by post, telephone, email and site visits
5. Maintain and develop existing and new customers, through active key account management and liaison with internal order-processing staff
6. Monitor and report on activities and provide relevant management information (MI)
7. Undertake market research, competitor and customer surveys
8. Maintain and report on equipment and software suitability for direct marketing and sales reporting purposes
9. Liaise and attend meetings with other company functions necessary to perform duties and aid business and organizational development
10. Manage the external marketing agency activities of telemarketing and research
11. Attend training and develop relevant knowledge and skills

Scale and territory indicators:
Core product range of 12 tool sets price range $80 to $450. Target sectors: All major multiple-site organizations having more than 500 personnel. Prospect database c.10,000 HQs of large organizations. Customer base of c.150 large organizations. Typical account value $20 to $50 p.a. Total personal revenue accountability potentially $4.5m p.a. Territory: USA

Under the CAREER acronym, there are a number of other words I could have used in R, including 'Replicable' or 'Repeatable'. The CV reviewer will be looking for indicators that the achievements, skills and experience referred to in your CV, as well as being relevant, can be repeated in the role for which you are applying. When an organization seeks an individual who is 'experienced in the role', what they are essentially saying is we want someone who has performed in this role before and can do so again at a competent level.

In order to pass this part of the CV sifting process, it is therefore critical that you:

- carefully read the job description and understand what types of skill and experience are required in the role
- match your relevant skills and experience in a way that specifically addresses the requirements of the role
- make it easy for the reviewer, who will be reading your CV at speed, to make the link between the requirements of the role and what you have to offer.

Seeking a second opinion

It is common practice in recruitment for a second opinion to be sought on CVs before the decision is made to invite a person to interview. In some cases, two individuals will work together to review all CVs. However, it is more common for one, usually junior, individual to undertake an initial review of CVs (removing those containing spelling errors as well as those that do not fit the job description), before passing on a much reduced pile of CVs to a manager or specialist who is normally closer to the role vacancy in question and who has a very clear idea of what is required.

It is also increasingly common for the initial phase of the recruitment process to be outsourced to a recruitment agency. In such instances, you have to negotiate this initial barrier before your CV gets in front of the final decision maker. Where you are aware that the types of role you intend to apply for are likely to pass through a recruitment agency as a first stage, you might find it productive to build a relationship with those agencies preferred by your targeted employer. Again, undertaking some initial research will be likely to identify such agencies. Consider making approaches to them before a specific role becomes available and they may be quite helpful in terms of offering guidance on the suitability of your CV. If it is what they believe their clients are looking for, they may offer to submit your CV not only to the prospective employer you had in mind but for other positions that are not advertised in the open press.

Recruitment agencies tend to receive payment for their services from the employer, normally expressed as a percentage of your starting annual salary.

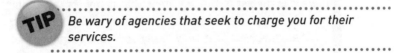

TIP *Be wary of agencies that seek to charge you for their services.*

Due diligence and cross-checking

The majority of checking and validation of what is contained in your CV and what you say at interview takes place through the referencing process once an offer of employment is made (the cost of checking all applicants in the early stages of the process would be too great). However, in instances where a CV is of particularly high quality and the reviewer wants some comfort that what is written has basis in fact, they may cross-reference your CV with the information about you that is available from social media sites and other sources before they meet you. Also, you should not underestimate the contacts that a reviewer may have within, and indeed outside, their sector. Such contacts might well know of you.

Whether you agree, or not, that social media sites or informal conversations should be used as a basis for determining your progression to the interview stage, these actions are a fact of life. As such, you should do what you can to manage your reputation across all sources, as far as possible.

How organizations sift through CVs

Here is the list of the key steps that many organizations take in sifting through large volumes of CVs to identify the individuals that they really believe are equipped for the role or job position in question:

1 Glance over

2 Read through

3 Validating your CV against role requirements

4 Seeking a second opinion

5 Due diligence and cross-checking

Summary

For many people, taking time to focus on their own skills and experience and using these assets to construct a powerful CV seems to be an uncomfortable process. It is tempting to bundle elements together quickly, using a document you prepared in the past or even simply 'cutting and pasting' from a colleague's document or from an example you found online.

The reality of successful CV design is that it requires some work from you in digging down deep to reflect on your strengths and main areas of competence. It's not something that many people take to naturally, but seek opinions from others who you trust to be honest with you. This will give you additional insight into your strengths and weaknesses and will therefore be helpful in giving you a further perspective on the roles for which you are best suited.

From this secure position and clarity of purpose, you can build CVs to address any future roles of interest to you.

Fact-check (answers at the back)

The ten questions at the end of each chapter will help you to assess your understanding. Try to resist the temptation to look back through the chapter as you answer the questions. There is only one correct answer to each question. If you make a mistake, look back through the chapter and reread the section to help you understand the idea better.

Let's see how much you have picked up from our thoughts on creating a successful CV.

1. The abbreviation CV:
a) Is a shortened version of Career Vector, meaning 'direction of career' ❑
b) Stands for the Latin phrase *curriculum vitae*, which translates as 'life path' ❑
c) Is short for Consultancy Vérité, meaning 'true consultancy' ❑
d) Was copyright protected by a recruitment agency in 1986 ❑

2. One of the primary purposes of a CV is to:
a) Give you something to talk about at the interview ❑
b) Manufacture a profile that the potential employer will find attractive ❑
c) Meet anti-discrimination legislation ❑
d) Demonstrate a strong match between your capabilities and the stated requirements of the role ❑

3. A small error in spelling or grammar in your CV:
a) Demonstrates in a positive way that you work at a fast pace ❑
b) Could lead to it being discarded in the initial 'glance through' ❑
c) Is of no consequence as the reviewer will focus on your obvious strengths ❑
d) Cannot be helped and is just one of these things ❑

4. Experience suggests that the percentage of CVs discarded at the first review stage is:
a) 50 per cent ❑
b) 90 per cent ❑
c) 25 per cent ❑
d) 10 per cent ❑

5. In the acronym CAREER, what does the A represent?
a) Artistic ❑
b) Altruistic ❑
c) Appropriate ❑
d) Authentic ❑

6. Getting hold of the relevant 'job description' or 'role profile' before constructing your CV is:
a) A waste of effort as it is purely your qualifications and experience that count ❑
b) Something that can be done only through a recruitment agency ❑
c) Essential, since it enables you to tailor your skills and experience to those required for the specific role ❑
d) Useful if you have the time to request and review it ❑

7. Demonstrating 'emotional intelligence' in your CV:

a) Can be an important differentiator as organizations are keen to employ individuals with good self-awareness and an ability to interact effectively with other people at all levels ❏

b) Is useful only where you are applying for positions in caring professions ❏

c) Is a sign of weakness ❏

d) Is impossible ❏

8. Use of the summarizing personal statement in a CV:

a) Is now totally discredited and should no longer be used ❏

b) When carefully constructed can provide a powerful, immediate and accurate understanding of your capabilities to the reviewer ❏

c) Is only used by people who lack genuine skills and experience ❏

d) Turns it into a legal document ❏

9. Leaving a gap in your employment history:

a) Is advisable if you have been unemployed or in prison during the period in question ❏

b) Should be avoided as it may lead to your CV being discarded without you being given an opportunity to explain ❏

c) Is so common during periods of economic downturn that it is no longer an issue ❏

d) Is a good ploy for getting an interview as the reviewer will be curious ❏

10. Once you have created your CV:

a) You may use it as a basis for constructing future role-specific CVs but be wary of using it unedited for other roles ❏

b) You can use the same document as often as you like as it contains the essential details of your skills and experience ❏

c) As you know it works, pass it on to your friends to use ❏

d) As you've used it once, you must destroy it immediately ❏

CHAPTER 2

The core elements of a successful CV

In this chapter we look in detail at the core components that make up a CV. We look at two main types of structure: the traditional approach and the 'achievement-based' approach.

Many organizations still have a preference for the traditional layout of CV, in which you list your personal and contact details, previous employments, educational qualifications and references – in that order. However, many applicants are finding success in restructuring their CV to convey their achievements in a way that is adapted and relevant to the role for which they are applying.

My view is that in following this second approach, you do not disadvantage yourself when presenting your CV to reviewers that prefer the traditional approach, while providing the opportunity to impress those organizations that prefer to see an achievement-based approach.

In examining the factors that will help you to construct your CV in a way that best represents your capabilities and suitability to the role you desire, we will look at a number of components:

- Structuring the content
- Personal statement
- Achievements
- Employment
- Education and qualifications
- References.

Structuring the content

There is, as you will be aware, a huge body of work advising on how best to structure your CV. Success depends on a range of factors including the preferred style of the person reviewing your CV, the culture of the particular sector you are interested in and the process used by the organization offering the role in shortlisting CVs for the interview stage.

The primary focus of your CV should be to secure you a place at the interview stage. The best way of achieving this objective is to help the reviewer see as quickly as possible on starting to read your CV that your skills and experience match the requirements of the position on offer. In my opinion, simply listing your employments and qualifications in chronological order under the traditional approach is like setting out the ingredients of a recipe and leaving someone else to combine the various elements in the correct proportions and order. Alternatively, by ordering your skills and experience into the correct combinations to match the requirements of the new role, you are making it much easier for the reviewer to see the links between you and the role. This gives you an advantage over applicants of similar skills and experience who have not adapted their CV in such a way.

Tempting as it may be, you should not try to use your CV to answer all the questions a prospective employer may have about you as these can be addressed at the interview. Such an approach will make the document too long and could lead to it being discarded.

 Every statement you include in your CV should earn its place in linking your capabilities to the role. If it doesn't, take it out.

The key elements

In order to get that green light to the interview stage, it is vitally important that you get the key elements of your skills and achievements across to the reviewer as soon as possible (you will find out later why I recommend that in most instances you should restrict the length of your CV to two pages). Remember that a reviewer's impressions start to form as soon as they pick up your document.

In the past, conventional wisdom was that a CV should be arranged in this order:

- Personal details (name, address, etc., date of birth)
- Employment history (in reverse chronological order, i.e. most recent role first)
- Education (school, further or higher education)
- Other qualifications and skills (driving licence, languages, etc.)
- Hobbies and interests
- References (names and contact details, usually of two references).

The above structure is, and will continue to be, seen by many as the conventional way of documenting your personal details, skills and experience. Many employers still expect to see a layout similar to that described above.

In my view, however, this approach contains one big flaw. It leaves the effort involved in linking your capabilities to the requirements of the role to the person reviewing your CV. During periods when the ratio of CVs to vacancies is tens if not hundreds to one, such CVs, unfortunately, are likely to be discarded in the first review. Simply put, you have to do some of the hard work to relate your skills and experience to the new position, and not leave it all to the person reviewing your CV. More likely than not, a reviewer will not expend the effort, preferring instead to look in more detail at a CV that has already begun the process for them. After all, such CVs tend to indicate a person who has studied and understood the job description and has already started to put forward aspects of their skill and experience that relate directly to the specific role in question.

More recently, there has been a tendency towards structuring a CV in a way that communicates your relevance to the available position as quickly as possible, making reference to aspects of your skills and experience in ways that match the requirements of the role.

The structure favoured increasingly today, under the 'achievement-focused' approach, follows this order:

● Personal statement
● Achievements relevant to the new role
● Employment history – most recent first
● Education and qualifications
● Contact details and additional relevant personal information.

The two main approaches to CV structure

There are two primary ways of structuring your CV:

Traditional

1 Personal/contact details

2 Employment history (most recent listed first)

3 Education/key qualifications

4 Other relevant qualifications and skills (e.g. driving licence)

5 Additional personal information

6 References

Achievement-focused

1 Personal statement

2 Achievements

3 Employment history (most recent listed first)

4 Education and qualifications

5 Contact details and relevant personal information

The achievement-focused approach helps the person reviewing your CV to quickly see the links between your capabilities and the requirements of the role. This is particularly important where your current position does not exactly match the one for which you are applying.

The personal statement

A relatively recent development is the personal or character statement I referred to earlier. While this element can have a very positive impact when used correctly, when not it can be seen as clichéd to the point that it is either ignored completely or becomes a point of amusement for the reviewer. I know of several organizations where the most outlandish and exaggerated of such statements are pinned on the wall. As such, I would advise that you carefully construct the statement that takes up this prominent space, seeking to inform the reader who you really are and how you can help their organization.

Let's explore the following contrasting examples to help get the point across. Which one would you prefer to read if you were reviewing CVs within a limited time frame?

Example 1

James is a dynamic, forward-thinking individual who grasps every opportunity open to him. He is a strong team player who is also known for his leadership qualities and is a true asset to any organization seeking to employ him. He is now ready to face his next big challenge.

Example 2

I am a qualified project manager with eight years' experience in the utilities sector, three of which were spent overseas. I have personally managed four projects with budgets in excess of $20 million, all of which completed on time and within budget.

I would hope that the question I asked before setting out these two examples was an easy one to answer. Before I dissect these very different approaches, just take a couple of minutes to compare them and note their differences. Which approach does your opening statement normally take?

It is worth investing time in your CV's initial statement since it is second only to the immediate appearance of your document (which we will cover later) in creating an impression on the reviewer. Bearing in mind, as we said earlier, that many reviewers take a matter of seconds to form an opinion, it is essential that your CV 'locks in' to what skills and experience the prospective organization seeks for the vacant role.

Let's now compare the two examples in detail to see if you picked up on the points I have in mind.

The two statements are of approximately the same length and therefore take up the same amount of space on the document. It is important that this initial paragraph is not too long. Interestingly, the first example runs to 50 words, whereas the second runs to 42 words. Lengthwise, I would say that both are acceptable.

Now, let's turn to the content of each of these statements. Which one gives the reviewer the most useful information at this earliest opportunity, in your opinion? You may argue that the first example is the most telling in that it gives insight into the applicant's character, determination and so on. I would agree that it is the most revealing, but not necessarily in a good way, and might lead to immediate discarding of the CV, and here is why:

● **It is too generic.** This first example could have been used in every CV sent out by our applicant James. It therefore fails one of the 'golden rules' of a successful CV, which is that it should be tailored to the position in question. Indeed, some commentators on this subject go as far as to suggest that a CV should be started from scratch for each and every new position for which you apply. In following this approach, you should therefore think carefully about what content goes in, and just as importantly, what content stays out. While I believe a CV should be tailored to each new job application, I do not think it necessary to start afresh each time, particularly if you have worded your achievements (which we will look at in more detail shortly) strongly. However, I do firmly believe that you should write a new and individually tailored initial or personal statement for each CV you submit.

- The first example speaks of James' personal qualities, yet provides no **context or example for such supposed personal strengths.** In comparison, the second example uses figures and timescales to indicate what level of activities the applicant has undertaken as well as their likely levels of seniority and responsibility (indicated by the size of budget they have managed). This approach tends to leave it to the reviewer to determine what qualities and skills a person has from a description of their achievements, rather than rely only on unsubstantiated claims made by the applicant themselves.
- This next point may be a personal bugbear of mine, but it is one that is mentioned by many reviewers I know. I refer to the **increasing tendency for people to refer to themselves in the third person** (James is a ...), when they have written the document themselves. Very few of us are in a position to have other people author their CVs for them and this is intended to be a document written by you and about you. There is absolutely nothing wrong in referring to yourself in the first person. Anything else is an unnecessary affectation.

To summarize on the personal statement, it should:

- relate directly to the role for which you are applying
- be no more than four lines / 50 words
- be written in the first person (I am...)
- contain specific, quantifiable information that is relevant to the role
- above all else, convey effectively why the reviewer should read further and consider you for interview, even after only having read your first 50 words or so.

It is a good idea to draft your personal statement when you start to build your CV and revisit it again once you have completed it, making any adjustments to ensure that the statement accurately reflects the main body of the document. This statement should strive to be a mini CV in itself, giving a true flavour of your distinguishing abilities and relevance to this specific role.

Achievements

After the personal statement, the next component to be added to your CV is a list of relevant achievements. This section of short paragraphs demonstrates succinctly to the reader that you have previously used your skills and experience to undertake aspects of the role for which you are now applying.

The technique is a simple yet highly effective one that assists the reviewer in connecting you with the role. It does involve you having a clear understanding of:

- the key components of your previous roles, such as:
  - key objectives and targets that you met
  - any budgetary responsibilities
  - any managerial responsibilities
  - how you approach planning
  - the degree of autonomy or freedom you had in your role
  - details of any improvements you made, how you influenced others, including your managers, to adopt your suggestions
- examples which demonstrate the above
- the primary requirements of the role for which you are applying, such as:
  - what similarities there are between your previous role and the new one
  - where there are clear similarities in the types of skill and experience required
  - where there are obvious connections between your achievements in previous roles and the requirements of the current role.

The key difference between the conventional method of setting out your CV and the achievement-based approach is in drawing out common aspects from your previous roles and applying them in a structured way to the new one. Imagine if you will that your career to date is like Rubik's Cube, the three-dimensional mechanical puzzle. When fully complete, each of this puzzle's solid coloured sides represents one of your various previous jobs. Under the traditional approach to describing your career to date, you would simply list each of these jobs in your CV one by one. However, under the achievement-based approach, it is as if you start to twist and rotate the various components of the cube, mixing up the small squares that made up each of the original sides. If you imagine that each job is made up of a series of elements, then you start to see the analogy. Each job is made up of a number of skills and sets of experiences that you can use to be successful in other roles, even if you have not undertaken that exact type of role previously.

You can take the Rubik's Cube analogy further, in that for some roles there are skills or traits that are not close to the surface in terms of their relevance for a particular role. However, slightly reconfigure the role and such skills might play a bigger part in its requirements, bringing about a change in emphasis in how you blend the description of your accumulated talents.

This approach can make you more confident in applying for jobs that do not, on the face of it, appear to be exactly the same as your previous roles. Start to see your previous roles as combinations of your various skill sets, which can be reconfigured and rebuilt to meet the demands of new roles. Never again see a job as a singular, set entity; instead see it as a combination of skills and capabilities, some of which you may be stronger in than others.

In adopting this approach, it is possible that you as an applicant might bring it to the attention of a prospective employer that their vacant position may benefit from certain skills or traits that they had not previously considered but which you possess.

Let's now look at examples of achievements and how to construct them. To remind you, the objectives of such paragraphs are to:

- capture examples of how your skills and experience have been applied to meet the objectives of your roles in the past
- lead the reviewer to conclude that such skills and experience can be applied to the new role.

Example 1
IT Migration Project: As IT programme leader, for 2 years from origination to completion, I led a successful €30 million project to migrate IT systems to a new platform. I reported directly to the main board and ran a core team of 15 project managers and 7 contract staff. All major milestones and budget targets were met.

Example 2
In-house sales training programme: As head of design on this project, I was responsible for the scoping and development of an 18-month duration sales programme for 400 sales representatives in three countries. A key part of my role was development of multicultural material acceptable to all territories. Feedback on the design component of the programme averaged 4.2 out of 5 with a 92 per cent response rate.

Example 3
Office relocation: Reporting directly to the CEO, I was responsible for the planning and execution of office relocation to a different city with a key objective of providing an uninterrupted service to clients. Critical aspects such as utilities, communications and personnel relocation / desk planning were under my direct control. Being able to plan and undertake this project internally saved the company $40,000 in external costs.

All these three examples of achievements included the following elements:

- Reference to the key objective or requirement
- The role of the applicant in the project
- Some indication of degree of responsibility – personnel or budget
- The outcome.

While the scale or size of each of the examples may vary, this is not important since it is the structuring of the content we are interested in. The use of different scales of budget are merely to indicate that the same structure can be used whether you are aiming for a board-level appointment or considering your first move upward in your career.

The reviewer is interested in how what you have achieved previously can be used for the benefit of their organization should you be appointed to the role. In each of the three examples, the applicant can be seen at the heart of the project.

Such an approach, if structured well, can convey key aspects applicable to many roles, including:

- a willingness to take responsibility and have experience in doing so
- experience in coming into contact with and managing day-to-day problems and issues
- experience of reporting progress to the next level of seniority and having an awareness of and experience in working to timescales and budgets
- a proactive and problem-solving approach to work, which can be picked up on by an experienced reviewer.

TIP

Using active words and phrases rather than passive ones tends to denote someone who prefers to shape their environment rather than let their environment shape them.

It should go without saying that wording in a CV itself is no proof of a proactive and committed individual, since anyone can place these words on a piece of paper. An experienced interviewer will investigate statements made in a CV to determine their accuracy. The role of a CV, you will recall, is to get you through to the interview stage by highlighting your relevant skills and experience as clearly and succinctly as possible. It should not be used to make claims that cannot be supported at the interview stage.

What the CV can do, however, is show your skills and experience in the most effective combination to demonstrate their relevance to the position in which you are interested.

I hope that you can now see the advantage of adopting this achievement-based approach over the traditional approach of reciting your past roles and positions in reverse chronological order. The traditional approach, while easy to adopt and even easier to reproduce for future applications, requires no real hard work on your part and as such is more likely to fail in making strong links for the reviewer between your attributes and the vacant role.

So, let us now take a moment to consider what we have built into your new CV. We have drafted a personal summary statement (which we will fine-tune once the CV has been completed) and we have given examples of achievements, using the guidance above, to demonstrate our suitability for the role. You should order these achievements, aiming to give four or five, in the order of most relevant first. If you believe, for example, that sales and marketing experience and results are key to the new role, you should list this most relevant of your achievements first.

Employment history

Although you have used the Achievements section of your CV to demonstrate the relevance of the skills and experience you have gained from your current and previous role to the one for which you are applying, it remains helpful to the reviewer, and indeed is still expected, for you to list your recent employments.

Starting with your current employment first, you should include the following elements for each listing:

1 Dates of joining and leaving that employment
2 Type of employer and sector
3 Your role – being specific but succinct

Again, there is debate concerning exactly what else to include in this section of your CV. I will go through each of these elements, explaining the rationale for including them or leaving them out before offering you my opinion as to which approach you should take. Ultimately though, it is your decision, based on the specifics of your situation and any stated requirements from your prospective employer.

4 Name of employer and your manager

Many applicants decide to include the name and address of their employer in relation to each employment entry. Others go as far as to include the name of their department and the name of their manager. This has tended to be the traditional approach but it is my view that such information should be left out since it fails one of my tests for inclusion mentioned earlier. You may recall me saying that each statement included in your CV should earn its right to be there. I hold the view that while the role you undertook, the type of organization you were employed by and the length of your time there are relevant to an understanding of your capabilities, these additional details don't necessarily improve your case. Indeed, the experiences of the reviewer in relation to one of your former organizations, whether conscious or not, may have a negative impact on how they perceive your CV. Of course, any negative perceptions of one of your previous employers (or indeed a previous manager) will still exist if revealed at the interview stage but at least, by being present, you will have an opportunity at that stage to identify and manage such potential objections. At the initial CV stage, this obviously isn't possible and any reviewer prejudices will go unchallenged.

There is one exception I can think of in going against this reasoning. If you have been fortunate enough to have undergone training or a spent a period of time working for a respected market leader in the sector, then mentioning the name of such an organization in your CV could possibly provide you with an advantage over those who haven't. In this instance, rather than including the name in the Employment section, I would include it as part of your initial personal statement.

TIP *Remember that you are trying to create a positive impression as soon as possible in your CV: use your best material first.*

5 Reason for leaving

Again, traditionally, this element is almost always included.
However, I question the right of this particular piece of
information to be in your CV. Can you think of any reason for
leaving that would be responsible for making you attractive
to a potential employer? In reality, although this element is
normally included, the reasons usually given are clichéd, such
as 'left to take up a more responsible position' or 'headhunted
by a competitor'. As such, this information is seldom given
any degree of attention by a CV reviewer, unless you provide
a negative reason such as having been dismissed for gross
misconduct. This raises the question as to whether you
should disclose such unfortunate circumstances in your CV or
whether it is acceptable to do so at interview.

The fundamental principle is that you should not be
dishonest or misrepresent yourself; this means giving the
correct response to questions you are asked on application
forms, pre-interview questionnaires and at interviews. This is
particularly relevant to questions around any criminal record,
financial circumstances, and you being what's known as 'fit
and proper' to undertake the role in question.

Be prepared to disclose any fact about yourself that
is material to a prospective employer's decision about
whether to employ you or not. The point I am making here
is that including a reason for leaving such as not seeing
'eye to eye' with your previous manager, without giving
yourself an opportunity to explain the background, could
lead to your CV being discarded at the review stage, but be
readily understood and accepted were it to be raised at the
interview stage. On the other hand, an applicant involved
in fraudulent activities applying for a role in a financial
management capacity is unlikely to be accepted regardless

of whether they disclose this issue at CV or the interview stage. (Remember, non-disclosure of material facts is likely grounds for instant dismissal months if not years after you are appointed, and will also seriously damage your future employability prospects.)

6 Salary

It is assumed that disclosure of your joining and leaving salaries at your previous employers are helpful to the new organization in seeing a rising figure, no doubt indicative of increasing responsibility. Again, I would question the benefit of automatically including your salary details in your CV.

The requisite combination of skills and experience should be the key factors in determining your suitability for the new position. For a whole range of reasons, it is possible that you might have been underpaid or overpaid in relation to your capabilities in the past; none of this is relevant to your current application. The new employer should have determined the market rate for the position in question and have made that figure known when advertising the role. If you believe you have the attributes to undertake the role set out by the employer in return for the specified remuneration, then your previous salary levels are an unnecessary distraction to the key equation.

7 Detailed job description for each role undertaken

The danger of detailing each and every role is two-fold:

- You increase the length of the document to the point that the reviewer discards it as being too long and repetitive
- The key information the reviewer needs is obscured by this unnecessary additional wording.

As we will cover in further detail later, a successful CV manages to convey sufficient information on your relevant skills and experience to get you to first interview. It also creates 'hooks' or points of interest that an interviewer will wish to explore further. You can set up these signposts within your CV to point to areas you would like to discuss further at interview and which further reinforce your ability to fulfil the requirements of the new role.

Education and qualifications

Where a degree or other qualification is key to the role, again follow my general advice to present your best supporting material as soon as possible, including reference to these in your personal statement or achievements. The most effective way of doing this is by beginning one of your statements with this information, before continuing to describe a particular achievement.

Example
With a PhD in molecular sciences, I was responsible for running a team of 20 researchers working on a 4-year £3.5 million project to investigate the role of temperature fluctuation on hydrogen fuel cell depletion.

In the Education and qualifications section, it is normally sufficient to list your qualifications as follows, from the highest level downward:

● Higher degree (PhD, Masters, etc.) – institution and subject
● First degree – institution, subject and level of award
● Schooling – name of school or college and summary of type and number of qualifications obtained.

It is unnecessary to provide details of your junior school. It is also unnecessary to detail every school qualification obtained; only include these if they are relevant (for example, a minimum qualification required in language or mathematically related subjects) or when specifically requested by the employer.

Contact details and additional personal information

Under this section, you should provide clear details of how you may be contacted, and include your:

● postal address
● email address
● contact telephone number.

You should provide brief details of any other relevant qualifications or experience in this section, such as language skills (your degree of fluency).

References

Unless they are specifically requested, I suggest you do not provide names and contact details of references. These are almost always only taken up just prior to, or even after, an offer of employment has been made. As such, these details are not normally required at the CV review stage.

Summary

You can significantly increase your chances of securing an interview if you can capture your suitability for a role in a well-structured, clear and brief CV. In this chapter we have suggested a structure that can help you accomplish this objective. We have also suggested what types of information you can exclude from your CV, either because you can provide it at interview or because it is irrelevant in determining your suitability.

In putting your CV together, you should:

- be very clear from reading the job description what the person reviewing your CV is looking for
- aim to include the most relevant of your skills and experience first
- consider using the achievement-based approach to demonstrate your suitability
- make sure that each piece of information you include adds positively to your case
- resist the temptation to turn your CV into a chronological narrative of your career to date.

Fact-check (answers at the back)

1. A reviewer tends to form an impression of an applicant from their CV:
   a) Within seconds of having read the first few lines ❏
   b) By holding it up to a light ❏
   c) After approximately five minutes ❏
   d) After having read the complete document ❏

2. The most effective way of structuring your CV, according to this Part of the book, is:
   a) Contact details; employment history; education and qualifications; additional qualifications; references ❏
   b) Starting with your junior school details and continuing from then on a chronological basis ❏
   c) Personal statement; achievements; employment; education and qualifications; contact and other relevant personal information ❏
   d) By comprehensively listing your complete career history and educational achievements in reverse chronological order ❏

3. The objective of the initial personal statement is to:
   a) Introduce the CV reviewer to you as a person ❏
   b) Give the CV reviewer an understanding of your personality and other non-employment and qualification-related information ❏
   c) Inform the CV reviewer powerfully and succinctly why your skills and experience make you suitable for the vacant position ❏
   d) Fill in space on an otherwise sparse CV ❏

4. Ideally, the initial personal statement should contain this number of words:
   a) 10 ❏
   b) 50 ❏
   c) 250 ❏
   d) 1,000 ❏

5. The most effective type of achievement description should *not* include:

a) A specific example of how you have used your skills and experience to achieve a specific objective ❏

b) Hard information such as budgets, timescales, performance improvement percentages or return on investment ❏

c) Statements which cannot be supported by evidence when requested ❏

d) A proposal as to how previous experience makes you suitable for the new role ❏

6. What is the key advantage of the achievement-focused CV over the traditional approach?

a) It allows you to produce a longer CV ❏

b) It provides the reviewer with an accelerated understanding of how your skills and experience can be applied to the requirements of the new role ❏

c) It takes minimum effort to produce ❏

d) Traditionally structured CVs are now discarded at the very first stage ❏

7. Which of the following, in the author's opinion, should *not* be included in a CV, unless specifically requested:

a) Previous salary details ❏
b) Previous achievements ❏
c) Details of language skills ❏
d) A contact email address ❏

8. Your reason for leaving previous employments:

a) Should always be given in your CV, even if it reflects negatively on you ❏

b) Is not a key consideration for determining your suitability for selection for interview and as such should not be included in your CV unless specifically requested ❏

c) Is one of the most important factors in determining your suitability for a new role ❏

d) Should always be portrayed as someone else's fault ❏

9. Your salary in relation to previous employments:

a) Is not a relevant factor in determining your suitability for a new role and should not normally be included in your CV ❏

b) Should always be disclosed in your CV as this gives your potential new employer an idea of your 'market worth' ❏

c) Should be inflated as far as possible using bonuses and benefits in order to get the best chance of a high salary from the new role ❏

d) Must never be higher than the salary applying to the new role ❏

10. References should be included in your CV:

a) Only if requested by the prospective employer in their pre-application communications ❏
b) Never ❏
c) Always ❏
d) As a matter of pride ❏

CHAPTER 3

The 'look and feel' of a successful CV

In this chapter we examine key elements of your CV such as the way it looks, as well as specific details of content and the impression these elements have on reviewers. We will look at the factors that make the best impression on reviewers, increasing your chances of passing to the next stage – the all-important interview.

A number of the elements covered in this chapter, such as correct spelling, apply to all CVs. For other elements such as whether to include a photograph of yourself or not, I give my opinion based on experience as to the best approach to take. In some countries, certain rules covered in employment law determine how an employer must conduct fair recruitment practices, such as not discriminating on the basis of age, gender, race, religion or other personal factors. While the responsibility lies with an employer to follow employment law, it would be useful for you as an applicant to have a basic understanding of what an employer is permitted to ask you about yourself under the employment and anti-discrimination laws applying in your country.

Let us now start to work through a range of issues that concern applicants and employers alike when it comes to deciding what makes a successful CV:

- Spelling and grammar
- Length
- Use of photographs
- Age and date of birth
- Physical construction of your CV
- Additional advice on CVs submitted via recruitment agencies.

Spelling and grammar

I cannot underline enough the importance of correct spelling and grammar in your CV. It must be capable of passing the 'once over' glance of an eagle-eyed CV reviewer and in getting past the first cut. A decision to discard a CV can be made in as little as a couple of seconds.

If you are aware that spelling may not be your strongest skill, or even if you think it is, please use a spell checker and ask a family member or friend to read your document for spelling and correct grammar. Many organizations view spelling errors as grounds for dismissing CVs at the first hurdle on the basis that the individual has had ample opportunity to construct the document correctly. The view goes that if an individual cannot get their CV right, their attention to detail may be suspect and therefore insufficient for the role for which they are applying.

Length

A good piece of advice on the length of CVs is that they are rarely criticized for being too short but are often discarded for being too long. If you haven't received the green light to pass to the next stage by the end of your CV's second page, you are unlikely to have changed the reviewer's mind by the end of page seven, if they were to ever get that far.

The secret of an excellent CV is that it captures the reviewer's interest by two-thirds down the first page and uses the remainder of the document to support the reviewer's impression that you should be asked to attend for interview.

In my personal view, therefore, a CV should be no longer than two pages. Any longer and you increase the chances that the reviewer will become irritated or impatient with your document. My own preference, when I have been required to deliver a CV or resumé for a piece of work or project, is to restrict myself to one single side of one sheet. My success rate with this technique, interestingly, is in excess of 90 per cent.

There are exceptions to this approach, where further detail on an applicant is required at this initial stage. For example, a medical doctor applying for a post with a different health authority in another region may need to provide a detailed list of qualifications, experience and skills that run to several more pages than the length recommended here. However, I think it is safe to say that those applying for such roles will be aware of the conventions applying to their particular sector. For the majority of roles, it is possible, and indeed desirable, to match your key achievements to the requirements of the new role within two pages.

Use of photographs

You should not normally include a photograph with your CV unless asked specifically to do so (perhaps if you are a model or actor where physical appearance is an element of the selection process). In many parts of the world there is specific anti-discriminatory or equal opportunities legislation that prevents an employer from discriminating against an applicant on the grounds of race, religion, gender, sexual orientation, political beliefs, disability or age. While most employers operate within such rules, the inclusion of your photograph may subconsciously influence an individual reviewer (who perhaps through unconscious bias may prefer to recruit people who look similar to them). It is therefore generally recommended that you leave your skills and experience to represent you rather than include a photograph. The caveat to this point is that in some parts of the world, the inclusion of a photograph with a resumé is expected and part of normal practice.

In practical terms, many employers and recruitment agencies will remove photographs attached to CVs prior to review because of the potential discrimination issue or because they simply get in the way of copying and storing the CVs. Some potential employers may even discard a CV containing a photograph as soon as it is noticed to remove any possibility that they might be accused of discriminatory practices. As we will see in a later chapter, increasing numbers of employers and recruitment agencies now ask for CVs to be submitted to them in electronic format. The inclusion of a photograph can increase the size of an electronic file significantly and may even lead to the rejection of the file by the intended recipient's firewall or email scanning software which blocks images.

It is true that in an increasingly social media focused world there will be images of you available to a potential employer and that these may be reviewed informally as part of the recruitment process. However, in taking that approach, an employer carries the risk of mistakenly retrieving the image of a person with the same name as you (this has happened), and therefore this would not be normal practice for an employer or recruitment agency that follows correct procedures.

Age and date of birth

The inclusion of an applicant's age, date of birth or both of these items was once common in the traditionally structured CV. It was usually the second piece of information to be included after an applicant's name. Again, the impact of anti-discrimination legislation in many territories has led to a decrease in the inclusion of this biographical information in the initial CV document. Many territories have specific anti-discrimination legislation regarding age, with it being illegal to take into account someone's age in determining their ability to fulfil the requirements of the role in question.

Again, there is continuing debate around how effective the removal of any age-related data from your CV will be in preventing a reviewer from estimating your age. It is argued that they can do this simply by looking at the length of your career or in calculating from such details such as the year you obtained your degree or graduated from high school. While this may be true, this argument misses a key point that, in most territories, the whole direction of employment procedures has changed to incorporate anti-discriminatory practices.

Therefore, many employers, Human Resource departments and recruitment agencies no longer expect you to include reference to age, and indeed even gender, in your CV application. When you do, unless asked specifically to do so, you are potentially causing your prospective employer a dilemma.

TIP *Including your age on your CV at best may be ignored but at worst could actually lead to discarding of your CV as the reviewer may have some preconceived idea about the age range of the candidates they are seeking.*

Age and its relationship to a person's ability to perform a role remains a 'hot topic'. Let's look at the issue from a number of perspectives and in doing so examine how best to manage it in your CV.

People at the younger end of the spectrum might be concerned that their lack of years in the employment market may go against them. Conversely, those who have many decades of work behind them may feel that they will be seen as 'too old', 'tired' or have other negative connotations around their chronological age. My solution to dealing with this potential stumbling block to your career development, which may be due as much to your own mindset as any bias of a potential employer, is to focus on your achievements.

Within the consultancy work I currently undertake for many organizations of all different sizes and sectors across the world, I am extremely privileged to have met extraordinarily talented people with fantastic skills and experience, any one of whom it would be an honour to have working beside me. To give you a taster, these include:

- an individual who due to the unfortunate premature death of their father inherited a chain of 25 grocery stores, and despite having no previous experience in retail or commerce, has gained the trust of both customers and staff – turnover and profitability continue to grow
- a poet with incredible insights into the human condition and a fantastic presence; someone who has performed at the White House for the President of the United States
- a gifted linguist and much in demand management trainer who has written numerous articles on a wide range of subjects and can play almost any musical instrument, including 18 different stringed instruments

- a gifted pianist who plays the most beautiful Beethoven, having conquered the difficulties of coming from a war-torn nation to become a professional musician.

Even in such short descriptions, I would hope that my words convey the talents of these people. You will obviously have noted that in no instance did I make reference to age, gender, race or religious beliefs. Such factors are simply irrelevant to a person's abilities to perform a role.

There is an old saying in recruiting about whether a person has 20 years' experience or one year's experience repeated 20 times. In other words, the age of a person is not a reliable indicator of the experience or skills of that person and should not therefore be seen as a basis for making such a judgement. I have encountered many people, young and older, who have managed to build an impressive range of skills and experience into their career. Equally, I have also encountered people of all ages who, even despite opportunities being open to them, have not fulfilled their potential or even come close to doing so. You should not use your age as either a reason or an excuse for not having done something, as potential employers will always be able to point to someone of a similar age who will have managed such achievements.

TIP *Remove your age from your mindset and it will not be an issue for your potential employer.*

Physical construction of your CV

Let's now spend some time looking at the basic presentation elements of a physical (as opposed to an electronic) CV.

Type of paper

The standard advice is to use good-quality white paper. Some writers on the subject even advise the use of a particular weight of paper. In reality, your original CV is photocopied many times or even scanned by the organization reviewing your application, so the key is to make the job of doing so as easy as possible.

Do not used coloured paper, since this can make copies or electronic scans of your document difficult to read. Additionally, this is seen as a gimmick and does not lead to your CV being viewed as preferable to that of anyone else's in the pile. In fact, the person responsible for initially administering the arriving CVs may even photocopy it on to white paper to make it uniform with the others.

Binding or securing your CV

For similar reasons of practicality, do not invest time or money in binding or placing your CV in a booklet format. Remember, your CV document should be in the region of only two pages in length and should be held together with one staple. Any additional binding or stapling simply makes the likely task of duplicating your CV for multiple circulation that much more difficult. Again, think about ways of reducing any barriers that get between your CV and the relevant decision maker.

Spacing and formatting

The aim in formatting is to make your CV as readable and easy on the eye as possible. Do everything you can to make the reviewer focus on the content of your CV. Refrain from using page borders or other unnecessary embellishments which take away from the impact of your content. The best formatted and presented CVs are the ones where the reviewer doesn't notice these elements. I would also suggest that you print your pages on a single-sided basis, not double-sided, making it easier for your document to be copied. This may not appear environmentally sound but remember that my advice is that your CV is restricted to two pages.

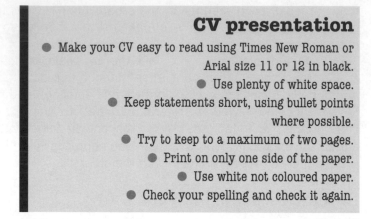

CV presentation

- Make your CV easy to read using Times New Roman or Arial size 11 or 12 in black.
- Use plenty of white space.
- Keep statements short, using bullet points where possible.
- Try to keep to a maximum of two pages.
- Print on only one side of the paper.
- Use white not coloured paper.
- Check your spelling and check it again.

Font

It is tempting when following advice to keep a CV brief to try to squeeze in more information by reducing font size. Do not give in to temptation and remember that quality and relevance of content is much more important than quantity. Aim generally for an 11 or 12 point font size and stay with either Times New Roman or Arial. Avoid scripted (handwriting simulated) fonts at all costs as these can be difficult to read, especially for a reviewer who has been looking through CVs for several hours. A CV that is difficult to read may just require too much effort, regardless of the calibre of the applicant, and the CV will be discarded.

A successful CV is an elegant one that creates the impression of plenty of white space within which you have placed carefully constructed statements in highly readable text.

Use of imagery

As well as incorporating a portrait photograph of themselves, some candidates also include further imagery of them undertaking various roles or tasks. Again, it is neither necessary nor advisable to include such images in a CV for the vast majority of job applications. This advice has as much to do with the practicalities of copying or scanning your document as it does about the minimal effect it has on someone selecting your CV for the next stage.

CVs submitted via recruitment agencies

All of the above guidance applies when you make a direct application to the organization offering the role. In cases where you are invited to make your application through a recruitment agency, bear in mind that they may copy and place your CV on to their own stationery for submission to their client organization. Such stationery may contain the recruitment agency's logo and contact details, so again leave good space around the margins of your original document to enable them to do this easily.

Agencies will also tend to ask you to submit a version of your CV electronically. Some people prefer to do so in PDF (portable document format, designed by Adobe Systems) in order to protect formatting and presentation of their material. However, as mentioned above, some agencies prefer to transfer your details on to their own format or stationery, which is difficult to do with PDF files. You may therefore decide to send your electronic version of your CV in a Word document format, so that the agency may reformat it to fit the available space on their document. It would be useful for you to ask them about their preference before sending it to them.

Summary

Having put a great deal of thought into the content and structuring of your CV, it would be unfortunate if it were to be discarded on the basis of a presentational issue. Sadly, however, this can often happen where a CV reviewer spots a spelling error or simply finds it takes too much effort to read your CV because of the way it is set out. To put it bluntly, even if you are genuinely the most skilled and experienced person for the role, a badly designed CV may mean that you never get the chance to prove this at interview.

A range of presentational aspects, if not undertaken correctly, can damage your chances of proceeding any further than the initial review of CVs. Such elements include:

- the length of your CV – being too long can be an issue
- spelling or grammar mistakes
- poor formatting – poor use of white space or a cramped feel to the document
- use of coloured paper or coloured ink
- including unnecessary photographs or images.

Fact-check (answers at the back)

1. The presentation and look of your CV:
   a) Says much about your personality and individuality. As such, original approaches are recommended ❏
   b) Is unimportant so long as you have the right skills and experience ❏
   c) Should be your primary area of focus ❏
   d) Should be structured so that it is the content that the reviewer focuses on, without any distractions ❏

2. The length of a CV:
   a) Is directly proportionate to your skills and experience. As such, the longer your CV, the more likely it is that you will be selected for interview ❏
   b) Is inversely proportional to the intelligence of the applicant ❏
   c) Should be kept to a maximum of two pages in most cases ❏
   d) Is unimportant – it is as long as it needs to be to get your point across ❏

3. Correct spelling and grammar:
   a) Is so 'yesterday's news' ❏
   b) Is vitally important in creating the right image for your CV ❏
   c) Is unimportant so long as you have the right skills and experience ❏
   d) Is only really important if you are intending to become a writer or journalist ❏

4. The most effective font is:
   a) Whichever one the potential employer uses most in its own material ❏
   b) Black, point size 11 or 12 in Times New Roman or Arial ❏
   c) One of the handwriting-based scripts that helps to personalize your CV ❏
   d) One that makes the most striking impression, leading the reviewer to pick your document from the pile ❏

5. You should include a photograph of yourself:
   a) Undertaking one of your specialist roles as this proves and supports what you state in your CV ❏
   b) Only if you are under 30 years old ❏
   c) In all CV submissions as this helps the CV reviewer build up a better picture of your suitability ❏
   d) Only when specifically asked to do so ❏

6. You should submit hard copy versions of your CV that are:
   a) Printed on both sides as this is environmentally friendly ❏
   b) Printed on one side only as this is generally easier to read and to photocopy where required ❏
   c) Printed on both sides if the length of your CV exceeds four pages ❏
   d) Printed on only the finest-quality paper ❏

7. You should include details of your age or date of birth:

a) At all times, as many roles are best undertaken by people of a certain age ❏

b) Only when specifically asked to do so ❏

c) Because employers need to ensure that they don't pay younger people higher salaries than is necessary ❏

d) To help employers meet any anti-discrimination targets ❏

8. Applying binding to your CV or placing it in a folder:

a) Is unnecessary since most reviewers will remove such covers to enable copying or to file in their own system (electronic or hard copy) ❏

b) Is a fantastic idea as it makes your CV stand out above the rest in the pile ❏

c) Is the new trend ❏

d) Expresses your individuality and will be a key factor in selection for the next stage ❏

9. Electronically submitted CVs:

a) Should always be submitted in PDF format to maintain their structure and to prevent them being altered ❏

b) Can be submitted in a range of formats. It is advisable to ask the recipient in advance which format they prefer ❏

c) Should be avoided in all cases ❏

d) Demonstrate your IT skills and give you a real advantage over people who only submit hard copies ❏

10. When submitting an electronic version of your CV to a recruitment agency:

a) Be aware that they may wish to adapt it to fit within their own format before submitting to a potential employer. A Word document format may be best in such cases ❏

b) You give up your rights to anonymity ❏

c) You should ignore all the guidance related to paper copies ❏

d) You increase your chances of being selected ❏

CHAPTER 4

Knowing your way around your own CV

The main aim of your CV is to help you pass through to the interview stage of the selection process. However, having achieved this goal, its role is not yet complete since the document itself will often be used by an interviewer to determine what questions they may ask you at the interview itself.

In this chapter we will look at the ways in which your CV can help you at the interview stage and how best to construct your CV to help you perform to your potential at a selection interview.

I do not intend to stray into interviewing techniques any further than is necessary to explain to you how a well-constructed CV can play an important role in a successful interview. We will look at such techniques as:

- 'hooks and trails'
- embedding key words and phrases
- critical incident interviewing techniques.

The CV and the interview

In preparation for an interview, a fully prepared interviewer will have gone through your CV, comparing its contents with the job description for the role in question. A key aim of theirs will be to assess your suitability and 'fit' against the roles and requirements of the position. To be successful, you should aim to make their task as easy as possible when it comes to your CV.

There still remain a small number of interviewers who ignore the CV once the interview stage has been reached. They prefer, instead, to use their 'gut instinct' to determine your suitability. Fortunately, these types are becoming less common and it is vitally important that you are able to navigate your way around your own CV competently and confidently, knowing where you can expand on material covered in your CV. (It should go without saying that a person who does not know their way around their own CV at interview will fail to impress.)

'Hooks and trails'

As you put together each element of your CV, in particular your personal statement and achievements, you should ask yourself the types of question an interviewer may ask you, based on the statements you make in your CV.

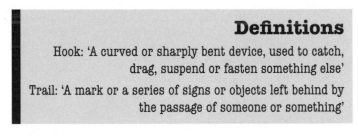

Definitions

Hook: 'A curved or sharply bent device, used to catch, drag, suspend or fasten something else'

Trail: 'A mark or a series of signs or objects left behind by the passage of someone or something'

Wherever possible, your statements should lead the interviewer to ask a question that gives you an opportunity to further demonstrate the fit between your skills and experience and the requirements of the role.

As we have said earlier, the CV is not intended to be an exhaustive and comprehensive record of your career and educational history to date. Each statement you include in your CV should indicate to the reviewer that you meet the requirements for the role. The information contained within each statement should reassure the reviewer that you have the necessary skill set and experience and lead them to a question that digs deeper into your suitability around that particular point. When such a question is asked, that is your cue to provide more detail on an achievement contained in your CV or to provide a further relevant example of an achievement that supports your suitability for that particular aspect. A request for more details or further examples as a result of statements contained in your CV should not come as a surprise to you. Be prepared with further examples and details.

In framing statements to go into your CV, think how you would answer questions such as:

● Tell me more about the work you did at...
● What particular challenges did you face in this role?
● I see that you regularly met your annual targets. What planning did you undertake each quarter to make this possible?
● How did you get into the position where you were responsible for a budget of £5 million?
● What are the main challenges in managing a 30-strong sales team?

Interviewers will use a range of open questions such as these examples. It will add to your chances of success if you are able to relate such questions back to key statements made in your CV, while being able to expand on them further.

Using the TED technique

One technique you can use to strengthen your CV and to increase your ability to navigate confidently around it is to ask a friend or family member to run the 'TED' exercise with you on your CV. 'TED' is a well-known questioning technique – you may have heard of it – which encourages a person to expand on statements they have already made, using this acronym which stands for Tell, Explain or Describe:

- **T**ell me more about...
- **E**xplain how you...
- **D**escribe an occasion where you...

Using your draft CV as the basis for discussion, your friend should review your CV (as of course they should be doing anyway to look for any spelling or grammatical errors) and then pick out a number of statements you have made. They should then use a number of the TED prompts to get you to expand more on those particular statements.

In following this technique, you can use your CV as the core of your approach, around which you build a series of additional examples to help support your application. These examples, which I again suggest are structured in the form of achievements, can be put together at the same time as your CV but not included within it. Instead, the use of key words or reference to such experience within your CV (i.e. the hooks and trails I refer to) will normally lead to an opportunity within the interview to use such examples. The alternative is to wait until the interview before thinking about forming such examples; not an approach I would recommend, particularly if you are also looking to demonstrate your planning and preparation capabilities.

Using the SMART technique

In Chapter 2, we looked at how to structure an achievement and how this approach was more likely to connect your capabilities to the requirements of the role than just a straightforward description of your employment activities to date. Although more commonly thought of as means of setting goals and objectives, you might wish to use this (slightly adapted) SMART acronym to structure your achievement examples.

To do this, draft and then test each achievement example against the following adapted SMART acronym:

- **S**pecific: make your example specific to a particular requirement of the role for which you are applying. Identify this requirement from the job description.
- **M**easurable: include figures such as budgets, cost savings and percentage increase in sales/profitability to quantify your achievement.
- **A**chieved: in this context, make it clear what the achievement was and how it can be related to the new role. Address why the stated achievement demonstrates your suitability for the new role.
- **R**elevant: are you able to verify the achievement you describe as well as your central role in it? Achievements that you observed 'from the touchline' but which cannot be linked to your actions, decision-making or involvement cannot be realistically used to demonstrate your impact on the new role.
- **T**imescale: include the time period within which your particular achievement was attained. This could be the duration of the project or the period over which you built the sales team or managed the cost reductions.

Embedding key words and phrases

As we have seen, 'hooks and trails' are intended to act as signposts within the CV leading to additional achievements or examples that you have constructed and can refer to at the interview stage.

The embedding of words or phrases of a particular type in your CV is intended to indicate to the reviewer particular characteristics that you wish to convey. For example, many employers are understandably keen to discover to what degree the achievements you describe in your CV can be attributed to your actions rather than to the input of others. To reinforce the idea that achievements were due largely to your own efforts, it helps your case if you are able to demonstrate your familiarity with key technical terminology or milestones. Such references should be used sparingly but if used in context can add plausibility to your submission.

Some employers are interested in any indicators that an applicant is proactive in shaping their own career and in having a problem-solving mindset. The inclusion of such words, sparingly, in your CV can start to reinforce that impression. Again, I remind you of my caveat that you should not seek to mislead within your CV. However, if you have been responsible for a particular achievement, it may be advantageous to use action verbs rather than document the achievement in a neutral or passive way (false modesty may not get your CV through).

Example 1 (passive)
The $10 million project in which I was involved was completed successfully two months before the due completion date.

Example 2 (proactive)
I played a significant planning role in the $10 million project, which was successfully completed two months before the due completion date.

Attention to the tense of verbs used by applicants is another indicator that reviewers sometimes use. This may sound a surprising approach but it is not uncommon for applicants to speak of what they would do in a certain situation, using future ('I will') or future conditional ('If this happened I would...') tenses, and for it to become evident subsequently that they had no experience in the area of interest. Consistent use of the past tense in a CV suggests that an applicant is used to describing events that have already occurred, and therefore that they have experience in that area.

Critical incident interviewing techniques

As well as determining whether your skills and experience are relevant to the role in question, potential employers are also subtly trying to find out more about you as a person and how you operate in different situations. You might think that this analysis takes place only from the interview stage. However, many organizations, and their appointed recruitment agencies, look for initial clues in your CV. Again, you should think about how you can leave hooks or trails that refer to such required qualities within your CV.

Many employers use the critical incident interviewing technique as part of the employment selection process. Essentially, at interview you are asked to think back to a situation you have been involved in and to describe how particular aspects such as people, decision-making process, risk management and budget as well as the problem itself were managed.

Prior to the interview stage, the employer will have identified a set of competencies that are central to the role for which you applied. At the interview itself, you will be scored against such competencies depending on your description of how the situation was handled and your role in such a situation. Again, this subject is best explored more fully under interview techniques but I raise it here as there are steps you can take when creating your CV to prepare for dealing with such a technique at the interview stage.

The person reviewing the CVs at the initial stage should be very familiar with the contents of the job description relating to the position in question. Additionally, they may also be aware of the detailed competencies the employer believes are required by the person best suited to fill that role. (These detailed competency requirements are sometimes, but not always, made known to applicants at the start of the process.) Therefore, in sifting through CVs at the first stage, the reviewer will already be starting to match what is seen on CVs against specific competency requirements that might not always be obvious to the applicant.

Not only does the achievement-based approach described earlier increase your chances of matching your profile to the requirements of the new role, but the actual words or phrases you use may also positively influence the reviewer to select your CV from the tens or even hundreds spread out in front of them.

Many organizations work to the premise that a person who consistently behaved in certain ways in the past is likely to behave in similar ways in the future, i.e. when employed by them. An employer is therefore interested in identifying particular traits, or patterns of behaviour, that are appropriate to the new role. By wording your CV in a certain way, you can start to indicate to the prospective new employer that you have one or more of these desired attributes.

From your CV, indicators of particular types of trait, such as extroversion, receptivity to change or need for affiliation, can start to give an employer some early impressions as to the type of person standing behind the CV. For example, a CV with many job changes in a short period of time might indicate a person who becomes unsettled or easily bored in a role after a relatively short time.

Definition

Trait: 'A distinguishing feature, as of a person's character'

'A component of a person's behaviour that is assumed to serve as an explanation of enduring personal characteristics'

The messages you give out from your CV can therefore be quite subtle and, indeed, subconscious on your part. For this reason, I suggest that you review your drafted CV from yet another angle to discover what other messages it might give out to a potential employer. Having reviewed the requirements of the job description, your CV may indicate that you possess the following attributes that might be seen as desirable by a prospective employer:

● an ability to plan and organize yourself and others
● a willingness to work on your own or as part of a team as necessary
● an ability to make sound decisions based on the information available
● an ability to communicate with people at all levels around you
● a tendency to see a job through to completion.

The way in which you structure your statements can give the reviewer a significant amount of information regarding such attributes. Please note the major distinction between simply stating that you possess characteristics such as those described above and providing details of achievements that indicate you possess such characteristics. The former approach is unlikely to be taken at face value while the latter will be seen as a good starting point.

Think of the approach I am suggesting here as using your CV as a highly effective set of signposts. You give the CV reviewer sufficient range and depth of information to reassure them that you meet the requirements for the role but leave sufficient room to develop the various themes at your interview with further information. In addition, the way that you construct your statements gives the reviewer an indication of the types of personality traits you may have, which in turn will provide guidance as to the type of roles to which you are best suited, or unsuited, as the case may be. In reviewing your draft CV, you should identify and be comfortable with the messages about you that your CV sends out.

TIP *Reflect on what impresses you about other people and use this insight to bring out your own best qualities in your CV.*

Using your CV as a navigation aid

Your CV is not meant to be a meandering narrative of your life story to date. It is a series of signposts that strongly direct the reviewer to the conclusion that you are right for the job. Since the reviewer may wish to explore some of the subjects you mention at interview, be clear on where your directions lead and what you need to cover if taken there.

Summary

In this chapter we have learned that a CV does not only convey information concerning your skills and experience. The way you set out your CV and the words you use can provide a potential employer with useful indicators as to your personality type, the types of role you appear to prefer and how you react to different situations. While such information is not comprehensive, it is part of the picture an employer builds up to determine your fit with the role for which you have applied. It is therefore extremely important that you understand what additional indicators your CV provides to your potential new employer and how you make best use of such indicators.

We also looked at how you can embed particular words or phrases in your CV to act as signposts to further discussions at the interview stage. These hooks or trails that you lay down should invite the interviewer to further investigate the areas you suggest. Of course, in adopting this strategy, it is important that you invest time prior to interview in constructing such additional achievement-focused examples.

Fact-check (answers at the back)

1. Wherever possible, the statements contained in your CV should:
   a) Make you sound as important as possible ❏
   b) Prevent the interviewer from having any need to ask further questions about your application ❏
   c) Rhyme ❏
   d) Lead the interviewer to ask questions that give you an opportunity to further demonstrate the fit between your skills and experience and the requirements of the role ❏

2. The aim of a 'hook' in your CV is to:
   a) Create a point of interest that can be opened up to provide further related information at the interview stage ❏
   b) Distract the reviewer from weak areas of your CV ❏
   c) Trick the interviewer ❏
   d) Remind you of areas on which you should ask questions at the interview ❏

3. The achievements you include within your CV:
   a) Should be a mix of those you are responsible for and those you could have achieved had conditions been in your favour at the time ❏
   b) Should be the most relevant and should also be supported with others you have available to you, should you reach interview ❏
   c) Should act as teasers to the reviewer with you saving your best examples to reveal at interview ❏
   d) Do not have to be genuine so long as they appear convincing, as no one ever checks ❏

4. A trait is:
   a) Some type of reward ❏
   b) A type of experience ❏
   c) A distinguishing feature of a person's character ❏
   d) A type of personality ❏

5. The 'T' in the acronym TED stands for:
   a) Trust ❏
   b) Tell ❏
   c) Topic ❏
   d) Team ❏

6. The 'E' in the acronym TED stands for:
   a) Explain ❏
   b) Expert ❏
   c) Entertain ❏
   d) Experience ❏

7. The 'D' in the acronym TED stands for:
a) Describe ❑
b) Document ❑
c) Detail ❑
d) Discuss ❑

8. The regular use of the past tense in your CV:
a) Suggests to the reader that you live in the past and are therefore unlikely to be suited to a newly created role ❑
b) Is indicative, but not conclusive, that you have been involved in the situations you describe in your CV ❑
c) Means nothing whatsoever and should be ignored ❑
d) Suggests you have just used an old CV ❑

9. Critical incident technique interviewing:
a) Is now totally discredited and should no longer be used ❑
b) Is designed to ascertain how you did or might act in particular situations or scenarios ❑
c) Is the term used for a particularly poor interviewing style ❑
d) Is used only for roles in which risk management plays a key part ❑

10. A CV with several job changes in a short period of time might indicate:
a) A person who becomes unsettled or easily bored in a role after a relatively short time ❑
b) An ambitious person who hasn't yet found the role that challenges or fulfils them ❑
c) A sector that is economically unstable with poor job security ❑
d) All of the above plus other reasons, so conclusions should be drawn with caution and supported by other evidence ❑

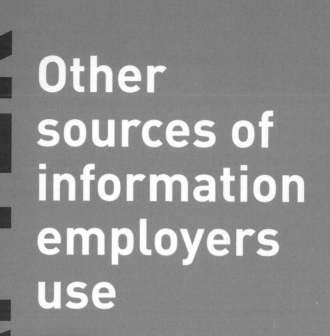

CHAPTER 5

Other sources of information employers use

In this chapter we highlight and consider other tools at the disposal of employers and recruitment agencies as they seek as much information as possible regarding your suitability for the position for which you applied. We devote a complete chapter (7) to the online world and its increasing impact on the application process.

Where once the CV was the main, if not only, pre-interview source of information open to employers in determining suitability for a role, this situation is changing rapidly. A successful applicant therefore not only needs to consider what goes into their CV but also how to reconcile what appears in their CV with what a prospective employer can discover from other sources of information.

Inconsistency is one factor that tends to set alarm bells ringing for an employer when seeking applicants for a vacant position. You therefore need to be informed and proactive in managing what the spectrum of sources indicates to your potential employer.

The other sources of information we will consider in this chapter are:

● the employer application form
● the personality or behaviour profiling test
● the 'fit and proper' questionnaire
● the handwritten covering letter.

The employer application form

Even if you are invited to submit a CV, a potential employer may also ask you to complete and return their application forms at the same time. This could be a hard copy but increasingly the online equivalent is being used. There is no evidence yet of widespread use of online analytics to observe the behaviours of a potential applicant's visit to the recruitment section of an organization's website. It may only be a matter of time, however, since the technology is already used elsewhere, before details are noted of which parts of the employer's site an applicant visited and how long they stayed, with this information used to add to the overall profile of the applicant.

Why organizations like application forms

In asking you to complete an application form, the organization is able to maintain some structure over the type of information you provide, more so than if it relied wholly on your CV, the contents of which are largely within your control. The information you provide is therefore likely to be more closely aligned to the information required by the employer since you will be guided by the headlines and questions in each section of the form.

Some application forms contain a declaration that the applicant is asked to sign, on the basis that the information provided may be more accurate and the applicant less inclined to exaggerate their skills and experience.

The application form may ask for information that is of more use to the organization were you to be eventually employed by them, such as your national insurance or social security number, date of birth and tax details. None of this information should be used in any way to determine your suitability for the role for which you have applied. Indeed, due to the anti-discriminatory legislation in place in many territories, requests for this and other types of personal information are now kept completely separate from the recruitment process so the organization can protect itself from any accusation of anti-discriminatory practices.

Additionally, you may be asked to complete a separate form asking for personal information such as your ethnic origin, whether you have any disabilities or your sexual orientation. Such a form is required in some territories as employers are legally obliged to maintain statistics as to the numbers of people they employ in particular categories, and this data is retained on an anonymous basis. Again, such information should play no part in determining your suitability for a role.

The personality or behaviour profiling test

Profiling tests are increasingly used to gain a richer picture of aspects of an applicant's profile such as:

● their preferred communication style
● whether they prefer to work on their own, in small groups or as part of a larger team
● whether they prefer roles that are well defined with tight parameters or whether they prefer more open-ended and less structured roles
● their tendency to complete tasks at a structured rate during the timeline available, or whether they tend to leave the bulk of the task until the last available opportunity.

These are only a few examples of some of the elements that such profiling can detect. On the whole, these tests are very well developed and consistently reliable in their findings. It is fairly difficult to deceive these profiling tools, and there is little point in doing so since their main aim is to align your personality and characteristics with a position that requires such a profile. If you end up in a position that requires you to behave in a way that is not aligned to your natural state, this will simply cause you stress, probably on a cumulative basis, leading to a likely move away from the role.

TIP *Always answer the questions related to these profiling tools as honestly as you can, because they can be very helpful to you in finding a role that fits your strengths.*

Possessed with the results of such a profiling test, which is usually shared with the applicant these days (ask for a copy), together with your CV, the recruiting organization is able to build a fairly accurate picture of the applicant. If you have undertaken a profiling exercise in the past, use the information gained from this source to inform and shape the messages arising from your CV to make them consistent.

Using profiling to enhance your CV

Personality profiling is becoming more common today as organizations keen to reduce staff turnover look more closely at the alignment between personality and approach to working and the role itself. Such increased understanding is not the sole domain of the employing organization: individuals can use profiling to identify how their strengths are better suited to some roles than others. Profiling tests are commonly available, most of them online. For guidance on which profiling test is best suited to your requirements, contact a local careers advice body or, alternatively, a reputable recruitment agency may be able to assist.

The 'fit and proper' questionnaire

You may already have encountered such a document if you are involved in any role that involves having access to an organization's financial affairs, are in a position where you have the capacity to contract on behalf of the organization that employs you, or a number of other instances where it is important for an organization prior to employing you to know that you meet what is generally known as 'fit and proper' standards. This means that you are required to declare specific aspects of your personal situation such as:

- a criminal record (different regulations apply in different territories as to what severity of conviction and as to whether 'time barring' can be applied after a certain period)
- your credit rating and levels of debt
- whether you are, or have been, declared insolvent or bankrupt
- whether you have ever been disqualified from holding the role of director or other senior position in an organization.

Again, the best approach to take with such a document is to answer it truthfully and honestly. In the event of an employment offer, the subsequent discovery of a misleading response will almost always be cause for instant dismissal, regardless of the amount of time elapsed since the declaration was made.

The handwritten covering letter

Many organizations still request that a handwritten covering letter accompanies the submission of a CV. It does appear that this is a declining request, in many instances simply due to the volumes of CVs received and the need to run the recruitment process as smoothly as possible.

Those organizations that do still request a covering letter do so for a number of reasons:

1 A handwritten document can provide information that doesn't appear on the CV. The letter usually details why the applicant is interested in the position and why, in their view, they are suitable for the position. This information tends not to appear in the more traditional CV, which details a person's employment and educational history. However, the achievement-based CV will tend to provide such information within the Personal statement or Achievements section of the CV, largely making the covering letter redundant.

2 The letter goes some way in indicating to the employer that the applicant has made an effort to tailor their application to the position in question as it should make specific reference to the

position being advertised by the organization. Of course, if you issue a standard covering letter to go with a generic CV to tens of employers, you will miss the whole point of the covering letter.

Whether it forms part of recruiting mythology or whether some organizations actually did this, it is said that handwriting experts would examine the script of the covering letter to determine further information about the applicant. If it were a commonly used tool, I suspect it is very much in decline today, due to the availability of profiling tests and applicant information available from a range of other sources online.

Summary

While the CV remains the key means of narrowing down candidates for a position, employers have an increasing range of other tools open to them in building up a profile of the applicant.

When applying for a role, it is no longer sufficient to focus on the content of your CV in isolation. You must consider the degree of consistency the information in your CV provides when compared to other sources of information available to the employing organization.

If in applying for your preferred roles you find that you are not reaching the interview stage, it may be that your skills and experience are not yet sufficient for that role. However, it may also be the case that the organization feels that your approach to working, or elements of your working style, is not compatible with the role for which you are applying. If you believe this is the case, it may be worth undertaking a personality or behaviour profiling test to gain a more comprehensive understanding of what types of role might be more aligned to your preferences.

Fact-check (answers at the back)

1. Potential employers:
a) Use your CV as the only source of information about you ❑
b) Ignore your CV and take more notice of what is said about you from references ❑
c Get most of their information about you from your online profile ❑
d Increasingly not only use your CV but also other sources of information, including online, to build up a picture of you ❑

2. Consistency across the various information sources available to the employer:
a) Is something you should aim to achieve ❑
b) Suggests you are boring and therefore unlikely to be selected ❑
c) Is not an issue as potential employers should not be using anything other than your CV ❑
d) All of the above ❑

3. The employer application form:
a) Is now only available in an online format ❑
b) Is used to prevent applicants from providing false information ❑
c) Is now illegal due to anti-discrimination legislation ❑
d) Is still used by many organizations in addition to your CV as it enables them to give more structure to the information they request from you ❑

4. In order to complete an application form effectively:
a) Read the document several times before you complete it to understand what information is requested and in which section this should be placed ❑
b) Read the job description carefully to help you make your answers relevant ❑
c) Write out or type your answers first in draft on a separate sheet of paper and ask a friend or family member to review your draft answers ❑
d) All of the above ❑

5. A handwritten covering letter:
a) Is requested in cases where organizations wish to study the applicant's handwriting for clues to their personality ❑
b) Can be a useful supporting document to indicate why an applicant believes they are suitable for a position and can add an extra dimension to the information provided ❑
c) Is seen as old fashioned – all covering letters must now be produced by word processor to demonstrate computer literacy ❑
d) Was last used successfully in 1998 ❑

6. When you are asked to undergo a profiling or personality test as part of an application:

a) You should answer the questions in the way you think the 'perfect applicant' should answer them ❏

b) You should refuse as this practice is seen as unethical ❏

c) Just be yourself and answer the questions truthfully and naturally ❏

d) You should answer in a way that is the opposite to what you really think as this makes the test results void ❏

7. It is useful for an organization to understand an applicant's preferred communication style:

a) As it provides some indication of how the person would interact with their manager and members of the team around them if successful ❏

b) So they know how to manipulate them at the interview stage ❏

c) As applicants who talk too much can be removed from the application process ❏

d) So their manager can get them to do things without them realizing it ❏

8. A 'fit and proper' questionnaire is generally used to find out:

a) Whether an applicant has a criminal record ❏

b) A person's financial position and creditworthiness ❏

c) Whether an applicant has been banned from holding a position of authority, such as Director of a company ❏

d) All of the above ❏

9. In completing a 'fit and proper' questionnaire:

a) You should answer the questions truthfully and honestly ❏

b) You should consult your legal adviser ❏

c) You should answer in a way that is not technically lying but does not necessarily tell a prospective employer the complete truth ❏

d) Your CV has indicated that you may have something to hide and the employer has issued this additional document ❏

10. If you find that you are generally unsuccessful in getting through to the interview stage:

a) Consider seeking advice from a person with experience in such matters, perhaps a manager you know who regularly reviews CVs ❏

b) Examine your online profile to see if there is anything that might possibly be putting potential employers off ❏

c) Try to get some feedback from organization or recruitment agencies you have approached on what you could improve ❏

d) All of the above ❏

CHAPTER 6

'Fuel injecting' your CV

In this chapter we will look at steps you can take to improve the information contained within your CV and to increase the chances of you becoming successful in reaching the all-important interview stage of the recruitment process.

This chapter will cover the following aspects of 'fuel-injecting' your CV:

- Following a project-based approach to CV composition
- Specializing rather than generalizing
- Using a recruitment agency to your benefit
- Submitting CVs electronically.

Following a project-based approach to CV composition

For individuals who operate within a mainly project-based environment, it is relatively straightforward to identify specific achievements, largely due to the fact that projects by definition possess structure, scope, budgets and timelines, against which that person's performance can be measured and determined. However, I have had discussions with a number of people who operate within non-project-based roles that are often referred to by the phrase 'business as usual' (BAU). This is the state of affairs within an organization or department where work is simply a continuation of tasks and undertaking of regular open-ended activities in line with the requirements of their role. The point being made by such individuals is that they find it difficult to express their achievements in quantifiable terms, since achievements are relatively difficult to identify when their work feels like one continuous process.

This is a valid point to raise. While more roles do contain a project-based component than before, this is not the case for everyone. For such individuals, I suggest that they examine their roles and activities more closely with a view to defining discrete components of their job that do contain project-like elements. A further step they can take is to volunteer for project-based work outside their day-to-day role.

Many organizations face rapid changes in their environment, regardless of the sector in which they operate, and are looking within their own organization for employees who can be seconded to projects. Taking part in such projects not only provides useful material for a future CV but genuinely stretches and expands the individual's skill set. A person who can demonstrate going outside their normal day-to-day role to gain further experience, project based or otherwise, will also be strengthening their CV for when it is required.

This area raises a further wider-reaching point. It is better to see your CV as a continuously developing document (remember the Latin definition as 'life path'), even when you do not need to use it.

Consider how you can strengthen your CV at regular intervals and do so by thinking about the types of activity in which you can become involved. Ask yourself how you can demonstrate proactivity and other desirable attributes long before you need to put your achievements to work in a submitted CV.

Specializing rather than generalizing

It may be tempting to portray yourself as a generalist, being able to turn your hand to a wide range of roles. However, since the development of social media and other powerful means of communicating your skills to the relevant organizations, it is now much easier to let those who need your skills know that you exist, even if you are not immediately available. This is true to the extent now that a specialist in any part of the world can have their CV noticed by organizations on a truly global basis. Having a rare or deeply specialized occupation no longer means that the chances of moving roles are minimal.

As an example of this increased visibility and marketability of those in specialist roles, I have a very good friend who for many years worked in the UK as a hydrogen fuel cell scientist at the forefront of research into this extremely important area. Continuing quietly with his work, he was being increasingly contacted by organizations around the world keen to use his expertise. Dave has now moved with his family to Vancouver and, as well as having a fulfilling new job, he has a fantastic and well-balanced lifestyle.

Using a recruitment agency to your benefit

You may become involved with a recruitment agency in a range of circumstances, such as:

- when a specific role is publicized in a newspaper, magazine or journal and you are invited to submit your CV to a recruitment agency acting on behalf of a named or unnamed organization
- where, after initial correspondence directly with an organization, you are directed to send your CV to their preferred recruitment agency which handles a number of the initial stages of the process on their behalf
- where a recruitment organization invites the submission of CVs but does not mention a specific employer or role.

In the first two situations, you are applying for a particular position and the employer is outsourcing all or part of the recruitment process to a third-party recruitment specialist. In responding to such opportunities, you should follow the same approach that I advocate in making direct application to a potential employer.

There is often discussion around the possibility that recruitment agencies have their 'preferred candidates' or 'favourites' and that it is therefore difficult for an 'outsider' to get their CV in front of an employer. My view on this potential criticism of recruitment agencies, and I have no reason to support or criticize them, is that if agencies do have preferred candidates for some roles, such individuals have probably worked hard to get into such a position legitimately by structuring their CV effectively.

Many recruitment agencies specialize in particular sectors in which they have built up a reputation with its main employers. Furthermore, many organizations have a preference for one or two recruitment agencies with whom they have built up a relationship, sometimes over many years.

 To increase your chances of passing successfully through the recruitment agency 'filter', it is best to approach the recruitment organizations that tend to be regularly involved with the roles and organizations in which you are interested.

Submitting CVs electronically

A significant number of organizations request the submission of CVs electronically. This enables them to:

- disseminate CVs to different personnel throughout the organization, often in different locations
- use search software to pick out relevant words or phrases of interest to them
- retain CVs for future positions, often loading them on to a database to enable future key word search.

Word search software

Use of word search software is an interesting development and one that you can use to your advantage. Potential employers and recruitment agencies who use this tool as part of their process claim that it helps them identify applicants who are more likely to be familiar with and experienced in the role in question. Their view is based on the premise that individuals with experience in that particular role are more likely to use specialist words or phrases in common usage by people who perform in that role. For example, a project manager may make reference to a particular type of software or methodology, or perhaps its abbreviated name, one that is only known to those who use it. Another example would be of an engineer or other technical specialist who may refer to a section of relevant legislation that would be known only to those who work within that environment.

TIP

To turn the word search method to your competitive advantage, include in your CV references to such specific components of the role that demonstrate your knowledge in this area. Of course, you must genuinely have experience in such matters, since you would soon be found lacking if questioned further at the interview stage.

This point reinforces my belief that you should focus your efforts only on positions that require your skills and experience. As we have previously discussed, you can blend and emphasize your skills and experience depending on the requirements of the role (remember the Rubik's Cube analogy) but you should focus where your skills are strongest. If you are applying for a role that is different, on the face of it, from those you have undertaken in the past, you must work hard to show the transferability and applicability of the skills and experience you possess.

Even if word recognition software is not being used, the appropriate inclusion of specialist words or phrases within your CV will normally be noticed, thereby differentiating your CV, by those assessing your CV manually but who have a clear understanding of the requirements of the role.

File formats

When asked to submit your CV electronically, you will need to give some thought to the most appropriate format to use. If submitting by uploading to a potential employer or recruiter's site, you will normally be provided with instructions. The most common options are as a Word document or as a PDF document.

Word documents are generally acceptable to use but on occasion these can become distorted or lose formatting when opened by a recipient who does not have the same word-processing software, or even a different version of the same software. It is unfortunate if this happens, because a formatting problem can change the look of your CV. It is for this reason that many people prefer to send a PDF as it in effect 'takes a picture' of your document and shows it the way you intended it to be seen. The potential drawbacks of this route are that it can make the file size larger than the word document equivalent; it is more likely to get stuck in an organization's firewall or anti-virus software; or the recipient may not have the necessary PDF reader – although this is increasingly rare.

If you are following the advice in this book to keep the length of your CV to two pages and not to include a photograph, then you should not need to compress the file before sending it. However, if due to its size and the limits of the recipient's email inbox, you do need to compress the file, an application such as Winzip will suffice in such cases. As an alternative, you can always upload your file using such software as 'Hightail', which notifies the intended recipient where and how to download the file.

As mentioned in Chapter 3 in relation to recruitment agencies, it is advisable to speak to the prospective employer well before any deadline about the best option for submitting your CV electronically. I would also advise that you do not leave it until the last moment to do so as others may be doing the same, leading to online congestion.

The covering letter

A related question is whether you should submit an electronic letter with such submissions. Again, this depends on any guidance given by the prospective employer. If you feel that the personal statement within your CV does not sufficiently represent your cause, you may wish to submit a covering letter of no longer than three-quarters of a page and as a separate document to the CV, so that the recipient can deal with it separately to the CV if they wish. Should you have the scanning equipment to do so, you may wish to compose, print off and scan your letter as a PDF, and then sign it to give it that personal touch. As an alternative, your covering words can simply take the form of an email, which is wholly acceptable today and not seen as too informal.

TIP *Make sure that you acquire a sensible and professional email address when applying for jobs, preferably one containing your name, rather than the once amusing one you used as a teenager.*

Summary

In a competitive jobs market, it is simply not sufficient to submit your CV to numerous organizations and 'hope for the best'. Organizations are becoming increasingly sophisticated in seeking out the most appropriately skilled and experienced people.

For their part, applicants must invest time and effort in analysing their own strengths and in communicating them effectively to organizations offering roles relevant to their skills and experience.

There are a number of steps you can take to increase the chances of matching your skills and experience profile to the roles you desire. You need to build and push your key messages through a number of routes and media, of which the CV is only one channel.

You also have to think ahead by seeing how your current roles and activities can be documented within a CV to show your suitability for new roles. You may need to decide what activities and roles to undertake if you are to be seen as shaping your career path. Passivity is unlikely to gain you access to the positions you desire.

Fact-check (answers at the back)

1. Having a specialism:
   a) Is a disadvantage as it significantly limits the range of positions for which you can apply ❏
   b) Is no barrier to job mobility, thanks to increased visibility through social media and business networking sites ❏
   c) Is seen as old fashioned, with most employers preferring generalists ❏
   d) Is a barrier to becoming a manager ❏

2. An advantage of being able to list project-type role experience is that:
   a) Employers tend to employ people who have project management experience ❏
   b) Such roles tend to have a stated objective, outcome, budget and other factors that can give a potential employer an indication of your performance ❏
   c) You will be perceived as someone who 'gets ahead' in life ❏
   d) You will get an automatic increase in your starting salary ❏

3. In this context, the abbreviation BAU stands for:
   a) Before Applicant Understanding ❏
   b) Behaviour Attitude ❏
   c) Business As Usual ❏
   d) Business Audit Unit ❏

4. Using a recruitment agency:
   a) Is seen as a sign of desperation by potential employers and as such should be avoided ❏
   b) Will guarantee you an interview, as they know the system ❏
   c) Will result in you getting a smaller starting salary than applying directly, in order to pay the agency's commission ❏
   d) Can be helpful, as you may get advice on how to structure your CV and on the types of role best suited to your skills and experience ❏

5. Many recruitment agencies:
   a) Specialize in particular sectors ❏
   b) Have built up a relationship and reputation with their key clients ❏
   c) Have advisers who can help with your CV ❏
   d) All of the above ❏

6. A recruitment organization inviting CVs but making no mention of a specific employer or role:
   a) Is operating illegally ❏
   b) Is recruiting for the security services and is not permitted to give details of the role ❏
   c) Is likely to be gathering a pool of potential candidates for future use but has not been asked to recruit for a specific role ❏
   d) Will only match you with a potential employer if you pay a fee ❏

7. The use of electronic CVs can have advantages for an employer, in that:
a) It enables them to circulate CVs to different personnel throughout the organization, often in different locations ❏
b) It allows them to use search software to pick out key words likely to be contained in relevant CVs ❏
c) It helps them to keep a record of unsuccessful applicants for a particular role, but who may be more suited to a future position ❏
d) All of the above ❏

8. Including key words or phrases in your CV that are specific to your role:
a) Is likely to be seen as unnecessary use of jargon and will lead to your CV being rejected ❏
b) Indicates you do not really know what you are talking about and have just copied them from the job description ❏
c) When done carefully can lead to your CV being 'flagged' by key word search software, as an indicator that you have experience in a particular role or specialism ❏
d) Is a form of cheating and is not to be recommended ❏

9. The following behaviours are likely to be viewed positively by a potential employer:
a) Proactive management of your career to date ❏
b) Criticizing previous employers ❏
c) Making it clear that the position you are applying for is only a temporary arrangement until something more suitable comes along ❏
d) Making suggestions when you first meet them on how to improve their recruitment process ❏

10. The following behaviours are likely to be viewed negatively by a potential employer:
a) Striving to make all sources of information about you consistent and accurate ❏
b) Looking to present yourself as 'You at your best' ❏
c) Being truthful, honest and frank about both your skills and your areas of development ❏
d) Doing whatever it takes to get the job ❏

CHAPTER 7

Managing your online profile

As well as the paper version of your CV, it is likely that you will also have left evidence of your profile online, either intentionally or without realizing it.

Until this century, other than following up references supplied by you or having an informal conversation with a contact at your current organization, the only source of information initially open to a recruiting organization was contained within your CV.

Now, with a range of social media available to them, an increasing number of organizations review these sources in addition to the CV itself. In this chapter we look at the impact of social media sites on the information presented in a CV and how employers are using such information to cross-check information contained in CVs. We'll focus on:

- the ethical debate
- LinkedIn
- Facebook
- 'blogging' sites
- Twitter
- search engines
- review sites and news sites.

The ethical debate

There is some debate as to the ethics of using social media sites as a means of supplementing the information available from your CV. Many would argue that social media sites belong to the family and leisure side of life and as such should not be used for work-related reasons. They would also say that the veracity of such sources cannot be assumed, particularly if comments were not posted by the job applicant themselves.

Those on the other side of the argument would suggest that the information on social media sites provides a useful supplementary perspective on you as a person. Additionally, while the CV provides a snapshot of your situation, social media sites indicate various aspects of your character over time and are arguably a better insight into your qualities than the (one would assume) carefully worded content of your CV.

TIP *As an applicant, you should always assume that a prospective employer, or recruitment agency acting on their behalf, will at some stage look at your online presence.*

There are therefore grey areas in what information employers think is acceptable to take from social networking sites, but most organizations would be comfortable taking into account information from a business networking site such as LinkedIn – in effect treating your entry as an additional online CV. It is important, therefore, that you do actively manage your profile on such sites to ensure that the information you present is consistent with what you provide in your submitted CV.

What this means to any and all of us who are likely in future to apply for an employed position, as well as self-employed individuals seeking work from other organizations, is that ongoing management and care of your online persona is vitally important.

Let's now take a look at what types of online information in social media and other sites may have a bearing on how potential employers see you.

LinkedIn

This increasingly popular business-related social networking site is well used by people in work across the world, both as a means of creating an online profile and for networking with people in a similar type of work or sector.

In addition to profiles of individuals, there are an increasing number of organizational profiles, often linking to people who have previously been employed by them.

There is a high degree of usage of this site among recruitment agencies and organizations looking to employ personnel, a proportion of whom use the premium package enabling them to search across and communicate with all individuals profiled on the site, not just those they know ('are LinkedIn to').

How to manage your LinkedIn profile

- Keep your profile up to date and current.
- Put the job role or skill set you most want to be known for in the primary description. It is this field that shows up when a searching organization uses a key word search to identify a potential pool of people for a vacant role.
- If you elect to attach a photograph of yourself to your LinkedIn profile (many people do), use one that shows you in a professional light – in other words, not one of you enjoying yourself at a recent party.
- Keep all comments and updates you make to this site professional.

Facebook

As the most used social network in the world, this site needs little introduction. Anyone you know under the age of 30 has a page on this site, as do increasing numbers over this age. With its undoubted benefits to people in keeping connected with one another in a personal capacity, it does carry some risk if personal information and comments 'leak' into the world of work. There have been a number of cases in the media of individuals being disciplined or even dismissed by their employer due to negative comments or details of activities incompatible with their employment becoming known to their employer.

How to manage your Facebook profile

- Ensure that your privacy settings are set to the level of exposure you require. You may be surprised at the high number of people who have open settings, allowing people they don't know, as well as their employer, to view their Facebook pages. Bear in mind that with your privacy setting at 'Everyone', this means not just everyone on Facebook but everyone with access to the Internet.
- Review images tagged to your name on a regular basis to find out whether there are any photographs of a negative nature associated with you in this way. You may have adequate privacy controls on your Facebook page but your friends may not. Even if you think there are no images on the site showing you in a negative light, it is useful to know whether there are negative images linked to a person with the same name as you. These may be seen by a possible employer who mistakenly believes the image to be of you.

'Blogging' sites

Such sites, shortened from 'web log', generally take the form of online journals, diaries or day-to-day observations of anyone who cares to post them online. These can be immensely interesting and, indeed, entertaining. However, many are extremely opinionated and statements made can at times veer into the slanderous and occasionally malicious. This is of course the prerogative of the 'blogger'. However, opinions you shared and views you offered some time in the past may be incompatible with the employment roles that you may now be seeking.

 While in no way wishing to restrict anyone's right to free speech, it is wise to carefully consider what you write and how it may be perceived by a potential employer in the future.

Twitter

Twitter is what is known as a 'micro-blogging' site through which you can instantly send your thoughts to the world in short messages of up to 140 characters. As many in the public eye have found to their cost, it is very tempting to message on Twitter (known as 'tweeting') in response to a hot topic or to someone else's message and come to regret your words later.

While it is possible to remove your previous messages, it is also possible that they may have been captured by someone else or forwarded to others ('retweeted') and therefore continue to exist on the Internet in association with your name.

Search engines

If you have never done so, you may be surprised by what comes up if you search for your name using an Internet search engine. Much of what appears will relate to people with the same name as you (which can lead to misinformation in itself). You may also find references to comments you have made, or attributed to you, that you would rather a potential employer did not see.

There is little you can do about search engine entries without spending a fair amount of time or money investing in help to push such entries further down the search pages. The best course of action is a pre-emptive one in managing your online presence to reduce the likelihood of a negative comment relating to you appearing on the first few pages of an online search of your name. It is worth noting that such a search can pick up images as well as written comments, reinforcing the need to maintain the correct level of privacy settings on your social networking sites.

Review sites and news sites

Even people who are careful in managing their online presence may miss this one. If you have ever left a review of a hotel, a car hire firm or anything else on either their site or a third-party review site, for example TripAdvisor, in your own name, the chances are it will appear in the results of an Internet search of your name. If the review was particularly negative or contained strong language, such an entry may create an adverse impression if seen by a potential employer.

The popularity of a site (i.e. the amount of Internet traffic it receives) will determine to an extent how visible your comment becomes, with high traffic-flow sites being particularly prominent. The message again is to think carefully before making such comments, taking into account the impact they may have on your online reputation and on anyone in the future who may use the Internet to build a further impression of your character or your tendency to comment on, for example, previous employers.

Similarly to review sites, any comments you make in your own name in relation to an online news story could come to the attention of a potential employer. Commenting strongly on press stories, particularly ones that divide opinion, while perfectly within your rights in most territories, can be perceived negatively by prospective employers.

Consider the potential impact on your online reputation of any comments you make on review sites and news sites.

Summary

Gone are the days when you could manage how a potential employer perceives you by controlling what went into your CV and how you presented yourself at interview.

Your cumulative online presence creates an increasing amount of material to help an organization piece together additional information on your character and activities. Of course, there are dangers in an organization using such information, both in terms of accuracy and in stepping over the line between a person's private life and their work. However, as we have mentioned, many believe that if you 'put it out there' then they are entitled to take it into account when assessing your suitability for a position with them.

Overall then, the key message is that the information you provide, either intentionally or unintentionally, makes an impression on those who are in a position to offer you a new role. Keep this in mind when you interact online and every time you consider posting a comment, considering how this might be perceived in the future.

Fact-check (answers at the back)

1. The contents of your online profile:
   a) Are your own business and no one, least of all a potential employer, has any business prying through it ❑
   b) Should be recognized as a potential source of additional information about you and, as such, managed carefully ❑
   c) Cannot be controlled, so why bother? ❑
   d) Get erased every six months ❑

2. LinkedIn is:
   a) A business networking site that also allows you to include your resumé ❑
   b) A dating site ❑
   c) Only available to people working in commerce ❑
   d) Run by a cartel of recruitment agencies ❑

3. A particularly useful aspect of LinkedIn is that:
   a) Skills and experience mentioned in your headline profile appear in key word searches ❑
   b) It is increasingly monitored by potential employers and recruitment agencies alike ❑
   c) It is free to use at its basic level ❑
   d) All of the above ❑

4. Twitter is:
   a) A social networking site, therefore potential employers are legally obliged to ignore anything you say on it ❑
   b) A social networking (micro-blogging) site that enables anyone to make brief comments in real time (including when tired, emotional or drunk) ❑
   c) What birds do, so why is it relevant to this subject? ❑
   d) Set up in a way that lets only people you allow to see what you say ❑

5. Facebook:
   a) For a fee, will allow organizations to review your entire profile regardless of your privacy settings ❑
   b) Has introduced a 'timeline' component to profiles which, if not managed, could reveal past activities that you'd rather a potential employer didn't discover ❑
   c) Is now the preferred means of creating and submitting CVs in Scotland ❑
   d) Will automatically generate your CV for you, using material you have posted ❑

6. Online images of you:
a) Cannot be identified if they don't have your name on them ❏
b) Will not influence someone considering employing you ❏
c) Can still identify you if a search of your name pulls up an image that someone has tagged with your name ❏
d) Only underline how professional you are at all times ❏

7. When you write online reviews of products or services you have used:
a) These may still be seen years after you made them ❏
b) These may appear high up in a search engine list, due to volume of traffic to the original site ❏
c) You should work on the basis that a future employer may read them ❏
d) All of the above ❏

8. Organizations that ask you to submit your CV online via their website:
a) Will give preference to such applications over those sent by post ❏
b) Will give preference to documents submitted in hard copy ❏
c) Are increasing in number, so it is advisable to familiarize yourself with such a process ❏
d) Insist your document is protected using 128-bit encryption ❏

9. Anything you read online about a potential employer:
a) Is likely to be true ❏
b) Is only put there by disgruntled former employees ❏
c) Can be useful in helping you prepare for the interview process but treat with caution ❏
d) Will also be known to them ❏

10. At www.myperfectcv.co.uk/ cv-examples, you will find examples of
a) Good CVs ❏
b) Bad CVs ❏
c) Job descriptions ❏
d) Covering letters ❏

7 × 7

1 Seven trends for tomorrow

- A successful CV stays current and reflects how the world is changing.
- Use of online CVs such as LinkedIn is increasing.
- Employers are looking for more multilingual employees.
- Jobs for life continue to decline, so think of yourself as 'Me Co.' or 'Me Inc.' with skills and experience for hire – in both the long and short term.
- New technology is driving change, with the increasing use of automated CV grammar and spell checkers at first sift. Will hologram CVs be the next thing?
- We'll have a longer working life as a result of our increased life expectancy. Consider developing skills and experience for next phase of your working life, doing something completely different.
- Prospective employers are looking for more succinct CVs, so make yours short and snappy (and two pages at most).

2 Seven great organizations worth working for

- PricewaterhouseCoopers, www.pwc.co.uk
- KPMG, www.kpmg.com
- Apple Inc., www.apple.com/uk
- UNHCR, www.unhcr.org.uk
- Google, www.google.co.uk
- Médecins sans Frontières, www.msf.org.uk
- [Insert your name here] Incorporated/Limited

3 Seven things to do today

- Manage your career and your CV proactively – it keeps you motivated. Ask someone who employs or recruits for a local employer to review your CV and give you honest feedback (you never know, it may give you an opening).
- Check the spelling and grammar in your CV. This is vital. Then get someone else to do it again.
- Check that your Facebook settings are not public – those 'party photos' may put off prospective employers.
- Consider having your LinkedIn photograph professionally taken – a portrait in business dress appropriate for your sector works best generally.
- Check what's out there about you on Google and other search engines, including images. Manage your online presence.
- In your current role, take on new challenges and consider additional qualifications. Recent additions to your CV generally impress, showing that you continue to develop yourself.
- Stay positive. There's a role out there for you – your future employer just doesn't know about you yet.

4 Seven inspirational people who probably didn't need a CV

- Einstein – He was not seen as being clever by his teachers; all relative, I suppose.
- Bill Gates – He saw an opportunity and made the most of it.
- Edith Cavell – Look her up. Hers is an amazing story of courage and selflessness.
- Steve Jobs – He had a vision where others didn't, and saw it through.
- Ghandi – This was a true leader who knew what his people needed.

- Nelson Mandela – He lived with a clear purpose and great dignity.
- The best teacher or mentor you ever had – If it's not too late, let them know.

5 Seven words and phrases to avoid in your CV (and what employers think of them)

- 'Motivated self-starter' – I will be the judge of that when I see what your timekeeping is like.
- 'Passionate' – This is one of the most inappropriately used adjectives, particularly when preceding 'about bookkeeping' or similar. Keep it real.
- 'Huge leadership potential' – You don't seem to have found anyone to lead yet.
- 'Capability to work unsupervised' – You wish.
- 'Creative talent' – You mean you don't like doing the boring day-to-day stuff.
- 'Can speak conversational Spanish/French' – You can order a coffee or a beer in a bar.
- 'Popular with managers and colleagues alike' – Hmmm.

6 Seven core skills every potential employer would like to see in a CV

- Effective communicator: you get across your point as accurately and efficiently as possible, recognizing that other people have different communication styles and preferences (some get to the point quickly, others are born storytellers). Communication style isn't an indicator of intelligence.

- Good decision maker: you can make the right decision, even where there is ambiguity in a situation and the guidance doesn't wholly cover it.
- Team player: you have an ability to work effectively with the people around you, including customers, colleagues, suppliers and supervisors.
- Ethical: you do the right thing ethically and morally.
- Self-aware: you know your limitations and can identify areas for development and do something about them.
- Empathic: you take into account the needs, feelings and aspirations of others in the decisions you make and actions you take.
- Modest: You are able to take honestly offered feedback in the spirit it was intended and use it to be better at what you do.

7 Seven aspirational entries in the CV of your life

- Learned all I could from my parents, friends, colleagues and teachers.
- Matched my talents, energy and experience to roles, not being afraid to move or change when it didn't work out.
- Passed on my accumulated knowledge and experience to those who were ready to receive it, without expectation of reward and with no agenda.
- Travelled as much as I could, seeking out different cultures and experiences (for example, going to the opera at least once).
- Didn't stress about issues or situations over which I had no control.
- Stayed true to myself while remaining sensitive to the feelings of others.
- Regretted nothing (helped by making the most of my time on this wonderful planet and making good life decisions along the way).

PART 2

Your Job Hunting Masterclass

PART 2
Your Job-Hunting
Masterclass

Introduction

In this Part of the book you will learn everything you need to know about successful job hunting. By the end you will find that you have a formidable store of practical information at your fingertips for dealing with the tough challenges that all serious job hunters have to face sooner or later.

Whether you are a newcomer to the world of work or a second, third or fourth jobber, you will find plenty here for you. Whether you are simply looking to better yourself, are facing redundancy or trying to break into an entirely new field – in fact, whatever your situation is – the task of finding opportunities that are consistent with the aim you have set yourself is still the same.

CHAPTER 8

Understanding today's job market

In this chapter you will learn about how the job market is made up of two sectors:

1 **The visible market:** the jobs that are advertised in newspapers, or on the Internet or anywhere else where they are open for everyone to see. Here the challenge is engaging and seeing off competition, especially where the jobs are good jobs

2 **The invisible market:** the jobs that are rumoured to be the best jobs; the jobs that, for one reason or another, employers keep to themselves. Here the challenge is finding out about these jobs and, when you have, knowing what to do to get your face in the frame.

Just as the visible and invisible markets are very different, so are the techniques you have to use to engage with them:

- **Reactive sourcing** is how you access jobs on the visible market
- **Proactive sourcing** is how you access jobs on the invisible market.

The terms 'reactive sourcing' and 'proactive sourcing' will come up again and again. It is important that you get used to the terms and understand what they mean and to what they refer.

The job jungle

Imagine you're setting off on a journey through the jungle all on your own. The first few steps you take will be bold ones until you find out the jungle is a strange place where there are no paths to follow and no signposts to show you the way. You press on regardless, hoping everything will be OK, but after a while you're thrashing around in the undergrowth hopelessly lost. Sooner or later despair takes over and all you want is the quickest way out.

Going out on to today's job market can be a bit like this. At times it seems impenetrable and hostile. At times it feels like all you're doing is going round in circles and achieving nothing. At times all you will want to do is sit down on the ground and put your head in your hands.

TIP

WARNING!

Discouragement *is what happens to people who thrash around in the job jungle with no clear sense of direction. In job hunting, discouragement is what you need to avoid at all costs.*

Job hunters' concerns

A few years ago we asked a random sample of candidates for junior to middle-management posts in manufacturing industry to list what concerned them most about today's job market conditions. This is what they came up with:

- the sheer volume of competition for good jobs – the difficulty in even getting interviews
- bad manners (employers not replying to applications or letting candidates know how they got on at interviews)
- the so-called invisible market – the rumoured 90 per cent of jobs that aren't advertised; how to find out about such jobs
- the risk attached to changing jobs; the fear of making bad moves and what could follow.

Understanding today's job market

So what's going on here and why do so many people see today's job market as such a 'difficult' place? Let's take a closer look and see what we can find out.

Few of us need any reminding that the world in which we live and work has changed very substantially in the last 20 years. Big smokestack industries have for the large part gone. Dozens and dozens of small start-up businesses have taken their place – to the extent that the small firm sector is now an important provider of quality employment (a fact no one should ignore).

Even with big firms, the need to cut costs has driven many of them to downsize and streamline. What's more, this downsizing and streamlining has been accompanied in many cases by breaking up once large structures into smaller, more manageable units (fragmentation).

How do these changes affect the way recruitment is handled?

Classic recruitment

We have coined this term to describe most people's conception of what the recruitment process involves. The following example will help you understand what it is.

Example: Company X

Company X has a vacancy for an IT Manager. Company X is a major player in the automotive components industry and it employs approximately 5,000 people spread across three locations. The instruction to proceed with recruitment is given to Company X's human resources department. Advertisements are placed in various newspapers and on the company's website. The vacancy is also given to two firms of recruitment consultants specializing in IT staff. As a result, 30 applications are received, from which the human resources department picks out 15 for preliminary interview. From these preliminary interviews, a shortlist of five candidates is put forward to the Chief Executive for final selection purposes. At each stage unsuccessful candidates are informed in writing.

Recruitment today

Big companies Classic recruitment still goes on, of course, but in many big companies where classic recruitment used to be practised, very different circumstances now prevail.

For a start, human resources departments suffered more than most in the various phases of headcount slashing we have seen in recent years. Viewed as peripheral to the core activity of businesses, they have, in some cases, been disposed of altogether while in others they have been reduced to mere shadows of their former selves. The result? We see recruitment today pushed more and more on to the shoulders of line managers, meaning the standard to which it is done depends on:

● how much time and what resources they can give it (bearing in mind they have other functions to discharge as well), *and*
● how experienced they are.

Time and resources are, of course, major areas of concern for all practising managers but, to add to the problems, the delayerings, restructurings and downsizings of recent years have left many of them with little or nothing in the way of administrative support. Witness the fact that the armies of secretaries and assistants who once used to surround senior managers in big companies have to all intents and purposes gone. Today the same senior managers are more likely to have to do their own fetching and carrying, take their own phone calls and, in some cases, do their own typing as well.

Small companies Small companies have never carried human resources departments (at least not as a rule). Recruitment has always been dealt with by busy managers with other responsibilities. What's different about small companies is that there are a lot more of them about.

Bad manners?

Why are employers so remiss about responding to applications these days? Has there been an outbreak of bad manners as some job hunters seem to think?

Not that we wish to excuse employers who don't reply to candidates' letters but the explanation, very often, is not rudeness but some hard-pressed manager faced with the problem of finding a replacement for a key member of staff who has decided to leave. What happens is this. An ad is put in the paper and maybe a few firms of recruitment consultants are contacted. Where the job is a good job, the result is a glut of applications. Bearing in mind that our manager is probably not too used to such situations, they respond by picking out a couple of letters which catch their eye then put the rest to one side with the intention of dealing with them later. Another crisis crops up followed by another and, like any good manager, they respond by prioritizing. As a result, jobs like replying to a bunch of unsuccessful applicants get pushed to the bottom of the pile from where they may never surface.

Quick fixes

Another facet of the downsized delayered world we live in is the way gaps in the ranks of key people quickly cause companies problems.

Example: Company Y

Company Y is a manufacturing plant employing 600 people. Previously, Company Y had a three-tier management structure:

Manufacturing Director

▼

Section managers (5)

▼

Cell managers (30)

Five years ago, faced with intense global competition and the urgent need to cut operating costs, Company Y decided to take out the section management tier from its structure, leaving cell managers reporting directly to the Manufacturing Director. As a consequence of this, wherever a cell manager's position is vacant, shop floor personnel have a direct line to the Manufacturing

The invisible job market

Classic recruitment is time-consuming and hard work. It has little appeal therefore to hard-pressed managers with vacancies that need filling fast and a thousand and one other concerns clamouring for their attention. So what happens in these situations? The answer is they do what all resourceful managers do; they look for short cuts.

Here is an example of a short cut:

'If we advertise positions in the press, we find ourselves inundated with response – 90 per cent of which is totally unsuitable. Rather than give ourselves this kind of hassle, we prefer first of all to see if there is anyone we know in the trade. If there isn't, we usually go to a few firms of recruitment consultants and ask them to put up a shortlist of candidates from their files.'

A vast and largely untapped invisible job market has emerged in recent years – jobs that are never advertised and are filled by one of three methods:

1 **Approach** – companies sourcing people through their networks of contacts within given industries or trades or using headhunters to do this task for them
2 **Recruitment consultants** – accessing candidates by asking firms of recruitment consultants to search their files for suitable candidates
3 **Previous applicants** – revisiting applicants for previous jobs, including unsolicited CVs.

There are other reasons apart from the ones we have touched on already for the growth in the invisible market. Let three senior executives from the new breed of small knowledge-based businesses explain:

'The people we're interested in won't necessarily be looking for another job. This is why advertising doesn't work for us.'

'We're seeking people with scarce and very defined skills. We find the only way of getting such people is by going to specialist firms of recruitment consultants.'

'Picking up a square peg in a senior management job is a major area of concern for us because of the damage it could do to a team-based business like this. When we recruit, therefore, we always enlist the help of headhunters. We feel happier about people who come to us with a headhunter's recommendation.'

The key points to pick out here are:

● the increased awareness today of the downsides of making poor selection decisions, particularly where the vacant slot is a position of responsibility; not only is there the damage to the business to be considered but also the prospect of litigation if the bad choice has to be exited quickly
● the impact of skills shortages on businesses: the widely held view that recruiting people with scarce skills calls for something 'special'
● the growth of headhunting as a preferred method of recruiting, particularly where senior executive appointments are concerned; the 'comfort' factor that headhunting offers.

There are just three things you need to appreciate about the invisible market:

1 it's big
2 it's getting bigger
3 you need to get in on it.

Reactive and proactive sourcing

The last job for this chapter is to introduce you to some useful terminology.

Reactive sourcing

This is where the stimulus is provided by the employer – usually in the form of advertising. Here you are responding to an invitation to put yourself forward and the quality of your response is what counts. Reactive sourcing is used to attack the visible market.

Proactive sourcing

This is job hunting aimed at the invisible market – where, to penetrate the walls and get your face in the frame, the stimulus needs to come from you.

Successful job hunting today means having the capacity to attack both the visible and the invisible markets, which in turn means using a 'mix 'n' match' of proactive and reactive sourcing. Too many candidates put all their effort into the latter (replying to advertisements), meaning they miss out on some of the better opportunities the market offers.

Summary

One of the reasons why candidates prefer to put their effort into reactive sourcing is because, on the face of it, it is easy. All you have to do is sit at home and flick through the local evening paper on jobs night, comb through the ads in your professional journals, check out a few websites and there you have it. Job done, or so you think, whereas in reality all you have looked at is a tiny fragment of what's out there for you. By completely ignoring the invisible market you have effectively put a barrier between yourself and what could be the best of what the market in its complete state has to offer.

The conclusion to what we have just done is therefore that the job market is like any other market. You don't dictate the way it works. It has its own rules and you have to learn to play by them or you will find yourself constantly in situations where, unless luck is on your side, you will end up banging your head on brick walls.

The message? Adapt your job hunting strategies to how the market works today and not to the way it was years ago. Learn to move with the times. Don't get left behind.

Fact-check (answers at the back)

1. The best jobs are found on the Internet. Do you...
   a) Agree? ❏
   b) Agree strongly? ❏
   c) Disagree? ❏
   d) Have no opinion? ❏

2. What percentage of jobs are never advertised?
   a) Over 90% ❏
   b) 75–90% ❏
   c) 50–75% ❏
   d) Under 50% ❏

3. You wrote off for a job that you saw advertised. Four weeks passed and you heard nothing. When you ring the firm's human resources department, you are told the job has been filled. Do you...
   a) Ask why your application has been unsuccessful? ❏
   b) Ask why they didn't let you know? ❏
   c) Ask both a) and b)? ❏
   d) Say thank you and goodbye? ❏

4. Where do you find invisible market jobs advertised?
   a) On the Internet ❏
   b) You don't find them advertised ❏
   c) In newspapers ❏
   d) Don't know ❏

5. Which of the following is an example of reactive sourcing?
   a) Registering with an agency ❏
   b) Calling companies to see if they have any vacancies ❏
   c) Looking at employers' websites ❏
   d) Sending in an unsolicited CV ❏

6. Which of the following is an example of proactive sourcing?
   a) Replying to advertisements in professional journals ❏
   b) Doing nothing ❏
   c) Asking round your colleagues and contacts ❏
   d) None of the above ❏

7. What is 'approach'?
   a) Replying to an advertisement and being asked to attend an interview ❏
   b) A friend asking you to help them find a job ❏
   c) What recruitment consultants do ❏
   d) Employers using their contacts to source staff ❏

8. In what order should you do your sourcing?
   a) Reactive sourcing first ❏
   b) Proactive sourcing first ❏
   c) Both at the same time ❏
   d) It depends ❏

9. You apply for 50 jobs and don't get a single interview. Do you...
   a) Keep going? ❏
   b) Take stock first then keep going? ❏
   c) Give up? ❏
   d) Go down the pub? ❏

10. You send in an unsolicited CV and hear nothing. Do you...
    a) Ring in and ask if it has been received? ❏
    b) As a) but complain? ❏
    c) Send in another unsolicited CV? ❏
    d) Do nothing? ❏

124

CHAPTER 9

Availability, accessibility and application

In this chapter you will learn three important rules for going out on the job market. They are:

- **Availability** The importance of 'being there' and being contactable when employers want to speak to you. The importance of being available to go to interviews at times when employers choose
- **Accessibility** The importance of making yourself understood to employers so it is clear to them who you are, where you are coming from and what you are seeking to achieve
- **Application** The importance of putting all your effort into job hunting and not treating it as something that you pick up when you feel like it and put it down again when you are less inclined.

These rules – known collectively as the **'Three As'** – are central to successful job hunting in the market conditions that prevail today, and in this chapter we will spend time looking at each of them more closely.

By the end you will be able to see for yourself where, without knowing it, you might be putting obstacles in the way of employers who are trying to engage with you. If you are, then before you go any further you need to take steps to clear the obstacles out of the way.

Availability

Being in the right place at the right time helps with most things in life and job hunting is no exception. Being there, being easy for employers to contact, and having the capacity to attend interviews as and when required all go a long way to ensuring successful outcomes in today's market conditions. This is why you need to audit your availability before you set foot into the job market, i.e. before lack of availability becomes the reason for you not having much joy.

How do you do this? Go through the following checklist and answer the questions as truthfully as you can.

Availability checklist

● How would prospective employers get on if they needed to get hold of you in a hurry? Would they have your email or phone numbers where they could contact you?

● Similarly, if the same employers needed to speak to you out of hours, would they have phone numbers or your home email where you could be reached?

● Could contacting you involve hassle in the shape of phones that aren't answered or lines that are engaged for long periods?

● What would your answer be if an employer needed to get you in for an interview in office hours some time within the next seven days? Would you be able to get the time off work or would it be difficult for you?

Going through this checklist will help you to expose flaws in your availability. Hopefully, it will also throw up some points for action such as:

● redoing your CV so that all telephone points of contact are included – by this we mean your home, work and mobile telephone numbers. In the case of your home number, it is advisable to give an indication of the time when you normally get in (e.g. 'after 6.30 p.m.')
● making sure all your phone numbers have voicemail
● making sure you check your email and voicemail messages regularly
● making sure you check for any missed calls

- introducing a few disciplines at home such as telling members of the family to keep their phone conversations brief, especially early in the evening (when people such as employers, headhunters and recruitment consultants could be trying to get through)
- always keeping back a few days' holiday in case you need to go for interviews
- cleaning up your answer tape – with the prospect of employers, recruitment consultants and headhunters ringing you up, now's the time to take those silly messages off your voicemail!

Make yourself available

Lack of availability sometimes has unusual causes. Often you are the last to find out about them.

Today the phone is used more and more for contacting job applicants. This is, in part, a reflection of the instantaneous, paper-free world we live in, in part the pressure on management time, and in part the increasing involvement of people like headhunters who do most of their business on the phone. As a consequence, interview lists are frequently decided on the basis of who can be contacted and who can't. Candidates who are difficult to get hold of are candidates who get given the miss.

Accessibility

A prospective employer needs to be able to see who you are, where you are coming from and what you are capable of doing in a very compressed period of time. Needless to say, accessibility has got a lot to do with the design of your CV. It has particular relevance to two situations:

1 **The visible market** – where you are applying for a good job which has been widely advertised. Here the problem is going to be competition. You will be one of many applicants and somehow your CV has got to stand out from the rest.
2 **The invisible market** – where you are mailshotting your CV to employers on the off chance that there may be something

suitable for you. Unsolicited CVs tend to get the 'quick read' treatment, so, again, they need to catch the reader's eye to prevent them from being binned instantly.

Revisiting your CV

It goes almost without saying that you won't get very far on your trip into the job jungle without a CV. If you don't have an up-to-date CV, then take steps now to get one prepared. If you already have one, now is the time to take a critical look at what you've got and to see how it stands up from an accessibility point of view.

Here to help is a list of common accessibility problems. If you recognize any of them in your CV, take the necessary action to put them right.

- **Too long (or too short)** Two pages of A4 is the recommended length for a CV. Anything over three sheets of A4 is suspect. Long CVs don't get read or don't get read properly. Equally, don't go to the other extreme and summarize your whole life on half a page of A4. CVs that are too short are no better than those that are too long.
- **Too inconcise** Long, rambling descriptions tend to lose the reader's attention and the detail of what you did in a job ten years ago isn't likely to be of much interest to anyone.
- **Too much jargon** Some recipients of your CV will be generalists, such as human resources managers and selection consultants. Bear this in mind and avoid using jargon that people from other backgrounds may not understand.
- **No clear statement of your aims** Someone who reads your CV needs to know what you're hoping to achieve by changing jobs. If you're looking for more money, for example, you need to make this clear by stating the figure you have in mind.
- **Poor presentation** This is usually the result of trying to cram too much information into too little space. Narrow margins, small font sizes of the sort that have readers searching frantically for their glasses (or conversely not bothering), lack of white space on the page – these are all factors which detract from your CV being a quick and easy read. The

answer? Edit furiously. Stick to presenting an overview and leave out the reams of detail.

- **Lack of logical order** CVs that 'jump about' fail on accessibility – for example, CVs that intersperse education and qualifications with information about experience gained during employment. Don't confuse your readers. Surprisingly, lack of logical order is one of the commonest problems with CVs.
- **Not customized** Don't use the same CV for every job application you make. Let the wonders of modern software help you customize your CV to the job you're applying for.

> **TIP** *Don't fight shy of making radical changes to the layout of your CV. Even if you've paid a small fortune to have your CV professionally prepared, don't hesitate to chop it about if you feel aims, achievements and qualifications don't come across sufficiently clearly.*

A useful image to have in mind as you go through your CV is that of some stressed-out, overworked senior executive given the task of wading through a hundred job applications with a view to picking out a few for interview. Just to add a bit of flavour, let's say our senior executive decides to leave this task till the end of the day when the telephone traffic has died down but when he won't be at his best for giving his full and undivided attention. Typically, he'll cast his eye over each application searching out key points that look OK (e.g. a certain type of experience). From this quick flick through he'll put the applications into three piles: the ones that interest him, the don't-knows, and the no-hopers. When he's finished doing this, he'll probably look at the 'yes' pile again just to make doubly sure he's picked out the right people.

If the number of applications in the 'yes' pile happens to coincide with what our senior executive views as a reasonable number of people to call in for interview, that will be that as far as the preliminary sifting process is concerned – i.e. the don't-knows will be joining the unsuitables in the turndown pile. If the pile is a bit thin on numbers, however, the don't-knows might just get a second airing.

The point to grasp? That even though not all recruitment will be dealt with in this way, your CV has still got to be capable of surviving this kind of treatment. It has got to hit our weary senior executive in the eye first time because, if it doesn't, it stands a good chance of ending up in a place where it is unlikely ever to see the light of day again.

Before leaving our senior executive to his after-hours reading, it is worth pondering on the fact that, once he's finished putting his interview list together, he could round off the evening by ringing the candidates he's picked out. Here is where your availability comes in: the ones he manages to contact will be invited for interview; the ones he doesn't may not get another chance.

Application

One of the big challenges you face on your journey through the job jungle is having the tenacity to keep going and not be put off by any of the difficulties that you encounter. This is partly to do with avoiding discouragement and partly to do with keeping your expectations in line. With the latter:

- don't expect to be invited for an interview every time you apply for a job (it won't happen)
- don't expect everyone to be nice to you.

Picking up on the second of these points, employers' standards vary enormously and not all the treatment you receive will be to your liking. The mistake, however, is to let bad experiences get to you so they become a source of discouragement and a reason for you throwing in the towel prematurely.

Employers who don't reply

Going back to the previous chapter, we saw the concerns about employers who don't reply to applications or don't let candidates know how they got on at interviews. We saw at the same time, however, that these omissions are not always manifestations of bad manners – as some job hunters seem to think – but evidence of organizations in turmoil or managers under pressure – in short, nothing very unusual in the modern-day business world.

The message? Don't get wound up about employers whose communication skills are lacking, and to some extent condition yourself to accepting this kind of treatment as the norm. Certainly don't let the general standards of employers' behaviour become the reason for you giving up because you feel you can't take any more.

> ## Unsolicited CVs
>
> Don't expect anyone to reply to an unsolicited CV – even if you enclose a stamped addressed envelope. Mailshotting prospective employers is an excellent way of accessing the elusive invisible market. The aim, however, is to sow seeds rather than chalk up streams of polite acknowledgements. Judge the performance of your unsolicited CVs on what matters – i.e. on the number of interesting interviews you are invited to attend.

Prepare for the hard knocks

Even if you can learn to live with employers who don't reply to your applications, because of its diversity the modern job market can still be a hostile and unpredictable place. Expect, therefore, your path to success to be littered with bad interview experiences and brushes with employers who don't seem to know what they're doing. Try to find ways of hardening yourself against the knocks.

Anything else?

What other preparations do you need to make before you set out on your job-hunting expedition?

Time off work

Having the capacity to take time off work to attend interviews is, as we have seen, an important part of your availability and, for this reason, you must always keep back a few days of your holiday entitlement.

The point stretches a little further, however. As part of your preparations for going out on to the job market, you must condition yourself into viewing your time off work as precious and something not to be squandered. An example of squandering time off work is using it to attend interviews for jobs that wouldn't interest you even if they were offered to you. We will be exploring this use of time off work in more detail in the next chapter when we will be looking at targeting – that is, making sure the jobs you're applying for are the right jobs.

For most of us, the time we can get off work is limited and even stock excuses like 'going to see the dentist' can start to wear thin after they've been used a few times. Not all employers will be happy to do interviews out of hours and this is certainly something you shouldn't be banking on.

Giving up smoking

While smoking in workplaces is banned in many countries where this book will be read, there is still concern on the part of many employers about the image of the business projected by the familiar huddle of smokers outside the front entrance to the offices. The question 'Do you smoke?' is therefore one that employers often ask at interviews or on their application forms. So much the better, for you, therefore, if you can answer truthfully 'No' – and better for your health too.

If you don't smoke, consider advertising the fact somewhere on your CV. Who knows, it might just tip the balance when it comes to deciding whether to include you on the interview list or not.

Summary

Availability, accessibility and application are about accepting the realities of life in the business world we live in today. Managers with positions to fill are often working under pressure so that candidates who are seen as 'difficult' won't hold much appeal. 'Difficult' in this context includes candidates:

- who don't return their voicemail messages the same day
- who want to attend interviews only at times when it suits them
- who start laying down conditions (e.g. 'I will only take time off work to come for an interview if you tell me what the pay is first')
- whose CVs are a jumble and need reading more than once.

Where a job is a good job and where it has been advertised (typical visible market situation), competition is always going to be an issue. Here is where you will score heavily if you can offer availability and accessibility.

The third of the three As – application – is about keeping going and not letting turn-down letters and bad interview experiences put you off. Don't expect the job market to be nice to you – not all the time.

Fact-check (answers at the back)

1. You miss out on an interview because the employer could not contact you. Do you...
   a) Feel it is the employer's fault? ❏
   b) Feel it is your fault? ❏
   c) At the same time as b), take steps to make sure it doesn't happen again? ❏
   d) Shrug it off? ❏

2. An employer asks you to go for an interview but you can't get time off work because you have used up all your holidays. Do you...
   a) Tell the employer you will attend only if the interview can be held on a Saturday morning? ❏
   b) Tell your boss you have a dental appointment? ❏
   c) Give the interview a miss? ❏
   d) Put your job hunting on hold until you have got some holiday back? ❏

3. What is the commonest problem with CVs?
   a) Too long ❏
   b) Lack of logical order ❏
   c) Poorly presented ❏
   d) Spelling mistakes ❏

4. You go for an interview and you are kept waiting for an hour because the applicant before you arrived late. Do you...
   a) Sit patiently? ❏
   b) Walk out? ❏
   c) Feel it is a bad reflection on the employer? ❏
   d) Complain? ❏

5. Which of the 'three As' is the most important?
   a) Availability ❏
   b) Accessibility ❏
   c) Application ❏
   d) All of the above ❏

6. What is the method of contacting job applicants that employers use most?
   a) Phone ❏
   b) Email ❏
   c) Text message ❏
   d) Letter ❏

7. You want to send out a batch of unsolicited CVs. Which of the following methods will guarantee you get a reply?
   a) Emailing your CV ❏
   b) Putting it in the post with a stamped addressed envelope ❏
   c) Sending it on a fax ❏
   d) None of the above ❏

8. You don't want to receive phone calls at work. Do you...
   a) Leave your mobile number off your CV? ❏
   b) Include it but indicate that it is only to be used after 6 p.m.? ❏
   c) Turn off the ring tone and pick up any missed calls and voicemail messages? ❏
   d) Keep your phone switched off when you are at work? ❏

9. When should you expect employers to ring you?

a) Between 9 a.m. and 6 p.m. on weekdays ❏

b) Up to 7 p.m. on weekdays ❏

c) At any time ❏

d) As b), but on Saturday mornings as well ❏

10. How many versions of your CV do you need?

a) One ❏

b) One for every application ❏

c) Five ❏

d) Ten maximum ❏

CHAPTER 10

Targeting the right jobs

In this chapter you will learn about targeting. Targeting is what gives your job hunting its sense of direction.

Targeting is simple – so simple that it is surprising that more people don't do it. Targeting is about being clear about what you are looking for, so you know from the outset which jobs you should be applying for and which you should be leaving alone. By targeting properly your effort is therefore focused and not spread out. You get out of the habit of seeing job hunting as an exercise in chalking up how many applications you can send off. Instead, you are selective and, as you will soon see, there are enormous benefits in this picky and choosy approach.

Targeting is an exercise that you need to carry out before you set out on your perilous expedition into the job jungle. Otherwise you run the risk of thrashing round aimlessly, and then, when you see what little progress you have made, you end up giving in. Worse still, you will see your expedition as wasted effort and it may put you off trying again.

The aims of targeting

Targeting has two aims:

- **Reducing failure** Not getting chosen for interview or going for an interview and finding you don't get put on the shortlist has a discouraging and demoralizing effect. The less of this you have to deal with, the better.
- **Reducing time-wasting** Job hunting is time-consuming. The time you give it has to be put to most effective use.

Targeting is about being *selective* with your job applications. Applying for hundreds and hundreds of jobs just because they happen to be there has no virtue to it at all. You succeed in doing nothing except:

- chalking up large numbers of 'sorry but no thank you' letters (inviting discouragement)
- frittering away your time off work time on utterly pointless interviews (loss of an important part of your availability).

Realism

Targeting needs to be done in the context of what the job market can reasonably be expected to deliver. If you set off in pursuit of unattainable targets, then, practically speaking, it is almost as bad as setting off with no targets at all.

Jobs you can't do

Although we're all entitled to have our dreams, there are some jobs that quite clearly we can't do because we don't have the necessary experience or qualifications. These jobs that are out of our range are usually self-evident to us, but occasionally we need reminding that we may be trying to take a step too far.

The signs of over-reaching? Inevitably, they are the number of applications where you find you don't even get as far as the interview list. The big danger in over-reaching, however, is that, if you carry on doing it, you finish up feeling dejected and discouraged. The answer is, therefore, to take stock from time to time. If your job hunting has been largely fruitless, ask yourself if you could be falling into the trap of applying for jobs you can't do. This is a case of acting on the feedback that the market is providing you with – feedback that's telling you you're trying to achieve something that's unattainable.

TIP *In a world where selection standards are not always consistent, there is the chance you could be offered a job that's beyond your capabilities. If you accept, needless to say, your celebrations are likely to be short-lived. Your lack of capability will be found out pretty quickly and it won't be too surprising if you find yourself on the receiving end of the short, sharp exit treatment.*

Jobs that don't exist

Incredible though it sounds, there are a lot of people out there pursuing jobs that don't exist or jobs that are in very short supply. Here are a few examples:

- Doug – who wants a job where he doesn't have to do shifts but where, at the same time, he won't have to take a drop in the high level of earnings he gets for working unsociable hours.
- Gaenor – who works in customer support and who wants a job where she can have every Wednesday off to go to college.
- John – who makes good money doing work he finds boring. John wants to make a complete change in career without having to take a drop in his earnings.
- Steve – who wants a senior management job where he won't have to put up with the hassle he gets now.
- Ruth – who wants a high-powered career in marketing without having to travel any further than ten miles from where she lives.

The conditions that Doug, Gaenor and the others are imposing on the jobs they're looking for effectively wipe out most, if not all, of the available market. What they are attempting to do really is dictate to the market and, not surprisingly, it doesn't work.

The lesson? Again, listen carefully to the feedback. What is it telling you? Could it be telling you, for example, that what employers have to offer and what you are looking for simply don't match up? If it does, stop what you're doing immediately and take stock. The mistake – and plenty make it – is to flog on in pursuit of these near-impossible aims year after year till discouragement sets in.

TIP *Feedback or experience is an important part of job hunting because, at the outset, few of us have any meaningful idea of what the market for our particular talents really has to offer. What all successful job hunters do is learn from their experience and, in this way, accumulate quite formidable stores of knowledge on the demand for people in their niche occupational area. Listening to feedback is therefore important. Ignoring it is something you do at your peril.*

Targeting benchmarks

Having dealt with the problems of targeting jobs you can't do and jobs that don't exist (or only exist in very small numbers), we want to turn our attention to looking at how to set about targeting jobs properly. To do this we need you to get some fixed points of reference, or benchmarks, in your mind. Targeting benchmarks will be there to help you when it comes to deciding which jobs to apply for and which to leave alone. They will help you to deal with people like recruitment consultants (people who will be using their contacts and know-how to search for jobs on your behalf). They also act as a fail-safe – making sure you take the right jobs and leave the wrong ones alone.

Targeting benchmarks can be broken down as follows:

- **The job** This should be the easy part. What are you seeking to gain from your job hunting? Is it promotion, for example? If so, what's the next job up the ladder?
- **The pay** More pay is often the reason why people look for another job. Pay is tricky and this is why we will deal with it separately (keep reading).
- **The area** How mobile you are clearly has a bearing on the kind of jobs you will be applying for. For example, are you a

truly global person who is happy to work anywhere in the world or, at the other end of the scale, do your partner's job and/or family commitments tie you to looking for work within commuting distance of where you live now?

- **The risk** Would you only be interested in a secure job with a big-name employer or would you be happy to entertain something with a little more risk attached to it (e.g. a start-up business)? Again, a lot here will depend on your domestic situation. Are you the sole breadwinner for your family, for example? Or does your partner have a secure, well-paid job, meaning, perhaps that you can afford to take a few risks?

- **The hours** Some jobs involve working strange or anti-social hours. How would you feel about this? Alternatively, are you just looking for something part-time or hours that fit round your other commitments?

- **The prospects** Are these important to you? If so, it will rule out any employers where the prospects are limited (e.g. very small firms in static- or low-growth situations).

- **Anything else?** What we're fishing for here is anything peculiar to you that will have a bearing on the kind of job you can go for. For example, do you have a medical problem that could preclude working in certain industries or environments? Or would your family circumstances make it difficult for you to have nights away from home?

Simple though it seems, this exercise in setting out your targeting benchmarks is what will give your job hunting the structure and direction it needs. Targeting, remember, is about being selective. This means that any job that falls short of your targeting benchmarks is a job you won't be applying for. Another way of looking at this is: the more focused you are on the target, the more chances you have of hitting it.

> **TIP** *Don't fall into the trap of scanning the ads and applying for jobs simply because they're there. If weeks go by without seeing a job that comes up to scratch, view it as evidence that your targeting is working.*

The problem of pay

Pay, as we noted a few moments ago, is an awkward area mainly because a conflict can and does arise between:

- your estimation of your own worth, *and*
- what the market is capable of offering at any one given point.

One of the bigger problems here is that, at the outset of job hunting, you will have little or no idea of what the market can provide – in short, whether the kind of figures you have in mind are going over the top, not enough or somewhere in between.

Sources of information on rates of pay

When setting your pay targeting benchmark, try tapping into three sources:

1 **the visible market** – the jobs you see advertised in newspapers, journals or on websites (jobs which call for people with similar skills and experience to yours)
2 **your networks** – contacts in your profession who may be able to give you some valuable inside information on what other employers pay
3 **recruitment professionals** – somewhere along the line you will be talking to people like recruitment consultants, people whose job it is to know about going rates.

From these sources you will be able to form a quick overview of whether the figure you have in mind is realizable or not. Incidentally, don't rule out the possibility of finding out that you're not so badly paid after all – meaning:

- if your only reason for changing jobs is more money, you may want to think again
- if your problem is something other than money (e.g. security, lack of prospects), you may have to contemplate stepping sideways (or even backwards) pay-wise.

Fine-tuning your pay targeting benchmark

Fine-tuning your pay targeting benchmark is something you do in the light of experience. For example, if the feedback you get from your job hunting suggests you may be asking for too much, then be ready to do one of the following:

- tweak your benchmark down a few notches
- stick with your original benchmark but realize that you're targeting just a narrow segment of well-paid jobs (top-end targeting)
- call off your job hunting altogether.

Targeting and accessibility

If you go back to Chapter 9, you will remember the point we made about making employers aware of exactly where you're coming from and what you're seeking to achieve. You will remember also that the main vehicle for this transparency and accessibility is your CV.

A common misunderstanding of the purpose of a CV is to see it only as the means of getting you interviews. While this is important, it is equally important that your CV conveys enough about you and your ambitions to enable employers to spot any mismatches between what you want and what they've got to offer. Don't, therefore, be tempted to use your CV to pull the wool over people's eyes. Present yourself exactly as you are and help employers to make the judgement as to whether the job is right for you or not. Getting interviews is no good if the jobs are time-wasters.

Summary

As you have found out, targeting is not just something you do at the start of your expedition into the job jungle. Rather, it is something that you keep doing as you go along. You keep adjusting the compass bearings. You learn from every job application you make. You listen to the feedback you get from every interview you go to. You listen to what people like recruitment consultants tell you. You pick the brains of colleagues who have been active on the job market recently.

From all these sources you put together a picture and you keep comparing the picture with the targeting benchmarks you have drawn up. If you see the benchmarks diverging from what you see in the picture, then it is time to take stock.

Here, always be prepared to be flexible and do not fall into the trap of setting your ideas in cement. Ideas get better if you give them a chance to develop, whereas fixed ideas can and do have a tendency to veer away from reality. Sooner than you know it, you are back to those jobs that you can't do or that don't exist.

Fact-check (answers at the back)

1. How should you measure the success of your job hunting?
   a) By the number of applications you make ❏
   b) By the number of interviews you get ❏
   c) By the number of jobs you are offered ❏
   d) By the number of jobs you are offered that match up to your targeting benchmarks ❏

2. You go for an interview and the interviewer tells you that you do not have enough experience. Two weeks later you see a similar job advertised with a different employer. Do you...
   a) Apply? ❏
   b) See applying as a waste of time? ❏
   c) Apply, see if you get an interview, then see what feedback you get this time? ❏
   d) Phone up before you apply, tell them about your experience and ask them what chance you stand of getting the job? ❏

3. What is the purpose of a CV?
   a) To get you interviews ❏
   b) To get you interviews that aren't time-wasters ❏
   c) To show you are professional ❏
   d) To make you look better than you really are ❏

4. You see a great job advertised where you do not have all the qualifications. Do you...
   a) Apply, tell the truth and let the employer decide whether you can do the job or not? ❏
   b) Give the job a miss? ❏
   c) Use a bit of spin? ❏
   d) Say you have got all the qualifications (i.e. tell a lie)? ❏

5. You have been for a lot of interviews but the salaries on offer never match up to your expectations. Do you...
   a) Adjust your targeting benchmarks? ❏
   b) Check your CV and make sure your pay expectations are clearly flagged up? ❏
   c) Do nothing (carry on with your applications)? ❏
   d) Blame employers for paying poor salaries? ❏

6. You want to find out if your pay expectations are realistic. Which of these sources will give you the best information?
   a) Recruitment consultants ❏
   b) Your human resources manager ❏
   c) Salary surveys ❏
   d) The Internet ❏

7. Jobs in start-up businesses are too risky. Do you...
   a) Agree? ❏
   b) Disagree? ❏
   c) Feel the answer depends on your personal circumstances? ❏
   d) Hold no opinion? ❏

8. You have been looking for a job for 12 months but so far you have only found two that match up with your targeting benchmarks. To find out where you may be going wrong, what do you look at first?
a) Your sourcing ❏
b) Your targeting ❏
c) Your accessibility ❏
d) Your application ❏

9. You are doing everything right but you are still getting asked to interviews that are time-wasters. What do you do?
a) Ring up each time and ask for more information over the phone ❏
b) Accept that sometimes this happens ❏
c) Take a break from job hunting ❏
d) Give the interviewers a piece of your mind ❏

10. Which of these is a sign that your targeting is going wrong?
a) Getting on shortlists every time and then finding the job is offered to someone else ❏
b) Applying for jobs and getting no interviews ❏
c) Getting interviews and then finding the jobs are not suitable ❏
d) Not getting replies to your applications ❏

CHAPTER 11

Attacking the visible market

In this chapter you'll learn about applying for jobs on the visible market – the jobs that are advertised and (if the jobs are good jobs) the jobs that are going to attract other applicants in large numbers.

In Chapter 8 we introduced you to the term 'reactive sourcing'. Reactive sourcing is what you do when you want to engage the visible market. It consists largely of keeping your eyes open and looking in the right places, notably at newspapers, journals and periodicals and on websites.

In this chapter we will look at these sources of visible market jobs in more detail and bring into play what you've taught yourself about targeting and being selective when it comes to choosing which jobs to apply for.

Now you'll learn how to engage and see off competition, because the first task you face on the visible market is to make sure that your application stands out from the rest. Take it as read that the crowd will be there, but by the end of this chapter you will know what to do to make sure that you are at the front of the queue and that you don't get ignored in the crush.

Sources of visible market jobs

Reactive sourcing is the term that describes the way in which you engage the visible market.

Reactive sourcing, remember, is where the stimulus is provided by the employer – usually in the form of advertising. How you respond to this stimulus determines how effective you are in engaging the visible market.

For convenience, we've broken down sources of visible market jobs into the following:

- ads in newspapers and journals
- the Internet
- other sources.

Ads in newspapers and journals

Advertising in newspapers and journals is still one of the most popular ways of recruiting people. 'Scanning the ads' is, therefore, an important part of job hunting. It is where most of us start out on our search for a new job.

The choice of **newspapers** can be baffling and, with job hunting in mind, it is sometimes difficult to know which ones to take:

- **Local papers:** These vary quite a lot in the quality of the recruitment advertising they carry but, on the whole, they are essential reading from the job hunter's point of view. Local papers frequently have 'jobs nights' or nights on which they feature jobs in certain fields (e.g. engineering and technical appointments).
- **National papers:** Some national papers have strong toe-holds in certain sectors of the market. Other than this, 'pick 'n' mix' your choice of national papers and ring the changes from time to time. The same goes for Sunday papers. Because of the cost, broadsheets tend to carry advertising for top jobs only.

Don't try to scan the ads in every newspaper. You haven't got the time.

- **Journals and periodicals:** Those that carry recruitment advertising divide into two types:
  - journals published by professional associations
  - trade journals of the kind that circulate in certain industries.

Verdict on journals

Good points: well targeted job wise (some journals put out by professional associations are regarded as top sources of jobs in their particular fields).

Bad points: tend to be national or international publications, meaning that the jobs will be 'anywhere and everywhere' (a less attractive feature for those who are targeting jobs in specific areas).

The Internet

More and more employers use their websites for sourcing staff – indeed, the day may come when all recruitment is done online.

Recruitment websites divide into two types:

1 sites run by recruitment specialists
2 employers' sites – organizations using their own websites to advertise vacancies.

Employers do not always use their own websites to advertise vacancies (some do, some don't). Don't, therefore, rely on them exclusively – as some job hunters have been tempted to do. See them, instead, as yet another way of accessing the visible market. In other words, see company websites as complementing your other methods of reactive sourcing.

Other sources

Advertising on the radio, advertising on electronic billboards sited in public places, advertising in newsletters put out by the local branches of professional associations – the methods employers use to attract applicants are almost endless. The message is: keep your eyes and ears open.

Deciding which jobs to go for

With any job you source, the first decision you have to make is whether to apply for it or not. Here is where you go back to your targeting benchmarks. Does the job match up to your specification or doesn't it? If it does, then the green light is flashing at you to get moving. If not, an equally strong signal should be beaming out to you to go no further.

Advertisements without salaries

Being selective about the jobs you apply for by running them across your targeting benchmarks is all well and good, but a problem you frequently have to face up to is the ad that makes no mention of salary other than the meaningless jumble of words such as 'negotiable' or 'commensurate with the responsibilities'. The job looks OK but, without any insight into the pay, how do you know whether it's worth applying for or not?

As we all know, pay is a difficult area shrouded in mists of secrecy. Why don't employers put salaries in ads? In most cases, the reason will be one of the following:

- confidentiality (not wanting the world at large to know what salaries they pay)
- their salaries are poor and they don't like to say
- they're fishing (they want to see what you're earning first so they can decide whether they can afford you or not).

So how do you deal with ads with no salaries? On the face of it, the sensible approach to the problem seems to be to ring up and ask. You don't want to waste anyone's time so, before you put an application in, could they give you a rough idea of the kind of figure they have in mind please? Sensible though it sounds, anecdotal evidence of this approach actually working is rather thin on the ground. Often all you get is a lot of cagey answers that don't move you forward very far.

Make your pay expectations accessible

Going back to Chapter 9, we stressed the importance of always making it crystal clear to employers exactly where you are coming from and what you are seeking to achieve. If pay is what is driving you, this means two things:

- stating your current earnings
- stating the level of earnings you're aspiring to.

In this case this information is what needs to figure prominently in your CV and be mentioned again in any letters of application you send in. Because of the secretiveness and sensitivity that surrounds pay and because of the special problems arising from ads without salaries, this kind of accessibility acts as a fail-safe to ensure that your application goes no further if the employer's ideas on pay don't fall into line with your own. In short, deal with ads with no pay as follows:

1 Check first of all to make sure all your other targeting benchmarks are met
2 Revisit your CV and satisfy yourself that no one reading it will get any wrong ideas about your pay aspirations
3 Put together an equally accessible cover letter
4 Send off your application and see what happens.

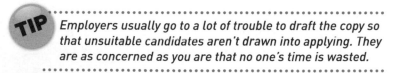

Conditioning your expectations

There is a snag with the above approach and it is this. Not many employers will own up to not being able to afford you so the likely response if the pay available falls way below your targeting benchmark is a standard 'sorry but no thank you' letter. Since 'sorry and no thank you' letters are a source of discouragement, when replying to ads with no salaries you need to condition your expectations accordingly. If you get turned down, tell yourself it's an even chance that the job's to blame – not you. This is all part of getting your expectations into line that we talked about in Chapter 10 under the subject of application.

Read advertisements properly

Ensuring that jobs match up to your targeting benchmarks sounds easy enough so why is it that so many people get it wrong? The reason in a lot of cases is not reading the ad properly or, rather, reading it selectively so that, consciously or not, we ignore:

- any stipulations that render us unsuitable – e.g. 'candidates must be able to converse fluently in Mandarin Chinese'
- job conditions that come into conflict with our targeting benchmarks – e.g. 'the work can involve anti-social hours including weekends'.

This blanking out of things we don't want to see usually happens when the job is a good job – typically one where a good salary is on offer. In the excitement to get an application off, we omit to go through the small print in too much detail or we see the bit that jars in our minds but decide to give it a whirl anyway.

Employers usually go to a lot of trouble to draft the copy so that unsuitable candidates aren't drawn into applying. They are as concerned as you are that no one's time is wasted.

Dealing with competition

Engaging the visible market means facing up to competition. The amount of competition you have to deal with depends on two things:

1 how good the job is
2 how widely it has been advertised.

Where there is a lot of competition, being suitable for a job is no guarantee that you will get an interview. What you also need to ensure is that:

● your suitability comes across in one quick read of your CV (your *accessibility*)
● you can be contacted without any fuss and bother, plus the fact you can come in for interviews quickly (your *availability*)
● any strong points you have are brought into prominence (your super *accessibility*).

We dealt with the first two of these bullet points in Chapter 9. Now let's look at the third.

Bringing out your strong points

Strong points mean your strong points vis-à-vis a particular job application. What this doesn't mean is what you see as your strong points generally. For example, you may have had a lot of very interesting experience with a certain brand of computer-aided design software but this won't cut much ice at all with an employer who uses a completely different package. The point here is to get you to see each job application as a fresh challenge. There will be more on this as we move on.

Strong points are the matches between what the employer is looking for and what you have to offer. A strong point could be the fact that you hold a particular qualification. Alternatively, it could be your experience with a certain technique or that living out of a suitcase for months on end is something you're completely used to. The clues to these matches can be found in the ad itself – in what employers have to say about themselves and in what they see as desirable attributes in candidates (another good reason for making sure you read ads properly).

Bringing your strong points into prominence

At the application stage you normally have three ways of bringing your strong points to the attention of an employer:

1 in your CV
2 in any supporting letters you submit
3 in any application forms you fill in.

● **Use their words:** This is one of the golden rules to getting across your strong points. In a world where there is an ever-increasing use of buzz words and jargon, a very real danger exists of the strong point you're trying to bring out falling on stony ground because it isn't understood or fully appreciated. The way to avoid this difficulty is by putting your own preferences to one side and always using the same buzz words and jargon as the employer (the same words as those used in the ad).

CV scanning software

Preliminary scanning of CVs is sometimes done by computer, meaning that your application could end up in the turn-down pile without it ever having been seen by human eyes. What CV scanning software is programmed to do is search for key matches between what appears in your CV and the specification for the job. It does this by identifying certain key words and phrases – all of which lends a new importance to the choice of terminology you use.

● **Customizing your CV:** This should present no problems if you keep a copy of your CV stored on your PC or on a memory stick. Simply get it up on screen and edit it. What you are seeking to achieve here is to bring your strong points into prominence without breaking the rule about keeping your CV short and concise. Be warned, however, that this may mean taking out some cherished piece of information to make the necessary space. Console yourself with the fact that this will mean the strong points will be more noticeable and it is these that have the most bearing on whether you get picked for an interview or not.

- **Cover letters:** The letter you send in accompanying your CV is another place to get across your strong points. Don't worry about repeating what's already in your CV.
- **Application forms:** Most larger firms have standard application forms and there's a fair chance you could be asked to complete one at the early stages of an application, i.e. before you know whether you've been granted an interview or not. Application forms usually have a section headed: 'Any other information you wish to add in support of your application'. Use sections like these to list your strong points.

TIP

As a general rule people give insufficient attention to filling in application forms. They dash them off quickly and this is a mistake. If an organization has provided an application form, remember next time you fill one in that it will probably get a better reading than the CV you spent hours preparing.

Follow the instructions

In the tailpiece to every ad you will find instructions on how to apply. These instructions usually include:

- the name and/or job title of the person to whom your application should be sent
- the form in which the application should be submitted (e.g. a current CV together with a cover letter)
- any references you should quote
- any closing date for applications
- how your application should be submitted – by post or email, or you may have to ring and ask for an application form to be sent to you.

What is important about these instructions is that you follow them to the letter and that you don't substitute your own ideas on 'what's best'. With large numbers of applicants and employers recruiting for more than one position at the same time, there is always the danger of individual applications getting mislaid or put on the wrong pile. Needless to say, you won't make a very good job of engaging the competition if you're not there to do it.

Don't procrastinate

Even though there may be no mention of a closing date for applications, don't let the grass grow under your feet when you're attacking the visible market. Remember, the world won't wait while you're finding the time to put the finishing touches to your CV or other distractions seem more pressing.

Application, the third of our three As, is the watchword here. Get moving!

Selection consultants

Finally, a passing acknowledgement of the fact that a lot of visible market jobs are advertised by firms of selection consultants. This reflects one or both of the following:

● the need for the employer's identity to remain confidential (not necessarily evidence that someone is about to get the sack)
● the need for expertise of the kind the employer doesn't have (expertise the selection consultants can offer).

With advertisements placed by selection consultants, is there a danger you could find yourself applying for your own job?

While this may be an extremely remote prospect, what is more worrying perhaps is that the application you sent off to Boggis & Associates, Selection Consultants, could somehow find its way into the wrong hands – namely the hands of your boss. Not knowing the identity of the employer behind the ad is a real area of concern for a lot of people. Could it be, for example, a company that is in the same group as your own?

Firms of selection consultants sometimes offer a confidential reply service meaning you can list out the names of any employers you don't want your details sent to. Failing this, ring the consultants up and ask them how else they can address your concerns. If you're still left feeling uneasy, then it may be best to give the job a miss. When job hunting, your first priority always is to look after the job you've got and never to put it at risk.

Summary

In this chapter you have learned the importance of being selective when it comes to applying for jobs that have been advertised. Yes, the jobs are there but just because they are there it does not necessarily mean you should apply for them. See first of all that they measure up to your targeting benchmarks. If they do, great; but, if they do not, then stick to your benchmarks and give them a miss. Remember: with job hunting you do not measure your performance by the count of applications you have sent off.

You have also taught yourself not to be put off when you know that you will be up against stiff competition. Take competition as read when you apply for any good job that has been advertised but, rather than occupying your mind with negative thoughts like 'What chance do I stand?', turn your attention instead to what matters – seeing what's good about your application and, more importantly still, seeing what steps you should be taking to make sure everyone knows what's good. In other words, let the need to engage and overcome competition stimulate you into giving your application your best shot.

Fact-check (answers at the back)

1. You see a good job advertised but you are concerned that there could be hundreds of applicants. Do you...
a) Apply? ❏
b) Feel you stand no chance and give the job a miss? ❏
c) Hand-deliver your application so it gets in first? ❏
d) Ring up and ask the employer how many applications they have received? ❏

2. A job that interests you is advertised but the salary indicated is £10k under the figure you are looking for. Do you...
a) Apply and hope you get an interview where you can negotiate the salary? ❏
b) Flag up your pay requirements in your application? ❏
c) Give the job a miss? ❏
d) Ring up first and try to negotiate a higher salary over the phone? ❏

3. You see an ad for a job but there is no mention of salary. Your main reason for looking for another job is so that you can better your pay. Do you...
a) Give the job a miss? ❏
b) Ring up and ask the employer to tell you the salary? ❏
c) Apply and hope for the best? ❏
d) Apply but make sure that your pay requirements are made clear in your application? ❏

4. What are your strong points?
a) Points about you that make matches with the requirements of the job ❏
b) Areas where you have had most experience ❏
c) Your outstanding achievements ❏
d) Your academic qualifications ❏

5. You are asked to fill in an application form and see a box headed 'Any additional information'. What do you put in this box?
a) Nothing (leave it blank) ❏
b) Your strong points ❏
c) That you work hard ❏
d) What your boss said to you at your last appraisal interview ❏

6. You are asked to fill in an application form and see straight away that most of the information requested is a repeat of the information in your CV. You have already submitted a CV, so do you...
a) Ring up and query why you are being asked to provide the same information twice? ❏
b) Send in another copy of your CV and write 'see CV' in the spaces on the form? ❏
c) Fill in the form carefully and send it back? ❏
d) Send in another copy of your CV and ignore the form? ❏

7. You see a job advertised by a firm of consultants where the identity of the employer is not revealed. You are concerned that the job could be with a company in the same group as your current employer. You do not want it to get back to your boss that you are looking for another job. Do you...

a) Give the job a miss? ❏

b) Ring the consultants, ask them to reveal the name of the employer, and give the job a miss if they refuse? ❏

c) Ring up the consultants, explain the problem and see if they come up with an answer? ❏

d) Apply and not worry about it? ❏

8. You see a great job advertised where applicants are invited to send in a CV. You realize that your CV needs updating but you are pushed for time. What do you do?

a) Burn the midnight oil ❏

b) Send in your CV as it stands ❏

c) Ring the employer, explain the problem and find out if they will hold the job open for a few weeks ❏

d) Update your CV and send it in late ❏

9. You see a job advertised but you know that there will be hundreds of applicants. Which of the following will help you to get an interview?

a) Ring up and say you will only apply if you are given an interview ❏

b) Take in your application in person and ask someone to see you ❏

c) Send in your application then ring up a few days later and ask to book an interview ❏

d) None of the above ❏

10. You see a job advertised on an employer's website but when you apply you get an email back saying the job was filled some time ago. Do you...

a) Email a reply to tell them to update their website? ❏

b) As a), but add on a complaint that your time has been wasted by their inefficiency? ❏

c) Do nothing but make a note never to apply for any more jobs with this employer? ❏

d) Do nothing and accept that websites are not always updated when they should be? ❏

CHAPTER 12

Attacking the elusive invisible market

In this chapter you will learn all you need to know about accessing jobs on the invisible market:

- the jobs that are not advertised
- the jobs that employers keep to themselves
- the jobs that are rumoured to be the best jobs.

Perhaps the most striking feature of the invisible market is its sheer size. Although there is no accurate count of how many jobs are filled without advertising, a conservative estimate would be around 90 per cent. In other words, the invisible market is far, far bigger than its visible counterpart and aspiring job hunters should not let this fact escape them. Furthermore, competition is rarely an issue. Because the jobs have not been advertised, it is unusual to find more than a handful of applicants for each one. In fact, there is a good chance of you finding yourself in the enviable position of being the only face in the frame.

So next you'll learn how to set about accessing the elusive invisible market – what you have to do and how you need to go about approaching employers if you want to prise out what they have chosen to keep under wraps.

Why the invisible market exists

Going back to Chapter 8, we picked out a number of reasons for the growth of the invisible market. Let's now extend this list to give you a complete appreciation of why the invisible market exists:

- the cost of advertising – laying out large sums of money with no guarantee that the outcome will be successful
- the resources and expertise needed to deal with response to advertisements – resources and expertise employers may not have
- the fear of making bad selection decisions coupled with the increased prospect of employers have to face litigation from people they have sacked
- the impact of skills shortages on recruitment
- the commonly held view that 'advertising doesn't work'
- bad experiences with advertising – a double whammy when the cost is also taken into account
- employers in a hurry – in a technology-driven age, the tendency for anything slow and ponderous to be viewed as intrinsically bad.

Invisible market methods

Against this background, more and more employers are turning to alternative methods of recruitment, notably:

- recruitment consultants (agencies) – people who are usually prepared to work on a 'no placement, no fee' basis and can put up shortlists of candidates at 24 to 48 hours' notice
- contacts – putting the word round in the trade or to selected individuals (e.g. people who work for competitors)
- revisiting CVs that are held on file
- using headhunters.

Accessing the invisible market

Let's now look at what you need to do to access this vibrant and expanding invisible market.

Remember proactive sourcing? Proactive sourcing is the key to getting to know about jobs that aren't advertised. Proactive sourcing is where you provide the stimulus.

Cold calling

This is one very obvious way of finding out if employers have got any vacancies that they're not telling the world about – simply by ringing up and asking them.

There is a right and a wrong way to go about cold calling. The wrong way is to ring an employer once, leave your name, phone number and a few personal details, then leave it to chance they'll remember you the next time a suitable vacancy comes up.

At best, a cold call reveals a snapshot of what's available in an organization at a particular point in time. Expect no more from it and you won't be disappointed. For instance, the chances of the person you spoke to remembering you in three months' time when a vacancy comes up are extremely remote. The scrap of paper where he/she wrote down your name will have disappeared a long time ago.

A model approach to cold calling

Done systematically, cold calling can be a very effective way of accessing the invisible market. Here is what to do:

● Start by picking **the right employers** – organizations that are likely to have the kind of job opportunities you are targeting. To an extent, this is inspired guesswork, but clues to suitable employers can sometimes be picked up from reading the job ads (e.g. companies that are doing a lot of recruiting).

● Get **the name of the right person** to speak to – e.g. if you're an accountant, ask for the name of the financial manager. Don't be fobbed off here with the name of the personnel or human resources manager – even though they may be the normal channel that applicants go through.

- **Keep it brief.** Remember, cold calls can be irritating, especially to someone who is busy. State simply who you are, what you're looking for and ask whether there's anything suitable for you at the moment.

- If you strike lucky, **keep the momentum going**. Suggest an interview and get in quickly – i.e. use your *availability* to maximum effect. Alternatively, if you find there's nothing doing, then, consistent with not outstaying your welcome, find out if the organization ever has the kind of job opportunities you are targeting. This, if you like, is your market research.

- End the call by **saying thank you**. Leave the door open for calling again another time.

- **Keep a record** of your calls, including the name of the person to whom you spoke and any useful information you picked up.

- **Give each call a score from 0 to 5.** Your 5s will be calls where the feedback has been encouraging (employers who are worth keeping in touch with regularly). Your 2s and 3s will be those who only have an occasional demand for talents such as yours. Give zero scores to employers who give you a hard time. Don't waste any more effort on them.

- **Work out a call cycle.** For example, put your 5s down for a call every two months or so, whereas your 2s and 3s won't need to be contacted quite so frequently.

- **Stand by to revise your ratings** (upwards or downwards) – each call reveals a little bit more of the picture.

TIP

Cold calling companies too frequently achieves little – the snapshot is still the same and you run the risk of getting yourself viewed as a pest.

Systematic and targeted cold calling eventually pays off. As the number of companies on your call list diminishes, the target will become more accurate and defined. Sooner or later statistical probability takes over from pure chance and you start to connect with good jobs. Patience and persistence are the watchwords here (all part of *application*).

Cold calling is a good way of getting to know about vacancies before they're advertised or put out to recruitment consultants – a case of getting in before the competition arrives.

Mailshots

Sending your CV off to prospective employers is another way of accessing the invisible market. Again, there's a right and a wrong way of going about it:

● **Don't expect a reply.** Whether employers should acknowledge every unsolicited CV they receive is a matter of opinion. The fact that many of them don't is, however, something you are going to have to learn to live with – a point we have touched on already.
● **Focus on the aim.** Rather than getting wound up about matters of no importance, such as how many standard letters of acknowledgement you do or don't notch up, concentrate instead on what really matters, which is:
  – that your mailshots may strike lucky and land on the right desk at the right time
  – failing this, that your mailshots have enough impact to ensure that they get put on the right file (the one revisited whenever vacancies for people like you come up).
● **Redesign your CV.** In Chapter 11, when we looked at attacking the visible market, we placed great emphasis on customizing your CV and, in particular, on setting out your strong points vis-à-vis each application. With the invisible market, this isn't quite so easy because there isn't an advertisement or job description to look at for clues on what to put in and what to leave out. The answer? Use your imagination and try to customize each unsolicited CV you send out to what you think the employer will be looking for.

Here are two important points to remember about customizing your CV:

1 Print off a second copy (one you can keep on file so you will have a record of what you've said to an employer if you're invited for an interview).
2 Don't neglect to do it, and take some time over it, because employers receive hundreds of unsolicited CVs and they automatically bin those that don't strike immediate chords with them.

Emails

An alternative to putting your CV in the post is to send it by email. What's best?

Go back to your aims. Once your CV has passed through the preliminary read test and, given there are no suitable vacancies at the moment, what you want to ensure is that:

● your CV is put on file
● when it is retrieved from file, it will still be in more or less pristine condition.

Emails fail on the first count because there is always the risk they don't get printed off. At risk of sounding prehistoric, therefore – and unless there are any overriding reasons for doing otherwise – put your unsolicited CV in the post.

Post or email?

A CV submitted by email would seem to win hands down where it is the practice to store details of interesting-looking candidates on an **electronic database.** One of the problems facing you, however, is knowing which employers do this and which don't. Since you will be sending your CV to individual named managers rather than to the Human Resources or the Personnel Department (where these computer-based systems tend to be located), the advice to 'put it in the post' still holds good.

Putting your speculative CVs in the post as opposed to faxing them or sending them by email is a good example of **keeping control** – playing an active rather than a passive role in ensuring your job hunting moves to successful conclusions; facilitating the process as far as you can rather than leaving it to chance or how some hard-pressed manager happens to feel inclined on the day. Keeping control has particular importance when accessing the invisible market. We shall see more of it as we move on.

Professional networking

Professional networking is another way of accessing the invisible market – using your circle of contacts in business as a source of suitable job opportunities – something most people only think to do when they're out of work or their jobs come under threat.

> **TIP** *More people find jobs by professional networking than by any other method.*

Networking is for everyone

A common misconception of networking is that it is the preserve of social climbers or extrovert personality types. Nothing could be further from the truth. Anyone in a career has his or her own professional network. Typically it consists of:

- work colleagues past and present – bosses, peers and subordinates
- other people you come into contact with in the course of your work – e.g., customers, suppliers, outside service providers
- people you know through your professional body – e.g. the local branch of the Chartered Management Institute
- people you meet through going on courses or while getting qualifications – people in similar lines of work to yourself.

*With the relatively small worlds that most of us operate in, sourcing jobs by professional networking carries the risk of our job hunting ambitions reaching the **wrong ears**. Take the case of Leonard. Leonard is a sales manager in the telecommunications industry. Leonard tried tapping into his contacts in the competition to see what jobs might be available but unfortunately his boss got to hear about it. The result? Leonard was in very deep trouble indeed.*

A model approach to networking for jobs

The key to networking for jobs successfully is keeping control:

- **Don't use your network contacts as sounding boards** for your grouses and groans. It will feed out entirely the wrong messages – i.e. that you're only looking for an escape route from your present difficulties and any job will do.

- Instead, make sure that the messages you feed out to your network contacts are **complete messages**. Give precise guidelines on the kind of job you're looking for – including the salary.

- **Set the parameters** by telling your contacts how far you want them to go for you. This would normally be to effect an introduction. In other words, you should make it clear that you want any detailed negotiations left to you (always better done first hand).

- **Stress the importance of confidentiality.** Lay down precise rules – like you want no discussions with any third parties without your prior knowledge and consent.

The lesson here is only to network with people you can trust – people you can rely on to look after your best interests and who won't compromise your position by indulging in tittle-tattle. Give a wide berth to those who don't meet these criteria.

Registering with recruitment consultants

A large slice of the invisible market is handled by firms of recruitment consultants (employment agencies). Recruitment consultants keep details of candidates on file and interested employers can access these details at short notice. Here are examples of two employers who chose to use recruitment consultants for different reasons:

Example – Company D

Company D's IT Manager unexpectedly handed in her notice halfway through a major project. With no suitable internal candidates to promote, Company D was faced with having to recruit someone from outside. The rigmarole of placing advertisements didn't appeal to Company D mainly because of the time it would take. Company D decided, therefore, to run their vacancy through a couple of firms of recruitment consultants specializing in IT staff to see if they had anybody on their books who would fit the bill.

Example – Company E

Company E's recently promoted Chief Accountant proved to be a total failure and they decided that he would have to go back to his old job at some stage in the near future. Before they broached this subject with him, however, they felt they needed to know if anyone more suitable was available on the market. A quick and confidential way of checking this out was to ask a leading firm of financial recruitment consultants to send in details of candidates they had registered with them.

Choose the right consultants

In picking firms of recruitment consultants to register with, you will normally find you are faced with a bewildering choice. You need to apply the following criteria:

- The consultants must deal with the kind of appointments you are targeting. For example, if you're looking for a management position in the construction industry, it is pointless registering with a firm of consultants who deal mainly in general office staff.
- They need to be effective, which is, in part, a reflection of their client base and, in part, a reflection of their general efficiency. (With firms of recruitment consultants, effectiveness should never be taken for granted!)

To go about finding the right firm of recruitment consultants for your needs, first look at their website to check that they deal with the right types of job. Then conduct further research in the following way.

- **Seek personal recommendations** – for example, does anyone on your professional network have any recent experience of dealing with a firm of recruitment consultants? If so, what information can they pass on?
- **Check the business telephone directories** – recruitment consultants often have display entries telling you what they do.
- **Scan the job ads** – recruitment consultants frequently run advertisements for vacancies that have been notified to them. From reading these advertisements over a period of time it is possible to tell which consultants are active in the areas of the job market you are targeting.
- **Ask** – if in any doubt, ring up firms of consultants, give them a brief run-down of the kind of job you're looking for and ask if they can help.

Registering with consultants

Registering usually involves filling in a registration form, sometimes attending an interview and sometimes doing some kind of test. Some firms of consultants offer the facility to register online. Once you have registered with a firm of consultants, they will be able to use their contacts and know-how to find you the kind of job you are seeking.

Keeping control

Those magic words again! Keeping control is the secret of success in dealing with recruitment consultants. Keeping control means doing the following:

● Make sure at the outset that they understand where you're coming from, i.e. go to great pains to explain your targeting, benchmarks and leave no room for doubt.
● Make sure that they know how to get hold of you. Recruitment consultants live in a fast-moving world where they have to get results both for their clients and for themselves (a lot of them are paid on commission). Needless to say, candidates they find hard to contact don't appeal to recruitment consultants one bit.
● Phone up or email consultants from time to time to find out how they are getting on. Not only will it remind them that you're still there but you might also pick up some interesting feedback (for example, that the salary you're asking for is too high). Prick up your ears for feedback. Feedback, remember, is what you use to give your targeting benchmarks their fine-tuning.

- It's very important to advise consultants whenever any information they are holding on you changes – for example, you get a new telephone number or you decide to tweak your pay targeting benchmark down a notch or two.
- Ditch any consultants who don't perform satisfactorily – especially consultants who waste your time by putting you forward for jobs that are completely wrong for you.

Summary

In this chapter you have learned how to access the invisible job market using methods that fall under the heading of proactive sourcing – sourcing where the stimulus comes from you. You have seen at the same time how the invisible market operates, why it exists and the rewards that await you if you can succeed in engaging with it:

- You will see what's really out there for you (the whole market as opposed to just the tiny slice of jobs that are advertised)

- You will find that there is little or no competition on the invisible market

- As a consequence, you will find that there is more chance of you getting the jobs

- You will find more flexibility when it comes to negotiating terms such as salary and perks

- The big message about the invisible job market is not to be put off by its seeming impenetrability. It does call for persistence but the effort usually pays off.

Fact-check (answers at the back)

1. How do you access the invisible market?
   a) By searching on the Internet ❏
   b) By proactive sourcing ❏
   c) By doing nothing ❏
   d) Don't know ❏

2. Which of the following is proactive sourcing?
   a) Sending out unsolicited CVs ❏
   b) Searching for jobs advertised on the Internet ❏
   c) Reading job ads in professional journals ❏
   d) Scanning the job ads in local newspapers ❏

3. Who is it best to speak to when you call an employer to see if they have any suitable vacancies?
   a) Whoever answers the phone ❏
   b) The Managing Director ❏
   c) The Human Resources Manager ❏
   d) The manager responsible for the areas of the business where the jobs for people like you will be ❏

4. You cold call an employer but when you ask if there are any suitable vacancies you are told 'no'. Do you...
   a) Strike them off your call list? ❏
   b) Say you will send them a copy of your CV? ❏
   c) Ask if they ever get vacancies for people like you and, if the answer is 'yes', say you will ring again? ❏
   d) Ask if you can call round and see them? ❏

5. You send in an unsolicited CV and hear nothing. Do you...
   a) Ring up and find out why? ❏
   b) Put it down to bad manners? ❏
   c) View the lack of response as normal? ❏
   d) Write a letter of complaint to the Managing Director? ❏

6. You want to put out feelers to one of your firm's major competitors to see if they could offer you anything. Unfortunately, your only contact in the competitor's business is someone you do not trust. Do you...
   a) Put your distrust to one side and put out the feeler anyway? ❏
   b) Speak to someone else (someone you don't know)? ❏
   c) Forget the idea? ❏
   d) Get a friend to speak to them for you? ❏

7. One of the recruitment consultants you are registered with phones you up about a position with one of their clients. Unfortunately, the position is completely unsuitable. Do you...
   a) Try explaining what you are looking for again and give them one last chance to get it right? ❏
   b) Tell them to stop wasting your time? ❏
   c) Take your name off their register (and say you want no more calls from them)? ❏
   d) View the experience as being part of the price you have to pay for dealing with recruitment consultants? ❏

8. Two recruitment consultants phone you about what appears to be the same job. The job sounds great but do you...

a) Let both recruitment consultants put you forward and, by doing this, feel you will be doubling your chances of getting the job? ❏

b) Tell one consultant you are not interested to prevent any complications about who introduced you to the client first arising later on? ❏

c) Tell the two consultants to sort it out between themselves? ❏

d) Give the job a miss? ❏

9. How do most managers find positions?

a) By replying to ads in the press or on websites ❏

b) By going to consultants ❏

c) By professional networking ❏

d) By being headhunted ❏

10. What is the best way of submitting an unsolicited CV?

a) By email ❏

b) In the post ❏

c) By fax ❏

d) Delivering it by hand ❏

CHAPTER 13

Getting headhunted

In this chapter you will learn how to get headhunted.

The world of executive search beckons where top appointments are filled by mysterious phone calls from complete strangers and over lunches in expensive restaurants – or so the story goes. But is there anything you can do to get your name on the headhunters' lists? Is it a matter of waiting for the approaches to come or can you exert any influence over the process?

By the end of this chapter you will have a clear understanding of why the market for executive search exists and how it works. You will learn what headhunters are looking for and how they operate. You will see how important it is that you project an image that fits in with what headhunters want to see in the candidates they put forward to their clients.

Building on this understanding, you will then learn how to deal with headhunters and how it is possible to talk up items in the package such as salary and perks.

Finally, you will learn what it takes to keep the approaches coming. Once you're on the headhunters' radar, what do you have to do to make sure you stay there?

The market for executive search

Executive search consultants don't come cheap, so the first point to grasp about headhunting is that employers don't go down this route unless there is a good reason. In most cases, the reason is that the job is a very senior job (e.g. a board-level appointment) where the person being sought is someone with exceptional qualities. Employers also use headhunting to recruit people with scarce and/or specialist skills.

What's in it for you?

Being headhunted is definitely something you can't afford to miss out on. There are two reasons for saying this:

1 Many of the best jobs are filled by headhunting
2 The money's flexible (it's up to employers to come up with an offer that's going to interest you).

How headhunters work

First, let's look at how headhunters work. Professional headhunters – or executive search consultants, as they are more properly known – thrive on their connections in the business world.

> ### Example – Company Q
>
> Company Q, a brand leader in the widget industry, is looking for a new Chief Executive to replace the present job holder who retires in 12 months' time. Company Q contacts RST & Associates, a well-known firm of executive search consultants, and briefs them on the kind of person they are seeking – ideally someone with several years' top management experience with a major widget maker. RST & Associates set about the assignment by tapping into their numerous contacts in the widget-making world. Soon they have a list of names – people their contacts have recommended to them. From here they proceed to ring up each name on the list to find out who's interested in making a move and who isn't.

What the example of Company Q shows is that, to get yourself on to the receiving end of a headhunter's approach:

● someone has got to know you
● more importantly, what they know about you has got to be good.

Projecting the right image

For the most part, by 'people who know you' we mean people who have come into contact with you in the course of your work. This includes:

● colleagues, past and present (bosses, peers and subordinates)
● external contacts such as customers, suppliers and professional advisors
● people who know you through your work on outside bodies such as professional institutions and trade associations.

With being headhunted hot on the agenda, it is people like these who can influence the outcomes for you by:

● mentioning your name at the right moment
● saying the right things about you.

This is where we ask you to focus your mind sharply on the image you project as you go about your day-to-day work.

The lifelong interview

An interesting contrast to draw here is between:

● the image you cultivate for going to interviews
● the rather less well-managed image you project to those who have dealings with you every day of the week.

With the first, you are extremely mindful of being on your best behaviour while, at the same time, taking great pains over your personal appearance. You will be guarded in anything you say. You will certainly be going to great lengths to keep any grey areas in your track record under wraps.

Not so, however, with the second. You will be more inclined to let your hair down and a few of the less endearing aspects of your character may even creep out.

What we're talking about here, however, is projecting an image *all of the time* rather than over the 45–90 minutes that's par for the course for most interviews. Harder? Of course it is – and this is what we mean by the lifelong interview. The consistency and application called for are not easy to achieve.

The lifelong interview in practice

- You don't have off days.

- You have to be 100 per cent reliable – you get back to people when you say you will and you complete your work to targets.

- Your appearance is always up to scratch (don't be the first to dress down).

- You refrain from running down your colleagues and your bosses behind their backs – you keep your opinions on people to yourself.

- You don't whinge and whine – you don't use your colleagues as a sounding board for your grievances whenever you feel you're being given a hard time.

- You learn to keep your flaws to yourself.

- You give some of the gloss you save for interviews to every day.

TIP *Is there anything on the Internet (e.g. on a social networking site) that could put you in a bad light? If so, remove it.*

Person perfect and work perfect

Headhunters get their business by reputation; hence they play safe when it comes to putting forward the names of candidates to their clients. Don't expect headhunters to be very interested in you, therefore, if:

- they know of any defects in your character, *and*
- your work record is not up to standard.

Rather, you must be seen as someone who is person perfect and work perfect and this is especially the case with top-drawer jobs.

Marketing yourself to headhunters

Headhunters have the reputation of being an aloof breed of people who move in elitist social circles – inaccessible to the Joe and Jane Ordinaries of this world. But is this true? Indeed, are there ways of bringing your credentials to the attention of headhunters so that you can enhance your chances of being the target of an approach?

Don't pepper headhunters with CVs

First, there is a wrong way to go about it. Don't pepper headhunters with copies of your CV – at least not until you've done some groundwork first. Headhunters (proper ones) receive thousands of unsolicited CVs, most of which end up in the shredding machine.

Think about where headhunters are coming from

Ask yourself why a headhunter should be interested in you. What do they stand to gain from having your name on their lists?

Headhunters are in business to make money – just like everyone else. What plays the biggest part in how they view you is whether they think they can make money out of you or not – in other words, whether they could place you with one of their clients.

Identify unusual areas of skill and experience

Headhunting assignments frequently involve finding people with unusual or special areas of skill and experience – people:

● who aren't in abundant supply, *and*
● whom advertising won't necessarily reach.

> ## Example
>
> Ask yourself if you've got any interesting areas of skill and experience. Take Garth as an example. Garth is the Financial Manager of a company that has recently gone through a major expansion programme. Garth, therefore, has a lot of knowledge of takeovers, mergers and acquisitions – a lot more than the average financial manager would have.

Use your connections

Play headhunters at their own game – by which we mean use your connections to access them. This is easy if you've been headhunted before. Speak to the consultant you dealt with previously and say you're ready to make another move. Explain what it is you're looking for this time.

> ## A plan of action for speaking to headhunters
>
> ● Use the phone for making contact.
>
> ● Quickly establish the connection: 'I got your name from Ruth Sykes. You placed her in a position with Wired Up Electronics six months ago.'
>
> ● Equally quickly, move on to where you're coming from and what you're seeking to achieve (your target). Do this in three sentences maximum.

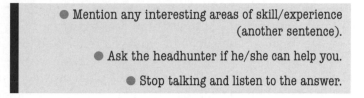

- Mention any interesting areas of skill/experience (another sentence).

- Ask the headhunter if he/she can help you.

- Stop talking and listen to the answer.

If you're not fortunate enough to have been the target for an approach before, find someone among your circle who has. With search becoming an increasingly preferred method of sourcing executive talent, there is almost bound to be someone you know who has been the focus of a headhunter's attention at some point in the past. Find out from them the headhunter's name, then follow the plan of action set out above.

There are a number of possible outcomes here:

- The headhunter may not deal with the kind of jobs you're targeting. If this is the case, ask if he/she knows a headhunter who does. Start again.
- The headhunter may ask you further questions. This is usually a good sign. Answer as concisely as you can.
- The headhunter may ask you to send in a copy of your CV, again a good sign.

Key points

- **Headhunters do most of their business on the phone**. You will do better communicating with them in this way than, for example, by writing to them or sending them emails.

- **Connections are important to headhunters.** The name-dropping you do at the start of your conversation will help to focus their attention on what you are saying.

- **Long-windedness is no way to a headhunter's heart.** By coming to the point quickly you will avoid losing the headhunter's interest.

The aim to your approach to the headhunter is twofold:

1 to see whether any of the headhunter's current assignments match up with what you're looking for (an off chance)
2 failing this, to ensure that when your CV arrives it is put in the interesting candidates' file rather than consigned to the batch to be shredded.

Visibility

Headhunters often source candidates from media reports on companies or from other sources that are in the public domain.

Examples

Sean specializes in corporate law and became the target for an approach following an article he wrote for a leading business magazine.

Gemma received three phone calls from headhunters after her name featured prominently in trade press coverage of the launch of her company's latest range of products.

Dealing with headhunters

Once you've got an approach from a headhunter, how should you deal with it? What's the best way of moving the approach forward?

Keep it to yourself

This is the first and most important rule for dealing with approaches. Don't succumb to the temptation to tell everyone. We say this for two good reasons:

● Approaches sometimes fizzle out. This can happen, for example when the company behind the approach changes its mind about recruiting.

- The fact that you've received an approach could send out a message to your principals that you're potentially a short-term stayer, with the result that they're going to think twice before spending any more money on your training and development.

Don't let it go to your head

After an approach there is a tendency to feel flattered. Someone out there has at last recognized your talents. While a certain amount of self-satisfaction is only natural, letting an approach go to your head is fraught with danger. For example:

- if the approach falls through – or you don't get the job for any reason – it could deal a crushing blow to your ego
- you could start to view the job with rose-tinted spectacles, meaning you fail to pick up on quite glaring mismatches with your targeting benchmarks
- feeling flattered tends to go with feeling grateful – not a good position to start from when it comes to negotiating the best possible deal for yourself.

Don't put up the shutters

Even if you're not looking to make a job move at the moment, always receive headhunters courteously and hear out what they've got to say. There are two reasons for this particular piece of advice:

1 Because of the cost factor alone, jobs filled by headhunting tend to be very good jobs – in short, without knowing it, you could be turning your back on the opportunity of a lifetime. As we all know, opportunity seldom knocks twice.
2 In today's uncertain world, you never know when you're going to need a headhunter. Keeping on the right side of them is therefore in your best interests.

State your position

Aware of the potential for time-wasting, a headhunter will seek to establish at an early stage whether you are in the market for making a move or not. Your response here should be on the lines of: while you're perfectly happy with what you're doing at the moment (true or not), you would always be interested to hear about any opportunities that would move your career forward. Then this cues you up nicely to trot out your targeting benchmarks – including the kind of package it would take to tempt you 'out of your tree' (irrespective of whether a figure has already been mentioned or not.)

> **TIP** *Employers normally enter into approaches with flexible ideas on the kind of pay and benefits package they would have to put forward to attract the right calibre of candidate. In short, there is usually plenty of latitude for negotiation. Don't, therefore, make the mistake of selling yourself short by naming a figure at the start that's too low.*

Remember:

- It is easier to come down than it is to talk your way back up
- With a top job, you could create the unfortunate impression that you're lacking in personal ambition (a bad point)
- Headhunters are used to talking salaries in truly astronomical figures without batting an eyelid. Sentiments like 'being too greedy' or 'going over the top' have little meaning to them.

Move the approach forward

It's usually in your best interests to move the approach forward as quickly as you can and, while the headhunter will probably want to engage you in formal selection procedures such as interviews and psychometric tests, you should endeavour to keep control over the pace at which events move. For example, if the headhunter says 'I'll get back to you', ask for some idea of timescale. If you hear nothing by the date you've been given, then get on the phone and chase them up.

Keeping the approaches coming

The first approach you receive may turn out to be a mismatch but there is a bigger picture here – one where you need the approaches to keep coming at you until eventually the right one turns up. What this means is cultivating headhunters and keeping them sweet. How do you do this? By incorporating some of the lessons we have touched on already, namely:

- **Be courteous.** Never shut the door in a headhunter's face and always hear out what they've got to say.
- **Be available.** Don't make headhunters' lives difficult by being impossible to reach.
- **Be reliable.** Go back to headhunters when you say you will. Don't leave them to have to chase you.
- **Be straight.** If a job's not suitable for you, say so. Don't string headhunters along. Wasting their time won't endear you to them.
- **Be positive.** Tell the headhunter what kind of job you are looking for and what kind of offer would tempt you 'out of the tree'.
- **Be engaging.** Encourage headhunters to keep phoning you.
- **Be proactive.** Keep up the contact by phoning them from time to time.

Summary

To some, the popular image of headhunting is that it is an extension of the 'old boy network' – the way top jobs in industry and commerce were filled a long time ago. In this chapter you have learned that this is not true. If you have got something to offer to prospective employers, if you have got the right skill set, if you have always done a good job, if you are seen as a safe pair of hands – then someone out there will be interested in you. The social circles you mix in, the school you went to or your family connections will not come into it.

You have also taught yourself that, if you want to get headhunted, you need to work on projecting the right image. More to the point, you need to see projecting the right image as something you do every day and not just on special occasions – like going for interviews – or when you feel like it. You have taught yourself to see what you do every day as you go about your business as your lifelong interview. It is the image of you that people carry forward and what will feature prominently the next time a headhunter is deciding whether to give you a call or not.

Fact-check (answers at the back)

1. Which of the following is a common reason why firms use headhunters?
   a) It's an inexpensive way of filling positions ❏
   b) They don't want the hassle themselves ❏
   c) It's quicker ❏
   d) They are looking for someone with exceptional qualities to fill a senior position ❏

2. You are quite happy with your current job but you get a phone call one day from an executive search consultant who asks you if you might be interested in a position with one of their clients. How do you respond?
   a) By saying no ❏
   b) By saying it depends on the money ❏
   c) By explaining that you're not looking for another job but, if the move was right for you, you would always be open to discussion ❏
   d) By taking the consultant's phone number and say you will get in touch if your circumstances should change ❏

3. Which of the following is most likely to interest a headhunter?
   a) Your salary expectations are not too high ❏
   b) You can count a number of celebrities among your circle of friends ❏
   c) You have only had one job since you left university ❏
   d) You have no blemishes on your work record or character ❏

4. What is your lifelong interview?
   a) All the experiences you have had at interviews you have attended ❏
   b) The image you project every day ❏
   c) Part of your learning curve ❏
   d) Don't know ❏

5. Which of these is an example of visibility?
   a) Coming to work every day in a different set of clothes ❏
   b) The kind of car you drive ❏
   c) Your blog ❏
   d) A quote from you in a trade journal about a new product your company is launching ❏

6. You receive an approach but a few weeks later the headhunter phones you to say that the position has been put on hold. How do you respond?
   a) By thanking the headhunter for letting you know and making it clear you would still be interested in the position if it came up again ❏
   b) As a), but add on that you would also like to be contacted if the headhunter got to know of any other interesting positions ❏
   c) By asking the headhunter why the position has been put on hold ❏
   d) By telling the headhunter not to ring you again unless the position he/she wants to talk about is more definite ❏

7. A headhunter approaches you about a job that does not interest you. Do you...
a) Pretend to be interested so you do not give the appearance of putting up the shutters? ❏
b) Tell them straight away that you are not interested and explain why? ❏
c) As b), but tell them at the same time what would interest you? ❏
d) Try not to commit yourself? ❏

8. Which of the following is the best way of boosting your chances of being headhunted?
a) Joining the right golf club ❏
b) Working on your lifelong interview ❏
c) Sending your CV to all the firms of executive search consultants you can find on the Internet ❏
d) Starting a blog ❏

9. What should you say when a headhunter asks you how much money you want to be paid?
a) Set out your targeting benchmark ❏
b) Add 20 per cent to your targeting benchmark ❏
c) Say you don't know ❏
d) Ask the headhunter what he/she thinks ❏

10. How do headhunters source candidates?
a) By using their contacts ❏
b) By going through banks of CVs that they hold ❏
c) By advertising on the Internet ❏
d) By getting candidates to register with them ❏

CHAPTER 14

Job offers and your career strategy

Congratulations, you have been offered the job but now you have to decide whether to take it or not. Should you be writing out your resignation or should you be thinking twice?

In this chapter you will learn what to do when the time has come for you to make up your mind. Will the job you have been offered be a good move or are you having second thoughts and, if so, why?

You will also learn that these last-minute worries about changing jobs are not always unfounded. Doubt about what you are doing has crept in from somewhere and, before you hand in your notice, it is sensible to ask yourself why you are hesitating.

Some areas of doubt can be cleared up quickly – often just by making a phone call. But sometimes your inner voices are telling you more. If you take the job you've been offered, are your new employers trustworthy? How well do you know them? They seemed keen to get you to take the job, even upped the salary, but could this be evidence of their desperation? If so, why are they desperate? Did no one else want the job?

The risk factor

Irrespective of how much research you do into prospective employers, a job move is still largely a step into the unknown. You don't know how you will fit in. You don't know how you will feel about the job in six months' time.

Fears like these serve to deter a lot of people. They turn down perfectly good offers of employment for the simple reason that they develop cold feet. This is clearly no good and a waste of all the time and effort they have put in.

Upsides and downsides

Accepting that there is a risk attached to any change of job, you need to view the risk in its proper context – by which we mean view both the upsides and the downsides together, then stand back and see how they balance up.

- **Upsides:** These are usually the advances in salary you make, the greater challenges and responsibilities the new job has to offer, and so on.
- **Downsides:** These are what happens when the job doesn't work out. You find yourself back on the job market. You could end up making a sideways or even a backwards move to escape from the pain. It could be several years before you get your career back on track.

Downsides are, admittedly, pretty frightening, but what most people neglect to do with their risk assessment is consider another set of upsides and downsides: those associated with turning the job down and staying where they are.

- **Upsides:** You have the security of working for an employer you know.
- **Downsides:** You continue to underachieve, stagnate, be underpaid – whatever it was that drove you out on to the job market in the first place.

Make your job moves for the right reason

There are two golden rules for taking a balanced view of the risks:

1 Don't make job moves for trivial or inconsequential gains (e.g. a small improvement in salary)
2 Don't be driven out on to the job market by minor gripes (e.g. your company car is overdue for a change).

Rogue employers

Not all the creatures you meet in the job jungle will have your best interests at heart. Indeed, the increasing diversity of today's market means that there is a far greater chance of you coming across a few slippery characters on your travels.

We all know of the odd hire-and-fire outfit (employers that are in a constant cycle of taking people on and laying them off), but there are some equally dangerous species about – people who will conceal important facts from you usually to get you to take the job.

How to spot a rogue employer

- Be on your guard the moment you feel you are being 'sold' a job. Good employers always point out the snags as well as the benefits. Rogues confine themselves to painting rosy pictures.

- Beware of employers who make big promises, e.g. on future pay increases – especially when they're not prepared to put their promises into writing.

- Sense danger if the answers to your questions are vague or evasive.

- Watch out for employers who give themselves let-outs – e.g. the offer is made conditional on the retention of a commercial contract.

- Be aware of employers who make you the offer you can't refuse (more on this in a moment).

- Trust your instincts. If you feel there's something fishy about an employer, let that be sufficient reason for you giving them a wide berth. Listen to those inner voices. They rarely let you down.

> **TIP** *Many jobs today (including management jobs) are short- term or temporary, and so you have to be very careful that what you are being offered is indeed a permanent position. Be warned that some unscrupulous employers try to disguise the fact that a job is temporary just to attract suitable applicants.*

Weighing up job offers

Though it hardly needs saying, don't act on any job offer until you've got it in writing. Don't, for example, spread it round the office that you'll be leaving soon. Don't, whatever you do, hand in your notice.

Read the small print

Job offers are frequently quite detailed and/or they come with supporting documentation such as job descriptions, standard terms of employment and information on items such as pension schemes and company cars. Read all of these documents, carefully making notes as you go along.

Pick out:

● any items that you feel need clarification
● anything at variance with information given to you at the interviews
● any items that appear to have been omitted.

What you are safeguarding yourself against here is not so much rogue employers but poor or inexperienced interviewers – people who don't get their facts right or leave out something important (important to you, that is).

Get all the information you need

Again, it scarcely needs saying, but don't accept any job until you've got all the information you need. In most cases this will simply mean a quick phone call to the person who made you the offer, but with really important issues such as the date on which a salary increment becomes payable or the details of a relocation package, it is advisable always to get the additional information put into writing. Any employer who is reluctant to do this should automatically be viewed with suspicion.

Revisit your targeting benchmarks

This, if you like, is your final fail-safe device. Does what you're being offered match up with what you set out to achieve by going out on the job market, or does it fall short in any significant way? Asking yourself this question exposes three potential dangers:

1 You could have allowed your career aims to drift (this tends to happen to people who have been on the job market for a long time). You could have lowered your sights without realizing it.
2 You could be allowing disenchantment with your present job to colour your opinion of what's being offered to you. You could be seeing the new job in a better light than it deserves.
3 You could be succumbing to enticement (read on).

'The perfect job?'

There's no such thing as the perfect job. This is said to warn you against:

● being over-pedantic when it comes to viewing job offers

● turning down good jobs because relatively unimportant aspects of the package are not in line with your expectations.

 For example, see where a major improvement in salary (higher than the figure you targeted) far outweighs a slight reduction in holiday entitlement or a more restricted choice of company car.

Enticement

With some employers quite desperate to acquire people with scarce or sought-after skills, the field is wide open for enticement or making an offer in the knowledge that the person on the receiving end will find it hard to refuse. Enticement often goes hand in hand with headhunting.

Enticement is perhaps the commonest reason why people make bad moves. 'I knew it was a mistake,' you hear them saying, 'but, with what was put on the table, how could I say no?'

Enticement can come in many forms: pay, perks and, these days, big upfront lump-sum payments or golden hellos.

All offers are refusable

Needless to say, a job with a fat-cat salary and a big flash car won't do you any good at all if it only lasts six months. You should beware of situations therefore where you feel you are being made an offer you can't refuse. OK, it could mean that you've hit the jackpot but it could also mean the employer you're in negotiation with is in dire straits and knows of no other way of getting you to take the job. The message? If the warning bells are ringing out at you, take notice of them.

With job hunting, all that glitters is not gold.

Job hunting as a part of a career strategy

Job hunting for many people is something they turn to in moments of desperation. They do it, for example, when their jobs are put at risk or when the pressure starts to get too much for them. They do it when the pay rise they banked on doesn't materialize or when they get passed by for promotion. Desperation puts pressure on people to go for quick solutions. They end up taking the first decent offer that comes along. This means that:

- they're not on the job market for very long
- they only ever see a fragment of the complete range of opportunities available to them
- they build up little or no experience.

Bearing in mind that these short spells of frantic job hunting are usually interspersed with long periods of inactivity, the result is a view of the outside world that is rather like a series of snapshots – one where you only see:

- what's in the frame
- what's happening at one particular point in time.

Keep the job opportunities coming

The two main messages are:

1 There's a much bigger market out there for your talents than you think
2 Source the bigger market properly and you could profit from it handsomely.

There is one final piece to the infrastructure we need to put into place, however, and it is this. You need to have an ongoing view of what the market has to offer, not one that starts and stops depending on how life happens to be treating you at the time. In other words, this is where you ditch the series of snapshots and go into moving pictures.

How do you do this? The answer is by employing some of the lessons we have touched on:

- **Don't be driven out on the job market by desperation.**
- **Keep in contact with the visible market** by scanning the ads regularly. As a matter of course, apply for any good jobs that catch your eye.

- **Keep up the proactive sourcing.** Keep up your presence on the invisible market by staying on the books of selected recruitment consultants. Mailshot selected employers occasionally.
- **Keep your networks open.** Let it be known to your contacts that you are always interested in hearing about opportunities.
- **Keep working on your lifelong interview.** Make yourself a more attractive target to headhunters by continuing to project a person-perfect and work-perfect image.
- **Encourage headhunters to keep calling you.** Don't put them off by being negative with them.

Because of the uncertainties of the world in which we live, good career management is about keeping options open and having irons in the fire all of the time. Keep up with what's happening in the job market. Turn job hunting into an everyday part of your life.

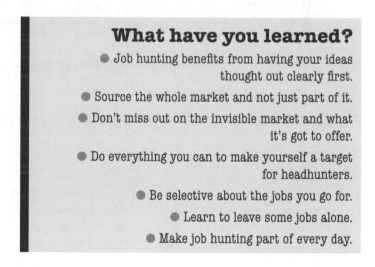

What have you learned?

- Job hunting benefits from having your ideas thought out clearly first.
- Source the whole market and not just part of it.
- Don't miss out on the invisible market and what it's got to offer.
- Do everything you can to make yourself a target for headhunters.
- Be selective about the jobs you go for.
- Learn to leave some jobs alone.
- Make job hunting part of every day.

A final word

When everything seems to be going against you, shooting off a few job applications immediately makes you feel better. You are doing something positive. Avenues are opening up. The world is suddenly a bigger and more exciting place.

Summary

In this chapter you have learned that the job jungle can be a place full of dangers, especially for the unwary. Some of the creatures you meet may appear to be friendly but, when you get close up to them, you may find out quickly that they are not what they make themselves out to be.

You have learned how to spot creatures who could do you harm. But at the same time you have learned not to be put off by employers who are poor interviewers or who give you half the facts because the explanation for these difficulties, in many cases, is pressure of work or lack of experience. You have learned that, where you feel you do not know enough about a job to decide whether you should take it or not, you ask!

Most importantly, you have learned that, while there is always a risk attached to changing jobs, you should see the risk in terms of its upsides and downsides. Where the upsides outweigh the downsides, it is time to stop agonizing and get on with the task of writing your notice out.

Fact-check (answers at the back)

1. If changing jobs is risky, what do you do to minimize the risk?
   a) Try not to change jobs too often ❑
   b) Nothing – take the risk ❑
   c) Assess the risk properly including the upsides and downsides ❑
   d) Take out more insurance ❑

2. An employer offers you a big salary, far more than the job is worth. What do you read into this?
   a) They value good people ❑
   b) They don't know what they're doing ❑
   c) They are desperate to get someone to take the job ❑
   d) The job won't be there for long ❑

3. A job is offered to you, but in the small print you notice a condition of employment that says you could be asked to work anywhere in the world. The condition wasn't mentioned in any of the interviews, so you phone up and ask for clarification. Even though you are told the condition does not apply to you, you are still concerned. Do you...
   a) Turn the job down? ❑
   b) Ask the employer to put what you have been told into writing? ❑
   c) Accept the job and try to put the concern about being sent anywhere in the world to the back of your mind? ❑
   d) Feel you don't know what to do? ❑

4. You find at the final interview stage that a job you've applied for is on a temporary contract for the first 12 months. When you query the arrangement, you are told by the employer that all their jobs start on a temporary contract. Do you...
   a) Withdraw your application? ❑
   b) Go back to the employer and see if they will make the job permanent? ❑
   c) See if you get offered the job? ❑
   d) Complain that you have been misled? ❑

5. You turn a job offer down because you found the owners of the business who interviewed you shifty and evasive. Now they keep coming back to you with bigger and bigger offers of pay. Do you...
   a) Trust your instincts and turn the offers down? ❑
   b) See how far they will go? ❑
   c) Call their bluff and name the offer that you would not be able to refuse? ❑
   d) Ask your partner to decide? ❑

6. You get offered a great job, but then you notice that you will have less holiday entitlement than with your current employer. Do you...
   a) See if you can renegotiate the offer to include more holidays? ❑
   b) Turn the offer down? ❑
   c) Accept the offer as it stands? ❑
   d) As c), but make it plain to your new employer that you have had to sacrifice some of your holidays? ❑

7. You are offered a job but when the negotiations are over you find that the salary falls a long way short of what you originally set out to attain (your targeting benchmark). Do you...

a) Accept the offer because you have not been able to find anything better? ❏

b) Turn it down and carry on looking? ❏

c) As b), but see if the feedback from your job hunting is suggesting that you need to adjust your targeting benchmarks? ❏

d) Turn it down and give your job hunting a rest for a while? ❏

8. You are offered a job but the offer is not very detailed. Do you...

a) Turn the offer down? ❏

b) Go back to the employer and ask them to fill in the missing detail? ❏

c) Take the risk, hand your notice in and hope you can find out all you want to know after you have started? ❏

d) Do nothing and wait for the employer to chase you? ❏

9. You applied for a job because it was advertised with a high salary. You have now been offered the job but on a lower salary than the figure indicated in the advertisement. Do you...

a) Turn the job down in disgust? ❏

b) Go back to your targeting benchmark and see how the offer compares? ❏

c) Ring up the employer and ask why you have not been offered the salary advertised? ❏

d) Feel you could have done better if you had inflated the salary quoted in your CV? ❏

10. What is a golden hello?

a) A pension arrangement for top executives ❏

b) A way of making tax-free payments to high earners ❏

c) An upfront payment made at the start of employment (or in stages) and intended as an enticement device ❏

d) A form of severance payment ❏

7 × 7

1 Seven good habits

- When you're applying for jobs, check your emails, voicemail messages and missed calls regularly.

- If you smoke, give it up. Not only will it do wonders for your health but it will also improve your chances of landing a job.

- Be tuned in at all times to pick up feedback. Use what you learn to adjust your targeting benchmarks.

- When you're looking for another job, keep it to yourself.

- Don't advertise your flaws.

- Trust your instincts, especially when it comes to weighing up prospective employers. Listen to what your inner voices are telling you.

- Keep in touch with the job market. Maintain an ongoing view of what's out there.

2 Seven key messages

- See the full range of what's out there for you. Source the whole market and not just part of it.

- Job hunting isn't an exercise in seeing how many applications you can send off.

- Don't miss out on the invisible market.

- When the advancement of your career is at stake, network with only the people you trust.

- Cultivate headhunters and do all you can to keep the approaches coming.

- Learn to see the risk of changing jobs in its proper context. Consider both the upsides and the downsides.

- Don't succumb to enticement. Proceed with caution when you feel you're being made an offer you can't refuse.

3 Seven surprising facts

- Around 90 per cent of jobs aren't advertised. Often, they're the best jobs.
- Most interviewers have never had any training.
- More candidates than you realize are turned down because they're too good for the job.
- Many applications are rejected for no other reason than that they arrive too late. The interview list has already been drawn up and it's tough luck on candidates who couldn't get their act together quickly enough.
- More top jobs are filled by professional networking than by any other method.
- More candidates than you think fail to attend their interviews. In many cases the employer is given no explanation.
- Unsolicited CVs sent to employers are often kept on file for years.

4 Seven things to avoid

- Don't thrash around aimlessly. It leads to time wasting and discouragement.
- Don't sour relations with your current employer by, for example, taking too much time off work for interviews. Make it your first priority to look after the job you've got.
- Don't apply for too many jobs at the same time, unless it's easy for you to get time off work.
- Don't cold call employers too frequently. It will get you seen as a pest.
- Don't register with too many firms of recruitment consultants or you could find yourself faced with too many requests to attend interviews.
- Don't confine your efforts to attacking the visible market.
- Don't try to pull the wool over employers' eyes.

5 Seven things to do today

- Carry out an availability audit, to make sure you're not putting obstacles in the way of employers who are trying to contact you.

- Check the greeting messages on your voicemails. Make sure they project an image that's consistent with the one you want to project to prospective employers.

- Revisit your CV to see how it stands up to the test of being a quick and easy read. Even better, get someone else to look at it (preferably someone with experience in recruitment).

- Remove anything from social networking sites you wouldn't want prospective employers to see.

- Start work on your lifelong interview. Identify where you may need to turn over a new leaf.

- Spare the time to draw up a list of targeting benchmarks.

- Rid yourself of any negative thoughts. Draw a line under the past.

6 Seven top tips

- Be selective when it comes to applying for jobs.

- Always keep back a few days' leave entitlement. Having the capacity to take time off work to go to interviews is an important part of successful job hunting.

- View the time you can take off as precious. Don't squander it on interviews that you know will be time-wasters.

- Make sure employers have always got a way of getting hold of you.

- Put unsolicited CVs in the post addressed to the person responsible for hiring people like you and in an envelope marked 'confidential'.

- Make your job moves count. Don't take risks when the gains in terms of advancing your career are negligible. Don't change jobs to settle scores.

- Always customize your cover letters and CVs so you can bring out your strong points vis-à-vis the job for which you're applying.

7 Seven trends for tomorrow

- Employers will increasingly use Internet search engines as a way of finding out more about the people who apply to them.
- Following on from the last bullet point, employers will be less willing to take people at face value.
- On the visible job market, more recruitment will tend to be done online. Conversely, job ads in journals and newspapers will have a less important part to play.
- The invisible market will expand further.
- There will be more jobs on temporary, fixed-term and zero-hours contracts, reflecting uncertainty in business circles about future trends. Various permutations of 'temp to perm' are expected to become more prevalent as employers seek to minimize their risks.
- As a result of age discrimination legislation, more people will exercise their right to go on working beyond what was once seen as normal retirement age. This will affect the supply side of the job market, in the shape of fewer opportunities for younger people who are trying to break into careers.
- As the world of work changes, the lines between what were once accepted areas of employment and self-employment will continue to blur. Tomorrow, thinking about a change of job could mean embracing the idea of working independently.

PART 3

Your Cover Letters Masterclass

Introduction

We are going to teach you everything you need to know about:

- putting together a good cover letter
- understanding the important part cover letters play in moving job applications to successful conclusions
- how to use this knowledge to your advantage.

Cover letters are what employers read first. If what they see interests them, they'll look at your CV. If, on the other hand, they see nothing that interests them they might give your CV a miss, meaning that's the end of the road as far as your chances of getting the job are concerned. The impact your cover letter makes is, therefore, vital. We will also be looking at the importance of correct grammar and spelling and how to avoid your application going nowhere for this reason alone.

CHAPTER 15

Making a good first impression

In this chapter you will learn about good first impressions and why it is important to make them.

Cover letters occupy a special place in the stages through which a job application passes on its journey from you seeing an opportunity that interests you to what you hope will be a successful conclusion. Cover letters are what employers read first. Up to when your letter comes out of the envelope or arrives in an email, employers know nothing about you. They have no preconceived opinions on your suitability for the job, so the stage is set for you to convince them that it is you and not any of the others they should be taking seriously.

A simplified view of cover letters is that they act as appetizers. If your cover letter does its job, your CV gets read. If your CV does its job, you get an interview, and so on. However, what this simplified view fails to take into account is how well-written cover letters can go on working for you right the way through to the final stages of selection.

The halo effect

The halo effect is the tendency to see some good points in a candidate at the start of the selection process and, from there on, to ignore any flaws which come to light. Professional interviewers are taught to beware of halo effects. They can lead to the wrong candidate getting the job.

The halo effect in reverse

What a lot of people don't realize is that the halo effect can work the other way round. Bad points can register at the beginning and, from there on, it is quite hard to make a comeback.

First impressions stick

The halo effect teaches us:

1 the importance of first impressions
2 how first impressions stick
3 how, once first impressions are formed, they are very hard to shift.

First impressions and cover letters

Cover letters occupy a unique place. They are what employers read first, so how they are seen, good or bad, will play an important part in determining what happens next. For example, a cover letter which arrives written on a scruffy piece of paper and full of spelling mistakes might mean the CV which accompanies it ends up being thrown in the bin without being read. Even if the CV does get a reading, an impression has already formed in the employer's mind and it hardly needs saying the impression won't be favourable and could be a strong factor in deciding who goes on the interview list and who doesn't.

Anyone who has worked in recruitment will tell you how common it is to find CVs which have had a lot of thought put into their preparation accompanied by cover letters which look like they've been dashed off in five minutes without anyone bothering to check them. In some cases it is difficult to believe the cover letters and CVs have been written by the same person.

> ## Key point
>
> It's no use spending hours crafting a great CV unless you are prepared to put the same level of time and effort into crafting an equally great cover letter. The two go together. One without the other doesn't work.

Make the most of the opportunity

There are still people out there who feel they can dispense with cover letters. They send in job applications attached to business cards or to home-made compliments slips. Alternatively, the cover letters they write consist of no more than a simple sentence or two, such as 'I wish to apply for the position of [ ]. A copy of my CV is enclosed. Yours sincerely'.

How such applications are received depends to a large extent on who reads them. Some employers may take the view that the person who sent in the application couldn't take the trouble to write a cover letter (a proper one); that would be a bad first impression. However, there is a much bigger point to be made here and it is this. A cover letter is an **opportunity** to make a good first impression, and missing the opportunity is a pity. Particularly in competitive situations (where jobs have been widely advertised and where there will be hundreds of other applicants), the need to score good first impressions is vital, and what better place to do it than in a cover letter?

An integral part of your CV

This is important. See your cover letter as an integral part of your CV – the front page, if you like. As we shall see later, a cover letter serves the function of drawing out and précising the key points in your CV vis-à-vis the job for which you are applying. Like the front page of a newspaper, you are saying to your readers 'These are the headlines but you'll find lots more interesting stuff inside.'

How a cover letter goes on working for you

We have seen how good first impressions have a vital part to play in moving job applications forward. We have seen how, once you've made good first impressions, they stay there and go on working for you. What we also need to consider is that, as a job application progresses, it brings in more and more people. For example, if you get put on a short list, the Human Resources Manager who saw you at the first interview will hand your papers over to another manager (perhaps the person who will be your boss if you get the job). The top item on your papers will be your cover letter, so now a fresh pair of eyes will be looking at it – someone else whose first impressions of what they see need to be good.

Bad English

Cover letters full of spelling mistakes, bad grammar, incorrect word usage and apostrophes in the wrong place don't go down well with employers. Now is perhaps an opportune moment to say a few words about how much damage job applicants inflict on themselves by not paying sufficient attention to their English.

When all is said and done, it is the responsibility of each one of us to make sure that anything we put in a cover letter (or, for that matter, a CV) projects an image which is consistent with the one we want to project. What we don't want to be seen as is someone who is careless or doesn't have the capacity to pay attention to detail, but sadly this is how cover letters and CVs riddled with mistakes come across. The people who put them together couldn't be bothered to check them properly and, to an employer, this doesn't say a lot for how the same people are going to get on when they're given some real responsibilities.

Later we will be coming back to the subject of making sure that what you're writing won't be sending shudders down the spines of employers who read it!

Spellcheckers

There is nothing wrong with spellcheckers but people can and do place too much reliance on them. A survey recently commissioned by the learning disability charity Mencap highlighted the fact that spellcheckers have given many people a false impression of their spelling ability. Because they've used the spellchecker they think anything they write is fine. They don't proofread, they don't get out the dictionary, they don't go to the trouble of getting a second opinion and the result is they let themselves down badly. The even bigger problem for these people is that no one ever tells them why their applications keep on ending up on the reject pile. They go on sending in letters and CVs riddled with mistakes.

> ### Warning!
> Don't run away with the idea that the problem of letters and CVs full of mistakes is confined to school-leavers and recent graduates. On the contrary, we see many examples of letters written by well-qualified professionals, people applying for senior and top management jobs, which are equally bad.
>
> **Footnote:** the grammar and sentence construction in some cover letters is so bad they don't make sense.

Standard cover letters

We have already looked at cover letters consisting of nothing other than 'Please see attached CV'. Almost as bad – for reasons we'll explain shortly – is the sort of standard cover letter people keep in template form in the documents stored on their computer. Even worse is the standard letter which is printed off with blank spaces which people then fill in with their not always terribly tidy handwriting.

What's wrong with standard cover letters?

Apart from the usual opening and closing paragraphs, they typically give a thumbnail sketch of the applicant: e.g. qualifications, background, current employment, main responsibilities. The constraints of keeping the letter to one page of A4 then tend to kick in, so the employer reading it sees nothing that's greatly relevant to the position they're seeking to fill. Once again the opportunity to score points is missed and the cover letter and the CV that goes with it stand a fair chance of ending up on the same pile as those of all the other applicants who don't seem to have anything interesting to offer.

To employers who see a lot of job applications, standard cover letters:

- are instantly recognizable
- suggest minimal effort has gone into preparing them
- project an image of someone who doesn't overexert themselves
- project an image (perhaps) of someone who is applying for jobs all the time, i.e. not the kind of person who will be a long-term asset to the business.

Again, the next chapter will have a lot more to say about making cover letters do what you want them to do. A prominent message will be the need to engage employers with what interests them, not bland personal statements of the kind which will make them want to switch off.

Pay attention to detail

To people who have never worked in recruitment, it may be surprising to learn just how many cover letters come in with the name of the people to whom they're addressed spelt incorrectly or similar mistakes in the spelling of the names of businesses and/or their addresses. We say surprising because, in the majority of cases, all the applicant had to do was copy what appeared in an advertisement.

Since there can be no other explanation for these lapses apart from carelessness, the message here is always, always pay attention to detail. Needless to say, people who make silly mistakes don't endear themselves to employers. In the world of business, silly mistakes cost money.

Using your cover letter to project a good first impression

So what you need to focus on when you design a cover letter is the impact it will make when it lands on someone's desk. Will it make a good first impression? Or will it let you down and put the kiss of death on your application?

Here is a list of dos and don'ts on presentation which will help you

- to avoid some of the more common mistakes people make
- to ensure your cover letters make a good first impression when they arrive at their destination.

Do:

✔ use black ink on standard white A4 paper

✔ stick to conventional fonts such as Arial or Times New Roman

✔ take care when printing off, especially on inkjet printers, where blots and smudges can become a problem

✔ take care with where you store the paper you use for your cover letters (and CVs). A waft of stale cigarette smoke or the smell of last night's fry-up as it comes out of the envelope at the other end won't do much for you on the first impressions front

✔ use a standard C4 white envelope

✔ keep it concise. Achieve conciseness by keeping it relevant

✔ stick to the default settings when it comes to the width of margins or the spaces at the top and bottom of pages

✔ leave a clear line space between each of your paragraphs

✔ remember to sign it.

Don't:

✗ use coloured ink or paper because neither looks good if for any reason your cover letter has to be faxed or photocopied. The same goes for email, where some of the businesses you write to might print your letter off on a black and white printer

✗ handwrite cover letters. It looks old-fashioned and, more importantly, you lose the capacity to draft, edit and make corrections

✗ try to catch employers' eyes by using fancy fonts and graphics. Keep it plain and simple

✗ in your efforts to get everything on one sheet of paper, try to save space by resorting to font sizes which will have your readers searching for their glasses (or conversely not bothering)

✗ fold your cover letter and CV to make them fit in a small envelope. They will forever bear the crease marks and it runs the risk of someone at the other end with a not too clean pair of hands trying to smooth them out

✗ try to squeeze more in by using every square centimetre of space available

✗ try to cram more in by cutting down on white space.

Summary

Making a good first impression will set your job applications off on the right track. We have just been looking at how cover letters, written with some thought and effort, are the starting point of a process which will hopefully end with you walking away with the offer of a job in your hand. The role of cover letters is often misunderstood. They are seen as serving no purpose other than providing the anchor point for attaching your CV. As a result, little attention is paid to what goes in them and a golden opportunity is missed for scoring important points right at the very start. An opportunity has also been missed for the same points to keep finding their mark with people who come into the selection process later on and who, by definition, will have a large say in whether you get the job or not.

Also you have seen how silly mistakes in cover letters can and do put employers off. The mistakes stick out like a sore thumb and are in most cases the result of carelessness and failure to check letters properly before they are emailed or put in the post. The idea is for people to catch employers' eyes with their skills and abilities, not their bad grammar and spelling mistakes!

Fact-check (answers at the back)

1. What is special about a cover letter?
   a) It is optional ❑
   b) It saves having to write a CV ❑
   c) It is what employers read first ❑
   d) It guarantees getting a reply ❑

2. What is the halo effect?
   a) The tendency to look for a candidate's good points ❑
   b) The impact you can create by arriving for an interview smartly dressed ❑
   c) The tendency to see good points in a candidate at the start of a selection process and thereafter to ignore any flaws that come out ❑
   d) The effect when one candidate for a job is streets ahead of the others ❑

3. With which of these statements do you agree?
   a) A cover letter is more important than a CV ❑
   b) A CV is more important than a cover letter ❑
   c) They are both as important as one another ❑
   d) It depends on the job ❑

4. What is wrong with sending in a CV clipped to a compliments slip and without a cover letter?
   a) It makes you look lazy ❑
   b) You miss the opportunity to make a good first impression ❑
   c) You won't get a reply ❑
   d) There is nothing wrong with it ❑

5. In a cover letter, which will damage your chances of getting the job?
   a) Spelling mistakes ❑
   b) Getting the employer's name wrong ❑
   c) Bad grammar ❑
   d) All of the above ❑

6. Who is to blame for bad spelling in job applications?
   a) The people who make the mistakes ❑
   b) The education system ❑
   c) Spellcheckers ❑
   d) Nobody ❑

7. When is it acceptable to send in a CV without a cover letter?
   a) When you need to get a job application off in a hurry ❑
   b) When you've got a great CV ❑
   c) When you're applying for a temporary position ❑
   d) It is never acceptable ❑

8. What is the best way of making your cover letter stand out?
   a) Printing it on bright coloured paper ❑
   b) Keeping it interesting, concise and relevant ❑
   c) Sending it by courier ❑
   d) Putting your photograph on it ❑

9. What is the best way of making sure your cover letter has got no spelling mistakes in it?
a) Run the spellchecker over it more than once ❑
b) Check it carefully ❑
c) Your spelling is perfect so there is no need to do anything ❑
d) Look up any long words in the dictionary ❑

10. What is wrong with using the same cover letter every time you write off for a job?
a) It looks lazy ❑
b) There is nothing wrong with it ❑
c) Most of the letter won't be relevant to the job for which you are applying ❑
d) Don't know ❑

CHAPTER 16

Making it work for you

In the previous chapter we looked at how cover letters can project a good first impression. Now we are going to look at what to put in them to get the right result.

A cover letter which does its job is one which prompts the reader to want to find out more.

It sounds simple and to some extent it is. Readers of cover letters (employers with positions they need to fill) want to find applicants who tick the boxes. Forget, therefore, the image of employers as people who don't read anything that doesn't jump off the page at them. Yes, most of them are busy people with all sorts of conflicting demands on their time but, if they see an application come in which offers a solution to a problem which is causing them pain (such as a hole in the ranks), then they're hooked. The tricky part, as you've probably guessed, is convincing the employers that you offer the solution and to do it in a cover letter. This is what we'll be focussing on in this chapter.

What we'll also be looking at is what it takes to make yourself 'employer friendly'. 'Employer friendly' means having the capacity to put yourself in employers' shoes, seeing it the way they see it and helping them with the job they have to do. The job in this case is sifting through applications to find ones which are suitable.

The 'one quick read' test

Though all employers are different in the way they process job applications, cover letters do in many cases have to survive quite robust treatment. Here it is worth noting that:

● Reading cover letters sometimes consists of little more than a quick flick through
● Cover letters are not always read from start to finish
● Cover letters are rarely read twice (once they've been put on the reject pile they tend to stay there).

What this means, especially in competitive job situations, is:

● What you have to offer has got to come across first time (it may not get another chance)
● What you have to offer has got to match up with what the employer wants.

Defining the message

So what are employers looking for? Which of your attributes will be the most compelling when it comes to booking your place on the interview list?

No one size fits all

All employers are different. Take two manufacturing businesses looking for someone to head up their human resources management teams. Business A is highly unionized and practically everything is determined by collective bargaining. Business B, on the other hand, is run on paternalistic lines with little union involvement and the main function of human resources management is to administer various welfare schemes. Experience as a hard-nosed negotiator would probably figure highly on the list of key attributes of the job with Business A whereas, with Business B, it would probably not.

Look at the ad for the job

So, given this diversity, how do you go about finding out what employers want? Where do you look to discover what they will find interesting?

A good starting place is the ad for the job, which tells you in outline terms what the employer sees as key qualities. Sometimes the ad will tell you how you can access a full-blown job specification, for example by downloading it from a website.

Where else to look for clues to employers' thinking

Ads, of course, don't tell you everything. They rarely, for example, tell you anything about the culture of businesses or other information which would give you some clues to their preferences when it comes to the people they take on. Suggestions on where else to look?

- **The Internet** is an obvious place. In addition to employers' own websites, you can tap into other interesting insights by searching round; for example, recent news items or, pushing the boundaries a little further, social networking sites.
- **Use your professional networks.** If you have been active in a career for a number of years you will have built up a circle of contacts who may be able to offer you some inside information. Best of all are contacts who work for the employer or who have worked for them in the past.

233

Make your strong points stand out

So, to summarize, what we have done so far is look at what employers want and what they will find interesting. What we are going to turn our attention to next is:

- what you've got to offer
- to what extent what you've got to offer and what the employer is looking for match up.

These matches, where they occur, are what we will be referring to as **strong points**. These strong points are what we need to come across when the employer submits your cover letter to the 'one quick read' test.

Strong points could include any of the following:

- You hold the right qualifications
- You have the right kind of experience
- You have received a particular type of training
- You have the kind of personal qualities the employer is seeking
- You live in the right place (you won't need relocating).

Remember

A reminder again that strong points mean strong points relating to the job for which you are applying and not what you may see as your strong points generally. For example, you may have a lot of experience in designing applications for a particular brand of computer software but this won't cut much ice with an employer who uses completely different systems. And when it comes to determining what employers will find interesting don't fall into the trap of substituting your own ideas for theirs.

Review your strong points

Now draw up a list of what you consider to be your strong points vis-à-vis the job application you're making and then count up how many you've got. Are there more than six? If there are then go through the list again to make sure they really are strong points. Be ruthless here. Don't let irrelevant information get in the way of the message you want your cover letter to deliver.

Keep the message clear and concise

If the job calls for a mechanical engineering degree and you happen to have one then here we have a strong point. Likewise, if the job calls for someone with experience of designing plastic injection mould tools and you've spent ten years in the trade then here we have another strong point. Simple though it sounds, all you have to do in your cover letter is list these strong points using no more than a few simple sentences to describe each. Break your strong points into paragraphs with a line space between each (bullet points are a good way of doing this).

What you have got now is the core part of your cover letter – one which is relevant and consistent with what the employer is seeking to find. The scene is now set for the employer to find out more by reading your CV. A case of job done? Well, almost.

Use their words

In a world of jargon and buzz words you frequently find employers using terminology which would not necessarily be the same terminology you would use. A tip here is to use the employer's terminology rather than your own to prevent any confusion arising.

Credibility and consistency

We frequently point out to people the importance of consistency in any documents they forward to employers. Why is this?

It is unfortunate, perhaps, but we live in a world where there are people who are prepared to bend the truth a little when they see some advantage for themselves. This bending of the truth often manifests itself in false claims of one kind or another, e.g. false accident claims. As a consequence, employers are on high alert especially when it comes to offering a job to someone. Anything in a cover letter or a CV or on an application form which doesn't ring true is therefore usually enough to ensure the application goes no further. The applicant, of course, is none the wiser.

A common way in which job applicants undermine their credibility is by allowing inconsistencies to creep into the information they present to employers. An example of an inconsistency is where different dates appear against jobs the applicant has held previously. One set of starting and leaving dates appears in the applicant's CV and a completely different set of dates appears in the same person's application form. The same goes for cover letters, where time spent in certain spheres of work may be at variance with what the applicant has said elsewhere. The explanation for these inconsistencies is usually carelessness but the impression that could form in some employers' minds is that they are having the wool pulled over their eyes.

> ## Key point
> Be careful that anything you put in a cover letter is consistent with what appears in your CV. Employers can and do compare the two.

What is a key achievement?

We mention this here because:

- Key achievements and strong points often get mixed up
- As a result, information gets included in cover letters which shouldn't be there.

Ask someone what they view as their key achievements and they might, for example, mention the fact that last year they raised a large sum of money for famine relief charities by competing in a number of marathons. An achievement, yes, but is it a strong point? The probable answer here is 'no, it isn't' unless of course our marathon runner happened to be applying for a job with a company which has recently taken a high-profile stance in promoting third world agriculture.

What this illustrates is how easy it is to start introducing your own agendas into cover letters and, again, letting irrelevant information get in the way of the message. It may be great you won first prize in a creative writing competition but, if you're applying for a job as an Internal Audit Manager with a firm of grocery wholesalers, it won't do a lot to promote your chances. By all means give achievements such as these a mention at the appropriate point in your CV because what you do with your life says a lot about you generally. But don't clutter your cover letters with information which isn't relevant.

Where you're coming from and what you're seeking to achieve

Employers will want to know why you're applying for a job with them. Central to their thinking will be the avoidance of mismatches. For example, if you're looking for advancement and the job is a downward step then there would be little point in taking your application any further. If, on the other hand, you're at risk of redundancy then it would be a different matter. Making your motives clear is therefore important.

Key point

Bringing you in for an interview and then finding there is a mismatch between what you are looking for and what the employer has to offer is a waste of everyone's time. The employer's time is wasted and, in your case, you may have taken time off work to go to the interview and/or booked a day's holiday. What this illustrates is that avoiding these mismatches is in everyone's best interests. Often the blame is the applicant's cover letter, which didn't make it clear where the applicant was coming from and what he/she was seeking to achieve.

So, if you're making the application because you feel you're ready for the next step up the ladder, then say so. If on the other hand, you're seeking to branch out into a different field, then, in the same way, make it clear. All it takes in most cases is two sentences tagged onto the first paragraph of your cover letter and a mention in what you have to say about yourself in your CV. Don't leave employers to guess at what's driving you.

Employer friendliness

All of which brings us neatly onto the subject of employer friendliness.

Employer friendliness is important at any stage in a job application and nowhere more so than in the design of a cover letter.

Conciseness and why it's important

Most of what we have done up to now is to do with ensuring that what goes in your cover letter is **relevant**, i.e. it falls in with what employers will be looking to see and will find interesting. Of equal importance, however, is keeping your cover letter **concise**. Why? If you go back to what we said earlier about the one quick read test, we drew your attention to the fact that cover letters are not always read from start to finish. If readers see nothing that interests them in the first few sentences, they switch off and go no further. OK, it doesn't seem very polite when you've gone to a lot of trouble to prepare the cover letter (and the CV that goes with it) but what you've got to remember is that your cover letter could be the sixtieth the employer has read that day, so anything that doesn't grab the attention straight away could finish up on the reject pile for that reason alone.

Careers advisors usually flag up the need to keep cover letters to one side of A4. The idea here is that one side of A4 will act as a constraint on writers of cover letters so they don't end up producing acres of script which employers will have to plough through. In many cases, employers won't bother.

Conciseness and relevance go together

Please remember this. A cover letter which conforms to the rule of one side of A4 maximum won't do much for you if it doesn't say anything relevant to the job for which you are applying. Similarly, a cover letter which is relevant but which rambles on for page after page won't do the trick for you either.

Help employers understand you

Put yourself in the shoes of an employer faced with the job of wading though a pile of job applications and it will help you see how important it is to engage with them quickly, concisely and in a way which will interest them. See the task they face and help them achieve it.

Summary

In this chapter we have been looking at what it takes to make a cover letter work for you in a world where, in many cases, employers are faced with large numbers of applicants competing against one another for a place on the interview list. We have seen the importance of tailoring your cover letters to the jobs for which you are applying and how different attributes you possess will strike different chords with different employers (they are not all the same). We have taught you to pick out which of your attributes make a direct hit with the requirements of the job which interests you and to treat these matches as your strong points – points which will give your cover letter the capacity to attract the attention of readers. At the same time we have looked at employer friendliness and the importance of conciseness, simplicity and making sure your letter is a quick and easy read.

A common complaint you hear from employers is how little effort many applicants make to match their skills, experience and qualifications to the requirements of the job. The ones that do make the effort stand out.

Fact-check (answers at the back)

1. Why is it important to keep your cover letters short?

a) It is the best way of making sure you don't make any spelling mistakes ❏

b) They will be quick and easy to read ❏

c) They take less paper and printer ink ❏

d) They don't detract from your CV ❏

2. What is a strong point?

a) Something the employer wants and which you have to offer ❏

b) Where you have better qualifications than those stipulated in the advertisement for the job ❏

c) Areas in which you have excelled in the past ❏

d) An outstanding achievement ❏

3. What is the best way of making sure your cover letter will be read?

a) Typing it neatly ❏

b) Using a larger than normal font size ❏

c) Making it interesting and concise ❏

d) Putting it in an envelope marked 'Urgent' ❏

4. What is the best way of ensuring a cover letter fits onto a single sheet of A4?

a) Keeping it relevant ❏

b) Reducing the font size ❏

c) Cutting out paragraph breaks ❏

d) Reducing the margins at either side of the page ❏

5. Why is consistency so important?

a) It shows you pay attention to detail ❏

b) It prevents confusion ❏

c) It saves unnecessary questions at interviews ❏

d) Lack of it will undermine your credibility ❏

6. When is a key achievement a strong point?

a) When it is relevant to the job for which you are applying ❏

b) When it receives attention in the media ❏

c) When it was mentioned at your last appraisal ❏

d) The two terms have the same meaning ❏

7. Why is it important to tell employers what you're seeking to achieve by moving jobs?

a) So they know you're ambitious ❏

b) To avoid mismatches ❏

c) To soften them up for discussions about salary ❏

d) It is nothing to do with them ❏

8. In the design of a cover letter, what is the best way of being employer friendly?

a) By addressing the person to whom you are writing by their first name ❏

b) By avoiding formal styles of address altogether ❏

c) By making sure your letter is a quick, easy and interesting read ❏

d) By sending it with a stamped, addressed envelope ❏

9. Which would you rank as the most important?

a) Keeping your cover letters concise ❏

b) Keeping your cover letters relevant ❏

c) Both a) and b) together ❏

d) Something else ❏

10. Why are cover letters not always read from start to finish?

a) The people who read them are too lazy ❏

b) There is nothing in the first few sentences which is interesting ❏

c) They are not important ❏

d) The CV that comes with them takes precedence ❏

CHAPTER 17

The structure of your letter

Judging by the questions we are asked, nothing causes people more problems with cover letters than how to set them out. For example, if the ad for a job asks you to send your CV to Gillian Smith do you start your letter with 'Dear Gillian' or 'Dear Gillian Smith' or is neither correct? After all you don't know Gillian Smith, so it would be more appropriate to stick to a formal style of address, but then how do you address her? Is she a Miss, a Mrs or a Ms? If you get it wrong, is she going to be offended, which wouldn't be a good start, would it?

This level of uncertainty about how to write a business letter correctly is perhaps a reminder that the art has declined substantially in recent years. The advent of email and other ways of communicating with people on business matters has had a great impact on letter writing and, sad to say, the impact has not always been good. For example, the days when every school-leaver going into an office job went to the local commercial college and learned the basics of good letter writing have long gone.

Now we are going to look at what makes a good cover letter in terms of its structure and, hopefully, at the same time clear up any areas of doubt in your mind about what's right and what isn't.

Making a start

Where you do have a big advantage over letter writers of years ago is in the access you have to modern technology. Today you can compose your cover letter on screen, spell check it, edit it if it's too long, alter it if you change your mind about anything and run off drafts as and when you please. So let's make a start with the modern version of a blank sheet of paper, a new document in whatever word-processing software you happen to use.

Fonts

We talked about fonts in Chapter 15 and advised you to stick to standard fonts used in business letters such as Arial or Times New Roman. Sometimes people get tempted to use fonts which fall outside the mainstream because they think it adds interest or says something about their personality. While we can understand the thinking here, what we would rather you do is add interest by making sure anything you say about yourself is relevant. Strange fonts have a tendency to be seen as the choice of strange people.

Font sizes

With font sizes our advice would again be to stick to the sizes you normally find in business letters (11 and 12 points came out as the favourites in a quick sampling exercise we carried out). As we said earlier, people sometimes reduce the size of their fonts so they can squeeze more onto the page. Don't do this because (a) it looks amateurish and (b) it can make letters and CVs difficult to read (i.e. not employer friendly). If you find you're having problems fitting everything onto one sheet of A4, the likely reason is that you're including information which isn't relevant (more on this later).

Margins

The default settings built into your computer software are fine. Don't change them. Don't see it as yet another way of enabling you to cram more onto the page.

White space

Text that is all crammed up, long paragraphs and paragraphs with no space between them are not inviting to the reader, whereas plenty of white space is naturally pleasing to the eye (employer friendly again). Two spaces after every full stop and a line space between paragraphs not only look professional but also encourage people to read what you have written.

Page heading

Start at the top of the page with your address. Many of you will already have a letter heading set up as a template in the documents on your computer. Most of the ones we have seen are excellent and an example appears at the end of Chapter 18. Again, avoid any temptation to unleash your artistic talents. A cover letter is not the place to do it.

Email and telephone points of contact

These should also be included in your page heading (again, see the example in Chapter 18). When employers are happy that you tick the boxes, they might want to invite you in for an interview. Often they will do this by ringing you up or emailing you, so, as part of being employer friendly, you can make it easy for them by having your phone numbers and email address where they don't have to search for them, i.e. in the heading at the top of your cover letter. Your email address and telephone points of contact will also, of course, feature in your CV but information as important as how to get hold of you stands repetition.

The date

A letter which isn't dated is worthless, or so we were always taught. More to the point, a cover letter without a date on it has the mark of one which the writer sends off every time he/she applies for a job. Put the date at the top of the page immediately underneath the letter heading with a line space in between.

Left-hand justification

Some people indent their paragraphs but most writers of business letters don't. There is nothing wrong with indented paragraphs except they look old-fashioned and for this reason are best avoided.

Name and address of the person to whom you are writing

The ad for the job will tell you the name of the person to write to or occasionally you may be invited to send your application to someone who is identified only by their job title, e.g. Chief Executive, Human Resources Manager or Consultant. The simple rule here is to follow the instruction to the letter. So, if you're invited to write to Gillian Smith, write to Gillian Smith. If, on the other hand, you're invited to write to Mrs Gillian Smith then do that. The same goes for letters to the Chief Executive or the Human Resources Manager. In some cases the person you're writing to will have a job title as well as a name, e.g. Gillian Smith, Human Resources Manager. Here again, follow the instruction and include both the name and the job title. Who knows, there may be more than one Gillian Smith in the organization you're writing to and it's important your letter finds its way to the right one!

Warning!

We've said it once but we'll say it again. Be very careful when you're typing in people's names and make sure you copy them correctly. The same goes for the names, addresses and postcodes of businesses. Mistakes are more common than you may think and, not surprisingly, the person whose name you've spelt incorrectly will notice it straight away. How they view your failure to get their name right will be very much a matter for them, but, needless to say, the first impression you make won't be good.

Forms of salutation

When you're asked to send your application to Gillian Smith, how do you address her? 'Dear Gillian' might possibly be seen as a bit familiar but then if you want to avoid this problem you run into another one. Is she Miss, Mrs or Ms? Many people faced with this situation resort to using 'Dear Madam'. OK, so there's nothing wrong with 'Dear Madam' but it's hardly engaging/employer friendly. There is also evidence to suggest that someone addressed by name is more likely to reply to you. Our advice? Start the letter 'Dear Gillian Smith'. It's professional, it's formal without being starchy, yet it's personal and directed at someone in the most fixating way, i.e. by using their name.

Writing to a man doesn't have the same complications as writing to a woman, so, if you're invited to send your application to John Phillips, you can address him as 'Dear John Phillips' or 'Dear Mr Phillips' – either is acceptable. Given this choice our preference would be for 'Dear John Phillips' because including his first name is more engaging.

But what if you're not given the person's name? What if the ad asks you to write to the Human Resources Manager? Does this mean addressing them as 'Dear Sir' or 'Dear Madam' but, as you don't know whether the Human Resources Manager is a man or a woman does this leave you with no choice other than starting your letter 'Dear Sir or Madam'? Perhaps it does and let's straight away say there's nothing wrong with 'Dear Sir or Madam' except it's not very engaging. One approach you might like to consider is writing to 'Dear Human Resources Manager'. It's a bit different and engages with the person you're writing to more than a starchy 'Dear Sir or Madam' would do. We'll leave it up to you.

Make it clear why you're writing

You're writing because you want to apply for a job so make this clear right away and, at the same time, make it clear which job interests you. We say this for the simple reason that organizations are often advertising more than one position, so confusion can and does arise. The fall-out for you is if your application (your cover letter and CV) ends up on the wrong pile. Unfortunately, in large organizations, where opening the post is often left to someone quite junior, this happens more than people think.

The best way to make your intentions clear is by putting a heading in bold at the top of your letter identifying the job for which you're applying. For example:

Re: Production Manager (ref: XX/999)

Not all employers will ask you to quote a reference but, if they do, put it in the heading where it will stand out (as in the example).

Your opening paragraph

In your opening paragraph:

- **Tell the employer where you saw the job advertised.** Recruitment advertising is an expensive item and employers like to know which publications/websites yield the best results. Feedback from applicants is therefore important to them and, from your point of view, it is all part of being employer friendly.
- **Explain why you're applying for the job.** This goes back to what we had to say in the previous chapter about making it plain (a) where you're coming from and (b) what you're seeking to achieve.

Example of an opening paragraph

I wish to apply for the position advertised in last night's *Evening Bugle*. I am currently employed as a Production Manager in the automotive components industry and I am seeking a new position because the plant where I am based is scheduled for closure in six months' time.

Your killer bullet points

Your killer bullet points are the strong points we looked at previously: the matches between what employers want and what you've got to offer – in other words, how you fit the job specification.

Registering your strong points doesn't call for anything elaborate. Two or three short sentences are usually sufficient – enough to whet the reader's appetite and focus his/her interest.

> # Warning!
>
> Intent on catching the reader's eye with what they consider to be their most winning features, some people resort to using capital (upper-case) letters, underlining or picking out key words in red. Don't do this because (a) it is not necessary and (b) it's the written word's equivalent of shouting, i.e. not very polite.

The example cover letter in Chapter 18 shows how to list your strong points.

Closing paragraph

All you have to do now is to tell the employer your CV is attached. At the same time say a few words about your availability, by which we mean:

● your availability to attend interviews
● your availability to start a new job.

> # Example of a closing paragraph
>
> A copy of my CV is attached. I am available to attend an interview at any time except between [ ] and [ ] when I am overseas on a business trip. My current employment is subject to four weeks' notice.

Availability

With availability here are a few dos and don'ts to consider.

Do:

✔ try to give employers as much leeway as you can with interview times

✔ give details of any holidays, dates when you can't attend etc.

✔ see it from the employer's point of view. If you are on a redundancy list and the date you've been given is still some way off, tell the employer what the position would be if they offered you a job. For example, are there any arrangements for early release?

✔ state the period of notice set out in your terms of employment.

Don't:

✗ say you're only available for interviews after 6.00 p.m. or on Saturday mornings. If you do, you won't find too many takers

✗ say you're available when you're not

✗ leave unanswered questions. For example if your branch is closing in six months' time, does it mean you can't start a job for six months?

✗ (if you're employed) make statements such as 'I could start a new job at any time', which gives the impression you would leave your current position without giving the proper notice. Understandably, employers don't warm to people who are prepared to act in this way; it's a bad first impression.

Signing off

All that remains now is to finish your letter by signing off in the proper way.

There are only two acceptable ways of ending a business letter: one is 'Yours sincerely;' and the other is 'Yours faithfully'. So forget 'best wishes' or 'kind regards' or anything else you may put at the end of a letter written to someone you have had correspondence with before.

'Yours sincerely' or 'Yours faithfully'

The rules here are simple. If your letter starts with a name (e.g. Gillian Smith) then you end it 'Yours sincerely'. If it starts 'Dear Sir' or 'Dear Madam' then the more formal 'Yours faithfully' is correct.

Sign your name

Leave five line spaces for your signature and then type in your name (first name and surname). Initials (e.g. J. Brown or, worse still, Miss J. Brown) look standoffish and old-fashioned when the general idea is to engage with the person you're writing to.

> # Warning!
>
> If your letter is a hard copy that's going to go in the post, don't forget to sign it.
>
> Though the reason is usually oversight, letters that haven't been signed have unfortunate connotations for employers. Rather like application forms which come back without being signed, the omission could suggest the information you've given in your letter isn't true.

Anything else?

Insert another line space after your name and then type in: Attached CV

This is another way of bringing your cover letter and CV together.

Footnote: staple your cover letter and CV together to minimize the risk of them being separated when they arrive at the other end.

Envelopes

In Chapter 15 we drew your attention to using a full-size white C4 envelope so your cover letter and CV don't have to be folded. Typing the employer's name and address on an envelope can pose a challenge and, even with the best of us, it can result in a few failed attempts! You can of course print off a sheet of labels in anticipation of having further correspondence with the employer. However, don't worry about hand-writing an envelope provided you do it neatly. In any case, envelopes are usually discarded once they are opened.

Mailing cover letters

The reliability of postal services is usually a question of where you live. However, to avoid any risk of your job application being delayed in the post (and arriving too late), it's well worth investing in whatever guaranteed next-day delivery service is available in your part of the world.

Emails

Some job advertisements ask you to submit your application by email. Email scores highly in terms of speed and certainty of getting there. If the email is addressed to a named individual it is also a safe bet that he/she will open it and read it straight away.

The normal way of submitting an application by email is to put your cover letter in the body of the email and your CV in a file attachment. Any problem with this? Yes: what can happen is the email and the file attachment get separated – the usual reason being the file attachment gets printed off and the email doesn't. So all the effort you've put into preparing your cover letter is wasted. To avoid this we suggest you do as follows. Put a copy of your cover letter (complete with your name, address, points of contact etc. at the top) in the file attachment with your CV. Effectively your cover letter becomes the first page of your CV and you will have done your best to ensure it is assembled in this way when it comes off the printer at the other end.

Keeping control

Keeping your cover letter and CV together in this way is an example of **keeping control**. In the context of job applications, keeping control means keeping your hand on the steering wheel as far as you can, so your applications go in directions which you want them to go in. In this case you will have kept control over what finishes up on the desk of whoever will be making the decision on what happens to your application next.

Warning!

The issue of not being able to open files attached to emails is a serious one. People who process job applications won't as a rule be IT experts, so an email attachment which won't open stands a reasonable chance of remaining unopened. Rather than leave this to chance we suggest you send a test email with a file attachment either to your work email address or to one of your friends or family.

Writing style and good English

We have had a lot to say already about how candidates let themselves down with spelling mistakes and bad grammar. Email has brought a new dimension to this problem with

255

some people feeling that it's acceptable to allow lapses to creep in when corresponding with someone by email. The first point to make, therefore, is that it isn't acceptable and just as much care needs to be taken. Email also, for some reason, encourages people to adopt a more relaxed (casual) style of prose. Here is where 'Hi' and 'Cheers' are sometimes used in place of more conventional forms of salutation and signing off.

As a job application progresses, you will hopefully receive emails from the employer inviting you to interviews and second interviews, and, who knows, an email offering you the job. Here you may find the employer starts off with 'Hi' and ends up 'Regards' or 'Best wishes', which is on the whole a good sign of someone seeking to engage with you. Where this happens it is perfectly acceptable for you to respond in the same way; indeed to do otherwise might be seen as unfriendly or standoffish.

Bad English, as we have said several times, is usually the result of carelessness and, as such, it can be corrected by paying more care and attention to what you write. A tip you may find useful is to avoid some of the more obvious grammatical clangers by keeping your sentences short. Wandering off into subordinate clauses invites trouble but even more of a problem, we find, is that the meaning starts to become obscure. Take it from us, readers of cover letters won't spend time racking their brains over whether you meant this or that or something completely different altogether.

Note

We'll be coming back to writing style and good English in Chapter 21.

Summary

You may already be well versed in the art of writing good business letters, so a lot of what we have looked at may be going over old ground. There is, however, usually room for improvement and practice makes perfect. The more cover letters you write, the better you become at it.

What we hope to have shown you is that, if you do it right, setting out a good cover letter isn't difficult and will score you points on the favourable first impressions front.

Also we have looked at the challenge you face when you are asked to submit an application by email. It looks straightforward enough but unfortunately there is more scope for something going wrong; hence the few words about the importance of doing the best you can to keep control.

You have now arrived at the point where you are ready to put what you have learned into practice. Now we will start by looking at how to put together a cover letter for attacking the visible or advertised job market.

Fact-check (answers at the back)

1. When is it correct to start a cover letter with 'Hi'?
   a) When you're sending it by email ❏
   b) When you're writing to a named person ❏
   c) If you're under 25 ❏
   d) Never ❏

2. How is it best to end a letter which starts 'Dear Gillian Smith'?
   a) Yours faithfully ❏
   b) Yours sincerely ❏
   c) Best wishes ❏
   d) Yours truly ❏

3. Where on a cover letter do you put the date?
   a) Under your address at the top ❏
   b) At the end ❏
   c) It doesn't matter where you put it ❏
   d) Under the address of the person to whom you're writing ❏

4. Why is it important to identify the job for which you're applying?
   a) It helps to show you're interested ❏
   b) It is a way of making sure your letter is read ❏
   c) It is a way of making a good first impression ❏
   d) The employer may be advertising more than one position ❏

5. Why is it bad practice to pick out key points in your letter with capital (upper-case) letters?
   a) It's not necessary ❏
   b) It doesn't create a good first impression ❏
   c) It is the written equivalent of shouting ❏
   d) All three of the above ❏

6. What's wrong with not signing your letter?
   a) Nothing is wrong with it ❏
   b) To some employers it might suggest you're not telling the truth ❏
   c) It could show you don't own a decent pen ❏
   d) Employers need to see evidence of your handwriting ❏

7. In an email, where is the best place to put a cover letter?
   a) In the body of the email ❏
   b) With your CV in a file attachment ❏
   c) In both a) and b) ❏
   d) In a separate file attachment ❏

8. What is the most common cause of spelling mistakes?
   a) Bad teaching in schools ❏
   b) Spellcheckers ❏
   c) Carelessness and not checking ❏
   d) Tiredness ❏

9. Why is it a good idea to keep sentences short?
a) There is less scope for grammatical errors ❑
b) It takes less effort ❑
c) Their meaning is usually clear ❑
d) They don't need to be checked ❑

10. How do you choose between sending in an application by email and putting it in the post?
a) It depends on whether you've got the employer's email address or not ❑
b) You don't. You do what the advertisement tells you to do ❑
c) You send it by email if you want your application to get there quicker ❑
d) Flip a coin ❑

CHAPTER 18

Attacking the visible market

In this chapter we're going to look at what to some people is the toughest challenge of all: designing a cover letter to attack the visible or advertised job market, where the issues will be engaging with and overcoming competition.

How many applications are received for a job will depend to a large extent on:

- How good is the job?
- How widely has it been advertised?

It goes almost without saying that a good job which has been given prominent advertising will attract large numbers of applicants. In recessionary times, these numbers increase several-fold, reflecting the fact that:

- good opportunities are thin on the ground
- more people are chasing them.

What this means from the employer's point of view, of course, is that every time they advertise a position they are faced with excessive numbers of people who are capable of doing it. The issue for the applicant therefore becomes one of how on earth are they going to make themselves stand out from the crowd?

Against this backdrop, the job of a cover letter takes on bigger proportions. It has to perform feats out of the ordinary, which sets the scene nicely for this chapter.

> ## Be aware of what you're up against
>
> Applicants for jobs usually have the disadvantage of not knowing what competition they're up against, in terms of both its quantity and its quality. In some cases they proceed blithely, hardly moving out of first gear, in the vain hope that the cover letter and CV they're used to churning out will be good enough. When the reply comes back saying they've not got on the interview list, they don't understand. As they see it, they've got all the qualifications needed to do the job – indeed they could do it with their eyes shut – so why haven't they been given the chance to go further? Usually people in this position blame the employer for not reading their cover letter and CV properly. What they rarely see is that the responsibility for not getting their message across rests squarely on them.

Checklist

We have prepared a checklist for you which should help to highlight where you may be going wrong with the cover letters you're submitting. At the same time the checklist will act as a revision exercise by picking out the main points you've learned so far.

Go through the checklist and put a tick against the questions to which you can truthfully answer 'yes'.

- Are your cover letters typed on one sheet of plain white A4 paper?
- Do you design a new cover letter every time you apply for a job?
- Are they set out in the way we described in Chapter 17?
- Other than using a spellchecker, do you check your spelling and grammar rigorously?
- Are you identifying your strong points?
- Are your strong points matched to the skills, experience and qualifications the employer is seeking?

- Is everything in your cover letters capable of being understood in one quick read?
- Do you check for consistency between the information in your cover letters and what appears in your CV?
- Do you always remember to sign your cover letters?
- Have you done background research into employers and taken the trouble to find out more about them?
- Are you getting your applications in the post promptly?
- With emails, are you including a copy of your cover letter in the file attachment with your CV?
- Are you making it clear to employers what interests you about working for them?

Defining the task you face

In every trawl of applicants for jobs which have been advertised, there are usually a few no-hopers, people who are not properly qualified to do the job but who thought they'd give it a shot anyway. However, take these no-hopers out and what employers usually find they are left with is a large number of people who, on paper at least, seem be quite capable of doing the job.

Most people these days are quite savvy when it comes to applying for jobs. They read books such as this one, they go on the Internet, and by and large they know what to do. So the task you face is a tough one. Somehow you've got to stand out from a crowd of people who in many cases will be every bit as good as you.

How employers see it

Employers faced with large numbers of applicants can afford to be picky and choosy when it comes to deciding whom to interview. On the one hand they won't want to miss the best applicant but on the other hand they are constrained by time so they won't be able to see everyone. What follows, therefore, is a whittling down of candidates done on the basis of who, on paper, matches the specification closest. Out at this stage go people with a question mark over what they have to offer – for example, people who haven't made themselves very clear in their cover letters and CVs. Phoning people up and asking them 'Did you mean this or that?' doesn't figure at all in this process.

> ## Key point
> In these highly competitive situations 'once' really does mean 'once' when it comes to counting how many times your cover letter will be read. It has to register with employers first time because it won't get another chance.

Who stands out?

What the decisions tend to rest on at this crucial stage is 'who stands out?' So back to the strong points which you've listed out in your cover letter. How do they measure up and, more importantly, how do they measure up when other people also have strong points to offer? Is it a case of whose strong points are strongest? Well, perhaps it is, but where we need to start with this is by asking two questions:

● How have you described your strong points?
● Have you undersold them?

What's different about you?

Let's take an example:

You are applying for a senior management job with an Italian-owned business where one of the main requirements is that you speak Italian. OK, you do speak Italian, but what's a safe bet here is that most of the other candidates can also speak Italian or they wouldn't have applied for the job in the first place. However, what's different about you is the fact that one of your parents is Italian so to you Italian is practically a first language. What's the betting no one else can say the same? So here potentially you have something which will make you stand out from the crowd. All you have to do now is mention it and what better place than in your cover letter?

Your unique selling points

What we're looking at here are your unique selling points or USPs. In a nutshell your USPs are:

- what mark you out as different from the rest
- what you need to bring out if you are going to be successful at engaging with and overcoming competition.

Why you want the job

How else can you make yourself stand out from the crowd? In your cover letter is there anything which will make employers warm to you where they may not warm to others?

Let's take another example:

Two people, Jack and Jill, both with more or less the same qualifications, apply for a job.

In his cover letter Jack says he is making the application because he is at risk of redundancy.

Jill, on the other hand, tells the employer she wants the job because she has read about what the company does and wants to be part of it.

In Jack's case, the impression he is creating is that he is in a tight corner and any job will do to get him out of it. The further impression is that he only applied for the job because of the situation he is in and not because of any great interest in it.

With Jill, she is telling the employer she wants to come and work for them and why. The message in this case is one the employer wants to hear.

OK, we may feel sorry for Jack because his situation is all too familiar to us – but what the example is intended to show is how statements like 'I'm looking for a job because I'm being made redundant in six months' time' don't make much of an impression when an employer has lots of other applicants knocking on the door – applicants who may be like Jill.

The message? Have something **positive** to say about why you're applying for a job – for example, say you want to come and work for the business because of its excellent reputation or because the position you've seen advertised fits in exactly with where you see your next move (or both). Give the employer something to get excited about, which you will only do if you feel excited about it too.

Say it with flair and conviction

This leads us to where a lot of cover letters fall down. The messages in them are flat. The words are just words and, take it from us, reading one cover letter after another can be a mind-numbing experience. Then thankfully one comes along which is lively and engaging and it stands out like a splash of colour against a grey background.

Writing is a craft, and learning to write in a way which will make readers' eyes light up isn't a gift which comes overnight. However, there is a lot we can all do to make what we write more engaging. Just as an experiment, what we would like you to do is to take an example of something you want to say about yourself and, giving it your best shot, write it in four different ways. Then in a few days' time go back to what you've written and see what you think or ask someone you know to give you an opinion. Hopefully what this experience will prove to you is that you can always better what you did first time, remembering that better in this context means better from the standpoint of making what you've written have a bigger impact on the reader. Though we're not expecting you to aspire to the standards of the world's great literary figures (at least not yet!) you can do wonders and even surprise yourself with a bit of effort and inclination. Most of all, see the job of engaging with your readers as important and something worth doing, something which will help to make you stand out.

Conviction

Delivering your messages in ways which readers find easy to follow and understand has the added advantage of making them authoritative and more convincing. For the proof, try reading a newspaper article written by a good journalist and see how many times you find yourself nodding along in agreement.

Making it interesting

If there is anything interesting about any of the experience you've had, then, provided it's relevant to the job, say so. Picking out points of interest like this is a way of making employers want to find out more about you by looking at your CV. If, for example, you've worked for a business in the past which has many of the same customers as the employer you're writing to now, then make sure to mention it.

267

What makes success?

Attacking the visible market is by its very nature difficult. Even if you do everything right the odds are still heavily stacked against you. For example, where there are 200 applicants for a job and only 12 are called in for interview, your chances of being one of the lucky ones are slim, to say the least.

Why are we saying this? For the simple reason that getting a letter advising you that you've not been selected to attend an interview can be a big setback, especially when you've built your hopes up. Not perhaps appreciating the scale of the task you faced in the first place, your thoughts immediately turn to where you may have gone wrong. Sooner or later the finger starts to point in the direction of your cover letter and CV. Your cover letter and CV were designed, after all, to get you interviews, so their failure to do so is automatically seen as a bad reflection on their effectiveness.

Although some kind of inquest into why your job applications don't appear to be enjoying much success makes good sense, it equally makes good sense not to leap immediately to the conclusion that your cover letters and CVs aren't working for you. Success on the visible job market is often more to do with the ability to keep going in the face of what seems like adversity. Tinkering with the finer points of cover letters is in many cases wasted effort which would be much better put into getting off the next job application.

Example of a cover letter for attacking the visible market

John Everyman has seen a position for a Factory Manager advertised in the local evening newspaper. The position is with a business which is part of a large multi-national and which makes aluminium extruded sections for the construction industry.

John Everyman
12 Acacia Gardens
Anytown AT99 9XX
Tel: xxx xxxxx
Mobile: xxx xxxxxxx
email – Johne@xxx.com

29 March 2013

Julie Robertson
Human Resources Manager
XX Extruded Sections Limited
PO Box xx
Anytown
AT11 1ZZ

Dear Julie Robertson

Re: Factory Manager

I wish to apply for the position advertised in last night's *Evening Bugle*. You will see from my CV (attached) that I am currently employed as a Cell Manager in a precision engineering company where I am responsible for 120 operatives working four on/ four off continental shifts. I am aware of XX Extruded Sections' excellent reputation and I would welcome the opportunity to talk further about joining your management team.

With regard to the requirements set out in your advertisement:

Modern manufacturing techniques Information on the training I have received is given in my CV. In my present job I have been closely involved with the introduction of fast tooling changes.

Qualifications I have a degree in mechanical engineering

Management experience I have been in my present position for five years and previously worked for eight years as Shift Manager in charge of a high volume production unit.

Additional information For five years post apprenticeship I worked on the design of a range of dies and tools including plastic and aluminium extrusion dies.

Apart from Monday morning when I chair production meetings I am available for interview at any time. My current employment is subject to one calendar month's notice.

I look forward to hearing from you.

Yours sincerely

John Everyman
Attached: CV

Key points to pick out from John Everyman's cover letter are as follows:

- It looks professional
- It is well written
- It makes a good first impression
- It is a quick and easy read
- Everything in it is relevant to the job for which he is applying
- He has told the employer what makes him a serious contender for the job
- He has done some background research into XX Extruded Sections and found out they too operate four on/four off continental shifts
- He figured correctly that mentioning his experience of managing four on/four off shifts would work in his favour
- He also figured that other applicants may not have the same experience or, if they did, they may not mention it
- The mention of fast tooling changes is neat. He has figured that non-productive time spent on changing dies and how to reduce it must figure prominently in XX's thinking
- He has worked out his experience in designing aluminium extrusion dies is another unique selling point. He sees it as

a safe bet that not many people applying for the job (if any) would have experience of both production management and the design of dies
- The mention of chairing production meetings on Monday morning is a nice touch. It shows his loyalty to his employer and that the discharge of his duties comes first.

Summary

In this chapter we have looked at the challenging task of designing a cover letter to attack the visible market, where it's not just what you have to offer that you have to consider but what other applicants have to offer as well. We have directed your attention to the following:

- What makes you different from the rest? What are your unique selling points and how do you get them across?
- What do employers want to hear you saying?
  - Why do people who are passionate about wanting the job stand out?
  - Is there anything interesting in your background (anything that would make the reader of your cover letter sit up and single you out)?

Finally, we looked at how to condition your expectations when you're applying for jobs on the visible market. You won't get an interview every time and to think otherwise is not being realistic. If, on the other hand, you are getting some interviews and the jobs are good jobs then it is probably a sign your cover letters and CVs are working.

Fact-check (answers at the back)

1. What is the visible job market?
   a) Jobs in the public sector ❏
   b) Jobs which have been advertised ❏
   c) Jobs in high-profile industries ❏
   d) Jobs which are only open to graduates ❏

2. What's the main job your cover letters have to do when you're applying for jobs on the visible market?
   a) Engage with and overcome competition ❏
   b) Cover up your defects ❏
   c) Make employers take you seriously ❏
   d) Draw attention to your qualifications ❏

3. In the context of job applications, what is a unique selling point?
   a) Where there is a match between the requirements of the job and what you have to offer ❏
   b) A point in your favour ❏
   c) An unusual requirement in a job specification ❏
   d) Where you have something to offer which none of the others do ❏

4. What's important about unique selling points?
   a) They make you look better than you are ❏
   b) They make you stand out from the rest ❏
   c) Employers are fooled by them ❏
   d) They make it easier for you to negotiate a better salary than the one advertised ❏

5. What's wrong with giving impending redundancy as your reason for applying for a job?
   a) Unscrupulous employers may see it as an opportunity to negotiate a lower salary with you ❏
   b) Employers don't want people who've been picked out for redundancy ❏
   c) It's not a good enough reason for wanting the job ❏
   d) There's nothing wrong with it ❏

6. In competitive job situations, which of the following will help you most with getting interviews?
   a) Telling employers you're the greatest ❏
   b) Sending in a cover letter printed on red paper ❏
   c) Provided it's relevant to the job, highlighting areas where you may have more to offer than other applicants ❏
   d) Telling employers about your sporting achievements ❏

7. What's good about cover letters that are well written?
   a) They stand out ❏
   b) They make you look clever ❏
   c) They make you look more assertive ❏
   d) They show you're serious ❏

274

8. What do you need to take into account when you send a cover letter to a 'generalist' such as a consultant or a human resources manager?

a) They'll be more fussy about bad grammar and spelling mistakes ❑

b) They may not be familiar with what you do or the terminology you use ❑

c) They take a long time to answer ❑

d) They are more likely to read the letter than someone who is busy ❑

9. When do you need to think about designing a new cover letter?

a) When you're not getting interviews ❑

b) When you're only getting interviews occasionally ❑

c) When the interviews you're getting are for jobs which don't interest you ❑

d) Every time you apply for a job ❑

10. When is it better to send a cover letter by email?

a) When it's hard to get to the post ❑

b) When you know there will be large numbers of applicants for the job ❑

c) When you're on the last minute to get it off quickly ❑

d) Only when the advertisement for the job invites you to use email ❑

CHAPTER 19

Attacking the invisible market

In this chapter we are going to look at designing a cover letter for attacking the invisible job market:

- jobs which aren't advertised
- jobs which for one reason or another employers keep to themselves.

There is no way of accurately measuring the size of the invisible job market but it's fair to say that it is:

- big
- bigger than most people think.

One way of accessing the invisible job market is by sending out speculative mail shots either by post or in email form. Designing a cover letter for this purpose is what we will be looking at now. The rules – as we shall see – are very different from the rules for attacking the visible market. Notably there is no job advertisement to look at:

- nothing to tell you what the employer views as important
- nothing to give you clues on how to prioritize your key skills and achievements.

What you want a speculative mail shot to achieve

The hope with a speculative mail shot is that your application ends up on the right desk at the right time.

- **Right desk** means the desk of whoever is responsible for hiring people like you
- **Right time** means when there is a need to recruit or a need to recruit is about to arise.

Failing this, what you want to achieve with your speculative mail shot is to ensure your cover letter and CV are put away in the **right file**. The **right file** in this case means the file the employer revisits when the need to recruit next comes up.

Revisiting previous applicants

Employers faced with a vacancy to fill often start by looking back at the details of interesting candidates they've kept on file. If they come across someone suitable then:

- The 'someone suitable' is asked in for an interview
- If he/she ticks the boxes, he/she gets offered the job
- No one else gets a look in.

What opportunities are you seeking to source?

A further point to consider here is that your speculative mail shot could connect with a vacancy which has already been advertised (one you've missed). In other words, the employer is already recruiting, so your application is added to the list. However, the idea behind a speculative mail shot is not to source jobs which are already out in the market place but to prise out two types of opportunity:

- **first**, where the employer is thinking about recruiting but hasn't got round to it yet
- **second**, where your letter and CV generates sufficient interest to get an employer thinking 'Can we create a slot for this person?'

We would add a third situation here which is typical of recruitment in recessionary times. Employers faced with a gap in their ranks hold fire and wait for signs of recovery to show before they commit themselves to hiring. An enquiry from someone who looks interesting can often tip the balance in these situations.

The task your cover letter has to perform

Employers are bombarded with unsolicited job applications and most of them are seen as time-wasters. Therefore – rather like applications for jobs which have been advertised – the first feat your cover letter has to perform is to make your application stand out from the rest. This is not easy when, as we said a little earlier, you start off with little idea of what qualities the employer sees as important. You are left fishing in the dark – or so it seems.

Tap into your professional network

Before sending in an unsolicited job application a question you need to ask yourself is 'Why is this employer going to be interested in me?'

Apart from seeing what's useful in the way of information out there on the Internet, a good place to start is with your professional network, the circle of contacts you have built up over the years. For example:

- Do you know anyone who works for the employer or who has worked for them in the past? If so, what can they tell you?
- Do you know anyone who has business links with the employer – for example a supplier?
- Do you know any of the employer's competitors?

The value of background research

Often it's just a case of making a few phone calls and, although at the end of it you may not have a complete picture, you will have more information than you started off with and hopefully enough to know what is going to interest the employer and what isn't.

Example: a few years ago we talked to a design engineer who was looking for a new job. Before she sent off a speculative letter, she found out from a contact in the industry what computer-aided design package the employer used. She then gave her experience of working with the package a prominent place in her cover letter and a few days later she got a phone call to ask her to attend an interview. Making the match, getting across a strong point, worked for her.

Intelligent guesswork

There is nothing wrong with intelligent guesswork, particularly in situations where the information available to you would otherwise be thin on the ground. In the example of John Everyman we saw how he guessed his knowledge of fast tooling changes would add weight to his application to XX Extruded Sections.

Whom to write to

The next question you face when you sit down to the job of writing a speculative cover letter is whom do you send it to?

With everything we've said so far about engaging with employers and being employer friendly, it goes against the grain to suggest we get over this problem by writing to the business rather than a named individual, starting the letter with 'Dear Sirs...'

Get a name

It's important with a speculative cover letter that it is sent to the **right** person and, as we noted earlier, right in this context means the person who is responsible for hiring people like you. So, for example, if you're an accountant the right person may be the Finance Director, or, if you're putting yourself forward for a job at the top of the tree, you may need to send it to the Chief Executive.

How do you find out the name of the person you want to write to? This is the easy bit. The names of key job holders are often on websites. Failing this, just phone up and ask.

Warning!

Phoning up and asking has a danger, and it is this. The person you speak to may, for no reason other than being helpful, give you the name of the Human Resources Manager or a personal assistant through whom job applications are normally channelled. Human resources managers and personal assistants don't hire anyone, except perhaps for people looking for jobs in human resources management. Note also that human resources managers have bigger piles of unsolicited letters on their desks than anyone else, whereas people such as finance directors won't be quite so inundated.

Explain your ambitions

Now you have:

- a name
- a list of what you're hoping the person you're writing to is going to find relevant and interesting.

What you need to do next is decide what you want to say about why you're writing to the employer, i.e. what kind of opportunities you are hoping they will have.

Case study

Jenny X, a young and highly successful key account executive with one of the leading names in the food industry, wrote off to a number of competitors with the sole idea of improving her salary. Because of her background and track record she had no difficulty at all when it came to getting interviews but, because she said nothing about her pay ambitions in her cover letter (or her CV), she found the jobs with the competitors were in money terms sideways or in some cases backwards steps. The result? She used up a lot of her holiday entitlement on going to interviews which were effectively a waste of time. The fault? Regrettably it was hers.

A lot of unsolicited letters we have seen are like Jenny X's: strong on what the candidate has to offer but weak/silent/unclear on what they're seeking to achieve. In Jenny X's case, our guess is she fell into the trap of not talking about money because she thought it might make her seem greedy and avaricious. However, what needs to be considered here is that without any information on what's driving candidates – where they're coming from and what they're seeking to achieve – employers won't have a clue. They too are left groping in the dark and this can and does lead to misunderstandings.

Key point

With a speculative letter everything is the other way round. It's you, not the employer, who designs the job specification. It's what you want, not what the employer wants. It's what the employer has to offer, not you.

Be open and explicit

Again, this is important, and Jenny X's case will serve as a good example. Money, as we know, is a sensitive subject but in her cover letter she needed to make it clear:

● that she was looking for a better salary
● what she was earning now and the figure she was aspiring to.

By being open and explicit, Jenny X would have saved both the employers and herself a lot of time.
Note: being open doesn't just apply to salary. It is equally important to be open about your other ambitions. For example, if you're looking for an upwards rather than a sideways move in terms of your position on the management ladder then again you need to say so.

Mark your letter and envelope 'confidential'

Here is a tip. If you want your letter and CV to be opened by the person to whom it's addressed and not someone else (e.g. a post room clerk) then the best way to ensure this happens is by marking the letter and the envelope 'confidential'.

Send out unsolicited job applications in small batches

Taking time off work to go to interviews may not be a problem for you if you're in one of these situations:

● you are unemployed
● you are in full-time education

283

- your employer is happy for you to take time off work, e.g. you're being made redundant and your employer is supporting your efforts to find another job
- your hours of work are flexible
- you work part-time or on shifts so you have free time during the day
- your movements aren't closely supervised.

Otherwise you need to be careful how many speculative job enquiries you send out in one go. If you don't, you can find yourself overwhelmed with requests to attend interviews, leaving you with the problem of having to negotiate time off work (which could be awkward) or (the worst situation) having to turn interviews down.

Key point

Because you don't have any idea how your speculative enquiries are going to be received, it is best to send them out in small batches – say two or three at a time with gaps of a few weeks in between. Another reason for this advice is that the job of putting together a cover letter and CV for a 'cold' mail shot calls for a lot of input in terms of both background research and time spent in front of the screen. Sending out enquiries in small batches will therefore be more manageable for you.

Put it in the post

When you've written your speculative cover letter you have to decide whether to send it in the post or by email. Our advice? Put it in the post. Why do we say this? For the simple reason that emails aren't always printed off. Say, for example, you're looking for a job as a logistics manager and you email your speculative enquiry to the Head of Operations in a large distribution business. The Head of Operations will read your email on screen, possibly with interest, but if there isn't a current vacancy for a logistics manager there is a strong chance he/she will delete it.

If you go back to what we said earlier, you will remember that one of the aims with a speculative letter is to ensure your details go into the right file. If your email isn't printed off then this of course won't happen. So the next time an interesting vacancy comes up your cover letter and CV won't be where you want them to be.

> ## Warning!
> Be aware that with emails busy people are very selective about what they print off. Whereas a reply to a job advertisement (one where you've been asked to submit the application by email) will be printed off, the same can't be said for a speculative enquiry. There is also the danger of your carefully crafted email being treated as spam, i.e. being deleted without being read, or, worse still, the file attachment with your CV not being opened because of concerns about unleashing viruses into the business's IT systems. We know of some organizations where emails with attachments from unknown people are filtered out automatically.

Don't expect a reply

One of the difficulties about sending off speculative job applications is that often you hear nothing back – not even an acknowledgement.

Whether employers should reply to everyone who sends in an unsolicited letter and CV is a matter of opinion. Some do, some don't, and this is a fact you are going to have to learn to live with. The biggest difficulty, of course, is not knowing whether your enquiry has been favourably received or not, whether it has been filed away in the right file or whether it has been fed into the shredding machine. In short, you get no feedback and this is the issue we will be dealing with next.

What is success?

With jobs which have been advertised, success can be judged by how many times you get on the interview list. However, with speculative job applications, measuring success isn't quite so easy. If your application has landed on the right desk at the right time and been favourably received, then you will probably find out by getting a phone call. If, on the other hand, you hear nothing then it could mean:

- **either** your application has been favourably received but the employer has no vacancies
- **or** your application has not been favourably received and it has gone somewhere it will never see the light of day again.

Focus on what's important

When evaluating the success of unsolicited cover letters, don't base your judgements on how many polite letters of acknowledgement you receive. Focus instead on what really matters, which is:

- connecting with opportunities which haven't yet surfaced on the job market
- making sure unadvertised opportunities never surface because you got in first.

Example of a cover letter for attacking the invisible market

Sharon Smart is in a sales job with a firm of distributors which services builders' merchants, DIY chains and garden centres. Sharon has seen her promotion prospects taken away by the appointment of a Sales Manager from outside the business. Being ambitious, she decides to see what the competition has to offer.

Sharon Smart
9 Quayside House
Nowhereville
WWxx xxx
Tel: xxxx xxxxxx
Mobile: xxxxx xxxxxx
email – sharonsmart@xxx.com

29 March 2013

CONFIDENTIAL

Jill Cleverly
Head of Sales
ABC Limited
Greenfield Industrial Estate
Greatly on Spree
GSXX XXX

Dear Jill Cleverly

Sales Management Opportunities

I am currently employed by Allproducts Distribution Services and I am writing to see if you have any openings in sales management for an ambitious twenty-nine-year-old graduate with five years' experience in the industry. My main reasons for feeling I am ready for a management position are:

- I spent three and a half years working a territory before being promoted into a key accounts role (the job I do now).
- The business I currently bring in accounts for approximately 30% of Allproducts' UK turnover.
- I am currently studying part-time for an MBA – a course I am on track to complete in six months' time.

A copy of my CV is attached.

I am available for interview at any time. My contractual period of notice is one month. My salary is £xxxxx per annum.

Yours sincerely

Sharon Smart

Attached: CV

Key points to pick out from Sharon Smart's cover letter are:

- It looks professional
- It is well written
- It makes a good first impression
- It is a quick and easy read
- Sharon has written by name to the person responsible for hiring staff in sales
- The mention of Allproducts' name in the first line of the letter will quickly grab attention
- She has made her ambitions clear. No one reading her letter will misunderstand why she is writing
- She has also flagged up her salary benchmark – again, to prevent any misunderstandings
- She has engaged ABC Limited with what will interest them most: her knowledge of the industry and the key role she plays in generating sales for her employer
- She has not fogged the message in the letter with any irrelevant information
- Mentioning the MBA is another way of flagging up her ambitions. No one would read into her application that she is just looking for another sales job like the one she's got.

Summary

In this chapter we have seen that designing a cover letter to attack the invisible market is a very different task from designing one to apply for a job you've seen advertised. With the latter the stimulus comes from the employer whereas with the former the stimulus comes from you. This is why it is important you make it clear to employers why you are writing to them.

Speculative cover letters can sometimes seem like a lot of effort for little return but what needs to be remembered is that if you do connect with an opportunity:

- there's a good chance it hasn't been advertised
- you may have got in before the competition arrives.

Focussing on the second of these two bullet points, the issue of what makes you different from other applicants doesn't arise in these situations but the challenge you do face is finding out enough about the employers to know what will interest them. Where the recipient of your letter isn't in the same line of business you may have to work a little harder to find the common threads that will draw you together.

Fact-check (answers at the back)

1. What is the invisible job market?
   a) Another name for the old boy network ☐
   b) Jobs which aren't advertised ☐
   c) Jobs on the black economy ☐
   d) Jobs on short-term contracts ☐

2. What is the biggest plus point with jobs you source on the invisible market?
   a) They're better paid ☐
   b) You don't have to submit a full CV ☐
   c) You can pick and choose when you go for an interview ☐
   d) Less or no competition ☐

3. Why is it important to find out more about employers before you write to them?
   a) You'll learn more about what they will find interesting ☐
   b) You can find out which ones reply and which ones don't ☐
   c) You can find out who pays the best salaries ☐
   d) To avoid time-wasters ☐

4. With speculative cover letters whom is it best to write to?
   a) The Chief Executive ☐
   b) The Human Resources Manager ☐
   c) The person responsible for hiring people like you ☐
   d) The company, i.e. not a named individual ☐

5. With speculative cover letters, why is it important to be explicit about the kind of opportunities you are seeking?
   a) It makes a good impression ☐
   b) It makes you sound focussed and ambitious ☐
   c) It makes you sound assertive ☐
   d) Employers won't know otherwise and misunderstandings might creep in ☐

6. What's the point of writing 'confidential' on the envelope containing your cover letter and CV?
   a) To stop nosey people reading it ☐
   b) To make it sound important ☐
   c) It's a way of making sure it's opened by the right person ☐
   d) It creates a good first impression ☐

7. Why is it best to put a speculative cover letter in the post rather than sending it by email?
   a) It might be treated as spam ☐
   b) It creates a better impression ☐
   c) It might not be printed off ☐
   d) You're more likely to get a reply to a letter ☐

8. Why is it best to send out speculative cover letters in small batches?

a) It's easier ❑
b) It avoids you being asked to attend too many interviews at the same time ❑
c) It is less stressful ❑
d) You won't make as many spelling mistakes ❑

9. What is it best to do when you don't get a reply to a speculative cover letter?

a) Complain ❑
b) Ring up and find out why ❑
c) Post your opinion of the employer's bad manners on a social networking site ❑
d) Nothing ❑

10. What's the aim of sending out speculative cover letters?

a) Sourcing jobs which haven't been advertised ❑
b) Sourcing jobs which have been advertised but which are still vacant ❑
c) Encouraging employers to find a slot for you ❑
d) All of the above ❑

CHAPTER 20

Cover letters for consultants

One way of attacking the invisible market is to get someone else to do it for you.

In this chapter we will be looking at the task a cover letter has to perform when its purpose is to get you on the books of an employment agency. We will start by giving you an insight into how recruitment businesses work and what drives the people who work in them. We will see how pressure to get sales is a significant motivator and how, to get results, you need to harness this driving force.

A lot of what we will be doing will be about making sure recruitment consultants understand you and how the responsibility of making this happen falls on you. A cover letter has an important part to play not only in making your ambitions clear but also in getting your relationship with a recruitment consultant off to a good start. If you tell them in clear unambiguous language what you want them to do for you then it stands a reasonable chance they will come up with the goods. If you don't then all kinds of misunderstandings can creep in, meaning your time on the agency's books will probably have nothing to show for it.

How consultants operate

One hard fact about agencies is they vary enormously in terms of both:

- their size
- their competence and professionalism.

Size isn't everything

Just because an agency is one of the well-known names doesn't necessarily mean it will be any good when it comes to finding you the job of your dreams. Small agencies, where often you find the consultant you're dealing with is one of the principals in the business, can and do perform very effectively.

No placement no fee

Agencies make their money out of successful placements. They place someone in a job and, when they do, they charge the employer a fee. How much do agencies charge employers? Fee structures vary but usually an employer would be looking at paying somewhere between 15 and 25 per cent of annual starting salary. Sometimes, depending on the seniority of the position, agencies' fees can be much higher. Conversely agencies who do a lot of business with a given employer often apply discounts. Some part of the fee is usually reimbursable if for any reason the employer and the person who has been placed part company in the first few weeks.

What drives consultants?

With the fortunes of agencies tied entirely to how many candidates they are successful in placing, it is perhaps not surprising to find that recruitment consultants are usually incentivized by having a large part of their salary paid in commission. Equally, perhaps it is not surprising to find that this arrangement brings out the best and the worst in people. On the one hand it is good to see consultants focussed on using their skills to get people like you the jobs they want. On the other it can and does lead to consultants putting sales in front of everything and, it has to be said, in front of what could be your best interests. In practical terms it means:

● Candidates who are seen as easy to place get the most attention
● Candidates who aren't get put to one side
● In the enthusiasm to chalk up sales, the finer points in candidates' instructions sometimes get overlooked.

To illustrate what we mean by the last of these bullet points let's hear what Eric has to say about his experience of dealing with an agency.

Eric

I am an electrical engineer with a lot of hands-on experience of maintaining high-speed PLC-controlled machinery of the kind found in the food-processing and packaging industry. I have reached the point in my career where I am looking to move into a more technical role – for example in research and development. With this in mind I registered with a firm of recruitment consultants who, according to what they say about themselves on their website, specialize in technical appointments. Imagine, therefore, my disappointment when they started ringing me up every few days with jobs in maintenance which had just come onto their books. Every time I spoke to a different person. Every time I had to tell them I didn't want a job in maintenance. Every time they apologized and said they understood but the calls kept coming till in the end I got fed up and told them not to ring me any more.

Understanding consultants

So what are we looking at here? Incompetence? Laziness? People who don't listen? People who style themselves as experts but who don't have a clue? Or was Eric to blame in any way?

Recruitment consultants come in all shapes and sizes. Some are good, some are not so good, and you need to take these variations into account when you sit down to the job of designing a cover letter to send to the ones you have chosen. Most importantly, with recruitment consultants you need to understand:

- who they are
- where they're coming from
- what they do.

Given this understanding, you stand a good chance of getting on with them. Without it you could end up like Eric.

Where agencies fit into the job market

Let's look next at where agencies fit into the job market. Apart from supplying temps (which most of them do), what function do they perform and why do employers use them? Here are three examples of employers who have decided to use recruitment consultants, in each case for different reasons.

Employer A

'In the build up to the half year accounts, our Head of Finance suddenly decided she was going to leave. Faced with the need to get someone on board quickly, we rang up three firms of recruitment consultants who specialize in financial appointments to see if they had anyone on their books who might fit the bill.'

Employer B

'Our experience with advertising for staff has been poor. We find we spend a lot of money on advertisements, then in most cases the people who apply are totally unsuitable. What we have done recently is run our vacancies through a few firms of recruitment consultants to see who is on their files. OK, it's an expensive way to hire staff but at least we don't have to pay until we've taken someone on.'

Employer C

'We don't have the time or resources to sift through hundreds of job applications. We prefer to hand over our vacancies to firms of recruitment consultants and let them come up with a short list for us. It costs but in our view it's worth it.'

Points to pick out from these three examples are:

- How employers in a hurry are attracted to using consultants. A file search can usually be carried out within hours of a request being made. This contrasts favourably with advertising, with which it can take weeks to arrive at a short list.
- How 'no placement no fee' enables employers to see who is available on the market without it costing them anything.
- How consultants offer a solution to overstretched, lean-look organizations, which are typical of today.

> ## Key point
>
> Dealing with consultants can be painful but, as the three examples demonstrate, they can provide an important means of access to an area of the job market which would otherwise be closed to you. The challenge with consultants is in getting them to perform for you, and we will be seeing shortly how the design of your cover letter has an important part to play in addressing this challenge.

Consultants' files

The more candidates consultants have on file the better their chances are of:

- finding suitable people to match their clients' needs
- offering their clients a choice
- making money for themselves.

The need to get as many candidates on file as they can explains the lengths consultants go to get people to register with them.

The sheer volume of people on file, particularly with the larger agencies, presents the first challenge to you. When the right job comes along, what can you do to make sure it's your name that comes out in the file search?

A further factor to bear in mind here is that file search in a lot of consultancies is done by computer. A possible explanation for Eric's bad experience is that a file search carried out by computer was matching him up with jobs which didn't interest him – a problem we will be returning to later.

What you want your cover letter to do for you

So, to summarize, when you sign on with a firm of recruitment consultants, the task you want your cover letter to perform is to ensure:

● your name comes out in the file searches
● you connect with the right opportunities.

Your CV has the same task to perform too but remember:

● It's your cover letter that's read first
● What's read first makes the biggest and most lasting impression.

Three assumptions

When you sit down to the job of designing a cover letter to send to a firm of recruitment consultants it is useful to start by making three fairly safe assumptions:

1 The point we have touched on already. Any agency you make contact with will be heavily results orientated. Your value in their eyes will be governed by one fact alone: whether they can place you in a job or not.
2 An agency is a busy place where new candidates are registering all the time. What this means is that your cover letter and CV will be subject to bulk processing, whereby once again the messages in them will need to satisfy the 'one quick read' test. They must be capable of being understood instantly because, if they're not, they could end up in the wrong part of the databank (another possible explanation for what happened to Eric).
3 Some of the tasks in an agency will be performed by people who have little or no understanding of what you do or the terminology you use.

Pick out your marketable talents

Focussing on what makes you attractive to recruitment consultants (what gets their blood racing), you need to use your cover letter to highlight anything in your qualifications, skills and experience which will make you marketable to their clients. Since you don't know their clients, this takes you back to fishing in the dark. The only clue you have is by looking again at why employers use recruitment consultants and going back to the three examples we used earlier.

- **Scarce skills and unusual experience.** Identify any scarce skills you may have or unusual areas of experience. Employers often go to recruitment consultants because they feel that (a) they're looking for someone special and (b) other methods of recruitment won't work for them. Is there anything in your portfolio which marks you out as different from most people in your profession? If there is, then make sure it is highlighted in your cover letter. For example, Shah is a management accountant but, because of his company's corporate development strategies, he has had more involvement with mergers and acquisitions than most people with his background.
- **Competence in core areas.** Employers who go to recruitment consultants are often looking for a safe pair of hands – for example, someone to steady the ship after a turbulent period or, as in the case of Employer A, someone stable and reliable to take over from a key member of staff who has departed unexpectedly and at a critical time. Such employers will be briefing consultants to come up with the names of candidates who are competent in the core areas of their job by virtue of their experience.

> ## Key point
>
> These marketable talents are the ones you need to bring into prominence when you design a cover letter for consultants.

Make sure consultants understand you

It is important consultants understand you because, as we saw in the case of Eric, they have a tendency to lock onto any talents they see as marketable and then, unless directed otherwise, pepper candidates with everything that comes onto the books which loosely seems to match those talents. Why is this a problem?

- Candidates' instructions can get ignored and in this way they gain no benefit from registering with the consultant. In Eric's case all he heard about was jobs in maintenance – jobs which didn't interest him.
- Sooner or later consultants get fed up with candidates who keep saying 'no'. They detach their effort. The calls stop.

How to get the message across

Your cover letter is the ideal place for you to tell consultants what you want them to do for you. How to do this?

- Don't use jargon because, unless the agency is specialized, the people who read your cover letter may not understand you.
- Keep the messages as plain, short and simple as you can. Reduce the possibility of misunderstandings.
- Be precise. Say exactly what you want and don't leave anything to the imagination.

Remember what you are trying to achieve here. If a job comes into the consultant's office which is right up your street, you want to be sure you trigger the retrieval systems. The file search has got to throw out your name.

Don't register with too many agencies

Registering with too many agencies can give you two problems:

● being asked to attend too many interviews at the same time, leaving you with the problem of getting time off work
● two or more agencies putting you forward for the same job.

One size does fit all

Contrary to everything we've said so far, the task of designing a cover letter for one agency is no different from designing a cover letter for another. Here is where you can use a standard model; in other words, there is no need to customize each letter.

Example of a cover letter for consultants

Robin Wrightly is a human resources manager in a business which is due to close in six months' time. Robin is emailing his CV to a consultant with one of the leading names in executive recruitment in the area where he lives.

To: Tim Fotheringay
From: Robin Wrightly
Subject: CV
Date: 29 March 2013

Dear Tim Fotheringay

I am seeking a position in human resources management paying £xx,xxx per annum plus and would like to be considered for any suitable opportunities.

From my CV (attached) you will see I have worked in all areas of HR including:

● pay negotiations with six unions representing staff and manual grades
● a 90% success rate in defending employment tribunal cases
● managing a programme of change which included new shift patterns and payment systems affecting over 200 employees.

I am available to attend interviews at any time. The unit where I am based is scheduled for closure in six months' time, which means all employees on site including myself are at risk of redundancy. Early release would be available to me if I was successful in finding alternative employment. If you require any other information at this stage please do not hesitate to ask.

Yours sincerely

Robin Wrightly
Attached: CV

Key points to pick out from Robin's email are as follows:

● It is concise and to the point. No space is wasted on information which isn't relevant

- In his first paragraph Robin makes it clear exactly what kind of position he is seeking and where his salary expectations lie
- From his experience he has picked out three areas which he thinks will make him more marketable
- He has recognized that not being able to start a job for six months might detract from his marketability. He has therefore included the few words about the availability of early release.

Summary

In this chapter we have been looking at designing a cover letter to use when registering with an agency. Here the challenge you face is engaging with the forces which drive recruitment consultants, namely:

- success in terms of placements
- the financial rewards that go with it.

We have asked you to focus on your marketable talents because these offer the key as far as consultants are concerned. They will see you as someone they can sell to their clients and make money out of, and this will fire their efforts to give their best for you.

Also we have stressed the need to send consultants off on the track you want them to follow and not one dictated by their ambition to chalk up more sales. Making it clear to consultants at the outset what you want them to do for you is an important element of getting off on the right foot with them and you can do this in your cover letter.

Finally, when you're dealing with consultants, expect to have to remind them about your aims from time to time because, they are apt to forget.

Fact-check

1. What is 'no placement no fee'?
a) An arrangement whereby you don't have to pay the agency any money if they don't find a job for you ☐
b) An arrangement whereby the employer doesn't have to pay the agency any money until someone starts in a job ☐
c) An arrangement whereby the agency agrees to work for free ☐
d) An arrangement whereby the agency is paid up front ☐

2. How do agencies make money?
a) They are subsidized by the government ☐
b) They charge fees to people who register with them ☐
c) Employers pay them retainers ☐
d) They charge fees to employers when they place people with them ☐

3. From a job hunter's perspective, where do agencies score?
a) They access areas of the job market which would otherwise be closed to you ☐
b) They write cover letters and CVs for you ☐
c) They don't score. They're a waste of space ☐
d) They have access to better-paid jobs ☐

4. What is the danger if you fail to give agencies a specification to work to?
a) They won't ring you ☐
b) They'll come up with the wrong jobs ☐
c) They'll refer you to a careers counsellor ☐
d) They'll put your CV in the shredding machine ☐

5. What will impress agencies most?
a) Outstanding academic achievements ☐
b) Your IT skills ☐
c) Talents that they can market to their clients ☐
d) Your references ☐

6. Why do agencies want people to register with them?
a) To attract government grants ☐
b) To keep them busy ☐
c) To draw visitors onto their websites ☐
d) So they will have more people on their files ☐

7. When can you use the same cover letter more than once?
a) When you're in a hurry ☐
b) When you're registering with agencies ☐
c) When you're writing off for places on graduate intakes ☐
d) When the job is with an employer you've written to before ☐

8. What is the danger if you keep saying you're not interested in the jobs agencies find for you?
a) They might charge you for wasting their time ❏
b) They might put you on a black list ❏
c) There is no danger (you're entitled to say you're not interested) ❏
d) They lose interest in you ❏

9. When dealing with agencies, what is one of the drawbacks with saying you're looking for an exceptionally high salary?
a) They may see you as someone who is going to be difficult to place ❏
b) You might look greedy ❏
c) No one will take you seriously ❏
d) You might look like someone who's just shopping round to see what's out there ❏

10. How do you judge the effectiveness of an agency?
a) By the number of times they phone you ❏
b) By the enthusiasm of their consultants ❏
c) By what they have to say about themselves on their websites ❏
d) By the number of interesting job opportunities they come up with ❏

CHAPTER 21

Moving into the future

In Chapter 16 we looked at how cover letters:

- are not just there to get you interviews
- go on working for you as the selection process moves forward.

Now we will take a closer look at how cover letters can influence:

- the directions interviews go in
- final selection decisions.

Also we will look at how you can learn from your job applications and get better at writing cover letters. Yes, practice does make perfect, but the confidence and style with which you write can play an important part in your life, which goes a long way beyond how good you are at turning out cover letters. We will look at what you can take forward from the experience of writing a cover letter. We will therefore see how you can apply what you have learned to writing the other letters you will need to, as the selection process advances. At the same time we will see how judgements of people are formed based on their ability to express themselves clearly and how, in an age when so much communication is done online, the need to write well is arguably more important than it has ever been.

Interviews

Imagine the scene. You have been asked to attend an interview, so along you go not exactly sure what to expect. The interviewer is usually sitting behind a desk and, in most cases, it will be someone you've never met before. Indeed, up to this point the interviewer's knowledge of you will be based almost entirely on what you've said about yourself in:

● your cover letter
● your CV
● your application form (if you've been asked to fill one in).

Interestingly, these documents will probably be sitting on the desk in front of the interviewer with your cover letter uppermost because, if you've been following the advice so far, you will have designed your cover letter so it is effectively the first page of your CV.

Interview questions

What candidates sometimes forget is that they may have more experience of interviews than the person who is interviewing them. And, when all is said and done, interviewing a complete stranger for a job can be a daunting task, especially to someone who isn't used to it. Many line managers have had no formal training in interviewing beyond perhaps going on the odd short course. What's more, they only occasionally get the chance to practice their interviewing skills (when there is a vacancy for staff in the area of the business they control). The result in many cases is an interviewer who is not too sure about what line of questioning to follow and so the natural inclination is to be led by what's in front of them – namely your cover letter.

Dictate the agenda

The information in your cover letter backed up by the more detailed information in your CV can determine to a large extent:

● the direction interviews take
● the topics that come up for discussion
● the questions that are asked.

So what we are seeing here is how a carefully crafted cover letter can have the power to dictate the agenda for an interview and, more to the point perhaps, an agenda which will be favourable to you, the applicant. Everything in your cover letter will be:

● relevant to the job for which you are being interviewed
● one of your strong points.

Straightaway the interview gets off to a good start, and the more time spent on talking about what makes you a great candidate for the job, clearly the better it is going to be for you.

The halo effect again

Just to remind you, the halo effect is where:

● a candidate makes a good first impression
● any flaws which emerge later are ignored.

Interviewers – particularly inexperienced ones – are very susceptible to halo effects. They make their minds up about candidates in the first few minutes and anything later on in the interview which doesn't fit in with the already formed favourable opinion will be either overlooked or relegated in importance.

Keeping copies of your cover letters

Some candidates put a lot of time and effort into rehearsing answers to tough interview questions which they think they are going to be asked. Where proportionately less time and effort is spent is on the job of revisiting the cover letter, CV and application form which they sent in. A pity? Yes it is, because, following on from the last point, by looking at what they said about themselves they might learn a lot more about the line of questioning they are going to face.

An even bigger pity would be if for any reason they hadn't kept copies of these documents because:

● they didn't save them
● they overwrote them
● they didn't run off hard copies.

Consistency and credibility

You will remember that we warned you about the importance of consistency between any information you put in a cover letter and any information you put in a CV. The point applies equally to interviews. Anything you say at an interview (for example, in response to a question you are asked) needs to be consistent with what you have said in your cover letter, in your CV and on any application forms you have been asked to fill in. This emphasizes again the importance of revisiting these documents before you go to your interviews and reminding yourself exactly what you did say. Remember: your credibility is at stake here and, once you lose it, it won't be easy to get back.

What went wrong?

Candidates go for interviews, psych themselves up before they go and feel at the end of it they've put in a good performance. Then they get a letter or an email telling them they haven't been shortlisted. 'What went wrong?' they ask themselves. 'Did I put my foot in it and, if so, where?' Here the answer could lie in something they said at the interview which:

● was at odds with information they had given elsewhere
● caused the interviewer to think twice.

Learn from the experience

Applying for a job – irrespective of whether your application is successful or not – is an experience from which you can learn valuable lessons.

In the case of cover letters, some people will have little difficulty in applying what they have learned, whereas others may struggle. Expressing yourself concisely doesn't come easily to everyone because, when you're talking about a subject which is familiar to you (such as your work), it is a great temptation to stray off the point and go into detail. This is fine where the detail is relevant – for example, in a competitive job situation, where it highlights something about you which makes you stand out from other applicants. However, if this isn't the case then your long rambling explanations will only serve to lose the reader's interest.

The art of précis

A précis is a short summary of a piece of writing. It gives the bare bones and nothing more. Someone reading a précis will see at a glance what the piece is about and, if it looks interesting, they will read it in full.

See a cover letter as an exercise in précis, in this case a précis of the **relevant** information in your CV. Pick out the main points, put to one side anything which isn't relevant and then say what you want to say in the smallest number of words possible.

Perfect the art of précis

It is easy to perfect précis. Take an article in a magazine or newspaper and sum up what it's about in three or four short sentences.

Writing a précis is an excellent exercise for:

● increasing your vocabulary
● improving your grammar and spelling
● expressing yourself clearly and concisely
● making you think.

Take the lessons forward

What can you take forward from the experience of writing a cover letter? How else can you apply what you have learned?

A cover letter isn't, of course, going to be the only letter you will need as the selection process advances. All being well, you will be invited to attend an interview and, if the interview goes to plan, you will be asked to go back for another one and/or at some point offered the job.

At each of these stages you may be called on to write a letter either to confirm you will be attending the interview or to say you will be accepting the job. All the etiquette you learned about in Chapter 17 will come into play again. However, do please note the following:

- If you're invited to an interview or offered a job, always remember to say thank you
- Always reply to letters/emails using the same terms of address as the writer's. For example, if they address you as 'Dear Mr/Mrs/Ms', do likewise when you reply to them. If on the other hand they're less formal (e.g. in an email, 'Hi' followed by your first name) then it's acceptable to write back in the same style.

Does it matter?

We pose this question because there are a lot of people out there who take the view that it doesn't matter if letters and emails are poorly written and/or full of bad grammar and spelling mistakes. So long as the people they've written to understand them, why get hung up about the odd bad construction or apostrophe in the wrong place?

Putting to one side the fact that badly written letters often don't make sense to the people who have to read them, the bigger point here is that the way you express yourself in written form is an extension of who you are. If your letters are ill constructed and messy, that's the image of you they project. If – as we mentioned earlier – they're littered with silly mistakes then the image of you that comes across is that of someone who's slipshod and careless.

Using your writing style to project the right image

We are, as we know, living in an increasingly image-conscious world, but what you also need to remember here is that:

● More and more business is conducted in written form thanks to email and other online forms of communication
● Less and less revolves around the use of the spoken word, either face-to-face or over the phone.

A large part of the image we project today is, therefore, determined by what we put into writing and how we say it. Writing which is snappy and straight to the point comes across as an outward manifestation of an organized and tidy mind, whereas writing which is messy and all over the place comes across as the exact opposite.

Warning!

Don't fall into the trap of thinking 'anything goes' just because you're saying it in an email. The standards of good business letter writing go right across the board. Bear in mind, too, that to be good and well-written doesn't mean it has to be stiff and formal. At the same time, don't lapse into the kind of conversational style which may be acceptable in emails to your friends and family. Equally, don't give business emails the same treatment as posting messages on social networking sites (another common fault). Remember, it's your image we're talking about here and you're the one who's responsible for it.

Build your self-confidence

So far we have portrayed people who can't put together a decent cover letter as people who either can't be bothered to go to the trouble or people who are careless and don't check their work. There is, however, another group of people who find having to put anything into writing daunting and something which they would prefer to avoid if at all possible. The problem in many of these cases is not bad teaching in the schools they attended but lack of self-confidence.

Designing a cover letter may be a small step to take but when your self-confidence is low:

- It is a step
- It is one going in the right direction.

Earlier we drew your attention to the link between a well-written letter and confidence in what the writer is saying. Someone who can express themselves clearly and in a well-thought-out manner is someone who has something important to say. Readers sit up and take notice, and being taken seriously in this way is a great boost to self-confidence.

> **Note**
>
> Even where self-confidence isn't a problem, the ability to communicate effectively in writing is a mark of quality which your bosses and colleagues will be quick to notice. In terms of your career prospects it will do you nothing but good.

Give the job the respect it deserves

Writing a good cover letter, picking out from your skills, experience and qualifications what's relevant to each job application you make and then linking these points together in a clear and concise fashion is something you can get better at. Partly this is a case of practice makes perfect, but that is not the whole story. What is equally and possibly more important is treating the job of writing a good cover letter with the respect it deserves. Even today, when most job seekers are clued up about what to do and have a lot of expert advice available to them, the cover letter is still the poor relation when it comes to presenting an employer with a set of credentials which will impress them. Still we find cover letters coming in which look as if they have been dashed off in ten minutes (or less) and show little evidence of having the same care and attention lavished on them as the CVs which accompany them. All of which brings us back to the point about the important part cover letters have to play in:

- getting CVs read
- moving job applications forward in the right direction.

The message? Attach proper importance to the job of writing a cover letter. Give it your best shot and not some half-hearted effort which will inspire no one to take an interest in you.

Summary

In this chapter we have discovered how a good cover letter isn't just one which gets you interviews. Far from it: as you move into the future it goes on working for you in ways which may surprise you:

- It can dictate what happens at an interview and lay down an agenda which will be favourable to you.
- It can prepare you for other letters you may have to write as the selection process moves forward.
- It can teach you how to express yourself clearly and concisely in writing.
- It can help you project an image which is consistent with someone who is organized and businesslike.
- It can help you to build your self-confidence.

The final message was to attach importance to the job of composing a cover letter. Put time and effort into it and take pride in it when you get it right. If you do, it will pay you back with interest and all the time and effort will then be worth it.

Fact-check (answers at the back)

1. Why do some interviewers find interviews daunting?
a) Because they don't know how to handle applicants ❑
b) Because they're not used to doing them ❑
c) Because they're useless ❑
d) Because they've had no training ❑

2. Why is it important to keep copies of your cover letters?
a) So you can use them again next time you apply for a job ❑
b) So you have proof you wrote one ❑
c) As a memento of all the effort you put into writing them ❑
d) So you can remind yourself what you said before you go for an interview ❑

3. What is a précis?
a) A short summary of a piece of writing ❑
b) Another name for a CV ❑
c) A French word for an interview ❑
d) Where there is a match between the requirements of the job and what you have to offer ❑

4. When does conforming to good business letter-writing standards not matter?
a) In emails ❑
b) On Fridays ❑
c) When you're not on business ❑
d) When you're in a hurry ❑

5. Why is it important to aspire to a good standard of business letter writing?
a) It isn't important any more (it went out with the Ark) ❑
b) It projects a good image ❑
c) It shows you've been to university ❑
d) It keeps you out of trouble with your bosses ❑

6. How can you get better at writing cover letters?
a) By applying for more jobs ❑
b) By getting someone else to write them for you ❑
c) By using specimens downloaded off the Internet ❑
d) By attaching greater importance to them ❑

7. Apart from confirming you will be attending, what is it important to say when you reply to an invitation to an interview?
a) To allow you five minutes in case you arrive late ❑
b) Get out the red carpet ❑
c) Thank you ❑
d) That you will want to be reimbursed for your travelling expenses ❑

8. Why is good business letter writing becoming more important?
a) The litigation culture and the need to put everything into writing so you can prove what you said in court ❑
b) Because of the increasing use of online communication ❑
c) It's cheaper to write than it is to make a phone call ❑
d) People don't do anything unless you put it into writing ❑

9. What can you learn from writing a good cover letter?
a) How to express yourself clearly and concisely ❑
b) How to write a CV ❑
c) How to make friends with people who don't know you ❑
d) How to be brilliant at everything ❑

10. What makes writing a good cover letter difficult?
a) Not having sufficient confidence in yourself ❑
b) Not having a good education ❑
c) Not applying for jobs very often ❑
d) Nothing does. It isn't difficult ❑

7 × 7

1 Seven good habits

- Proofread everything carefully.
- Use a dictionary. Don't rely on spell checkers.
- Pay attention to detail.
- Make the effort when it comes to matching your skills, experience and qualifications to the requirements of a job.
- Remember to sign any cover letters you put in the post.
- Never undersell yourself. See where you have something special to offer and make sure everybody knows about it.
- Learn from experience.

2 Seven key messages

- Cover letters are what employers read first. The impression they make is one that lasts.
- Design a new cover letter every time you apply for a job. Make sure everything you put in it is relevant.
- Cover letters designed to attack the visible job market need to address the issue of engaging and overcoming competition.
- A good cover letter carries on working for you right the way through to the final stages of selection.
- Have something positive to say to employers about why you want to work for them.
- With speculative cover letters it's you not the employer who designs the job specification; it's you who has to tell the employer what you're looking for.
- Treat the job of writing a cover letter with the respect it deserves.

3 Seven surprising facts

● The number of cover letters riddled with mistakes that are written by well qualified professionals.

● How many CVs are binned before they're read because the cover letters that come with them contained nothing relevant or interesting.

● How often a CV which has had a lot of thought put into its preparation is accompanied by a cover letter which has the appearance of being dashed off in five minutes.

● Cover letters aren't always read from start to finish.

● How many cover letters arrive with the names of people they're addressed to spelled incorrectly.

● How many well-qualified candidates fall by the wayside because they fail to pay sufficient attention to their cover letters.

● How many candidates send in CVs without a cover letter. How they miss a great opportunity.

4 Seven things to avoid

● Inconsistencies in the information you give to employers of the sort that will serve to undermine your credibility.

● Cluttering your cover letters with information that isn't relevant.

● Making your cover letter uninviting to read by trying to cram too much information on the page.

● Sending a cover letter without a date on it.

● Using capital (upper case) letters, underlining or picking out key words in red.

● Forgetting to sign cover letters you're putting in the post.

● Allowing the standards to lapse when you're submitting a cover letter by email.

5 Seven things to do today

- Ditch any standard templates you've been using.
- Read up on apostrophes. Make sure you know when and when not to use them.
- Write a short précis. Pick an article you have seen in a newspaper or on a website and summarize it in two or three paragraphs.
- Check your stock of A4 paper and envelopes. Make sure you've got a spare cartridge for your printer.
- Let someone who is qualified (e.g. a secretary) have a look at a sample of your typing. Satisfy yourself it comes up to acceptable business standards.
- Play a word game.
- Start taking a pride in anything you write.

6 Seven top tips

- See a good cover letter as the best way of creating a favourable first impression.
- Keep your cover letters concise. Achieve conciseness by making sure everything in them is relevant to the job for which you're applying.
- When submitting your CV in a file attachment to an email, include a copy of your cover letter in the same file.
- Keep your sentences short so the meaning of what you're saying is clear. Write the way you speak when you're designing a cover letter. Aim to be businesslike but, at the same time, engaging and friendly.
- With speculative cover letters, always send them to the person responsible for hiring people like you. Put them in an envelope marked 'confidential'.
- Always keep copies of cover letters you send to employers. Don't delete or write over them in case you're invited to an interview and you need to remind yourself what you said.
- See a good cover letter as what can make the difference when you're up against stiff competition.

7 Seven trends for tomorrow

- Employers and employers' organizations will continue to wage war on job applicants who can't spell. Expect more from prominent business leaders.

- A greater tendency for job applicants to use standard templates for cover letters thanks to the glut of material available on the Internet or from other sources; this gives an opportunity to people who can produce cover letters designed for purpose.

- In an online and image-conscious age the need to write well will command an ever-increasing level of importance.

- As the world of jobs becomes more competitive, a good cover letter could be what makes the difference.

- Greater focus on cover letters; more interest in what they say about the people who write them and their ability to communicate effectively and concisely.

- The trend of bringing cover letters and CVs together in one document is set to grow.

- Cover letters and CVs will increasingly be used by self-employed people as a way of selling their skills; a cover letter and a CV is a good way of advertising credentials to potential clients.

PART 4

Your Job Interviews Masterclass

Introduction

Have you ever wondered why some people seem to succeed almost effortlessly whenever they go for an interview? Perhaps they are just 'lucky'. We think not! Their performance, and ultimately their success, is the result of thorough personal preparation.

You, too, can improve your ability and success through a combination of thought, training, practice and experience.

You are now making the first significant investment in improving your interview performance to increase your chances of getting the job you want – congratulations! Now read on ... and good luck!

CHAPTER 22

What to expect from the interview process

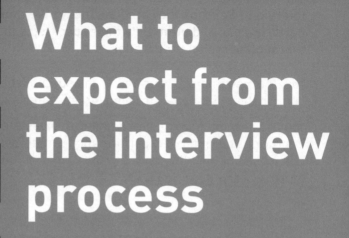

You opened the post this morning to find you have been invited to an interview – great news! You feel good. You are high, elated and you congratulate yourself. You imagine yourself in the role; it's exciting, an ideal job for you. You read the letter again and, as the reality of the interview becomes your focus, you are bombarded with less positive feelings and thoughts, such as:

- I hate interviews
- I can't remember the last time I was interviewed
- I really want this job – I hope I don't let myself down.

It is not uncommon to feel a degree of trepidation in anticipation of an interview. The trick is not to let this weigh you down.

After all, we suspect you've experienced being interviewed, not just once but many times in your career. Most career transitions – such as selection, promotion or other forms of career development – will have been punctuated by interviews. You are therefore likely to be familiar with the process. As interviews follow a relatively common format, you will already have some of the skills and knowledge required to make you successful. In this chapter we look at how to use this experience in your next interview.

Learning from past interviews

Think back over past interviews and answer the following question honestly: *Did I present myself in the best possible light?*

While we would hope that your answer is 'yes', it is more likely to be 'no' or 'not quite'. Even if, as a manager, you are an experienced interviewer, having undergone training on skills, techniques and questioning, you may not be so skilled at being interviewed.

Take some time now to think about some of your previous experiences as an interviewee. Think firstly about those where you have been less successful; what happened and what can you learn from them? What would you do differently if you encountered a similar situation? Note or record your findings. Now think about your successful interviews. What did you do that led to a positive outcome and what can you repeat when you go along to your next interview?

The following comments from interviewers reflect common problems:

● I know a lot about his employer, but very little about him
● She seemed very nervous and aggressive
● He stumbled over all the questions related to his personality
● I'm not sure how long he would stay
● She seemed too good to be true
● There was no substance in what he said
● It was difficult to get a word in edgeways.

We will help you focus on the known rather than the unpredictable factors, exploring questions such as why, in what way and by whom:

● Why: interview objectives
● In what way: types of questions
● By whom: the interviewer or interviewers.

Interview objectives

If you have been invited to an interview – well done! Your invitation is based on the limited knowledge the interviewer has of you from your application, a previous telephone interview, personal recommendation or your past achievements. They already believe that you could be the person they are looking for. The interview is therefore an opportunity for interviewers to extend their knowledge and complete their picture of you.

You will have your own agenda. The interview is an opportunity for you to discover further information about the job and the organization. Based on that information, you can reach decisions about match and suitability.

The interview is a two-way process: treat it as such. The **interviewee's objectives** are to:

- progress to the next stage and the final shortlist
- gain the initiative – an offer or a commitment
- present yourself in the best possible light
- make known your talents and expertise
- fill gaps in your knowledge about the job and the organization
- meet future colleagues/managers
- be clear about whether or not you would accept the post.

The **interviewer's objectives** are to:

- find the most suitable person
- encourage you to express yourself fully
- look for specific skills and achievements
- sell the job and the organization
- assess your initial impact and social fit
- appoint the right person.

You will both have independent objectives with a degree of overlap. Spend time before the interview clarifying your objectives. You may even want to rank them; having gone through this process, you can be much clearer about whether the interview matches your objectives and, if not, for what reason.

Interview structure

The whole of the recruitment process requires careful planning. It involves drawing up a job description and person specification, designing the advertisement, compiling the information pack, and then selecting who to interview and shortlist. The interview itself must also be carefully planned.

Be aware that interviewers will have clarified their objectives in general and decided on a format and a set of questions for each interviewee. No two interviews are the same. Your personality, application, CV, and experience will be different from others', as will the areas that require further exploration because they are of particular interest or concern. While interviews are not the same, there are similarities, and there is a process which is common and accepted.

The process can be likened to a sandwich. It is built on some 'warm-up' questions to help you both settle down and feel as comfortable as you can.

The middle and main section of the interview will constitute the filling in the sandwich, the most important ingredients, where you will be asked a variety of questions, checking and clarifying match and suitability.

In the final stage there will be time for your questions, closing with a summary of the interview and an indication of what will happen next: a second interview, a meeting with other staff members, or a letter telling you the result of the interview.

Some organizations provide their interviewers with a standard form to assess certain aspects of the interviewee and their performance. They will have a rating scale for each competence and make direct comparisons between candidates. Depending on the post available, these may cover the following:

● skills
● knowledge
● behaviour
● motivation
● fit with team
● fit with culture
● career aspirations.

Types of question

During your interview you will encounter a number of different types of question. If you can recognize these and the reasons they are being asked, you can concentrate on your replies. We will give you further guidance on responding to questions in Chapter 26.

The better the questions, the better the interview. Questions can be categorized as follows:

- open
- probing
- closed
- hypothetical
- leading
- difficult
- negative
- discriminatory.

Open questions

These are where interviewers give you the chance to talk. They want to hear your ideas and see how you develop an answer. Open questions usually start with:

'Who', 'What', 'Where', 'When', 'Which', 'Why' or 'How'.

For example:

- 'What levels of budget responsibility have you had throughout your career?'
- 'How did you implement your people strategy?'

Questions such as these allow you the opportunity to sell yourself. They require a level of preparation on your part. Think about the key themes that are likely to be covered in the interview, focusing on those which you consider will be of interest to the interviewer and most relevant to the job.

Probing questions

When interviewers are particularly interested in your reply and want further information, they will use probing questions to focus in on the subject.

For example:

- 'Tell me about your research to date.'
- 'How did you manage the change?'
- 'What made you respond in that way?'

It's rather like a funnelling process where the interviewer moves from general questions to specific examples.

Closed questions

These are direct questions that tend to pin you down to a factual reply or to a 'yes' or 'no' answer.
For example:

- 'Were you responsible for managing a budget in your last job?'
- 'Are you familiar with Investors in People?'

Questions such as these can inhibit you and restrict your freedom in presenting information. For example, you may not have been responsible for the budget in your last post, but you may have had budget responsibilities in the past. If you are not able to communicate this information, it may reduce your chances of being successful. Always try to highlight relevant previous experience. Just because an interviewer asks a closed question, it doesn't mean they only want a one-word answer. Use your initiative and be prepared to provide a fuller answer.

Hypothetical questions

Hypothetical questions are just that, encouraging you to imagine how you might handle the unknown. They also provide an opportunity for you to demonstrate how well you think and the quality of your judgement. The interviewer will suggest a hypothetical situation and ask how you would deal with it.
For example:

- 'What would you do if ... ?'
- 'How would you deal with ... ?'
- 'What would you expect from a perfect manager?'

These can tend to be difficult questions to answer, especially if complex scenarios are being presented. If you are not careful, you can end up tying yourself in knots, especially if you concentrate too much on trying to work out what kind of answer you think they might want. Try to relate these questions to your own experience and, if you are not clear about the complete details of the situation, ask for more information.

Leading questions

These are the opposite of hypothetical questions, as the interviewer steers you to the kind of answer they expect.

Leading questions do not give interviewers much of an idea about you, though you will have an insight into their thinking. Generally it is best not to rock the boat; go where the questions are leading and check if you are unclear.

For example:

- 'As you have had experience of budgeting, I'm sure you wouldn't ...'
- 'With regard to Investors in People, you are obviously aware of the problems with ...'

Difficult questions

These take many shapes and forms. Give yourself a moment to think, rather than trying to start answering immediately. Don't be evasive; you may have some ideas about areas of questioning that are likely to cause you difficulty.

Anticipate what areas interviewers might cover and be ready for them. It is important to have some kind of answer ready rather than clamming up and leaving interviewers to jump to their own, possibly incorrect, conclusions.

For example:

- 'I see you have a gap of three years in your employment. What did you do during that time?'
- 'This job requires a professional diploma. How are you going to make up the shortfall in your qualifications?'

You don't know which questions will take you by surprise. Whatever they are, take your time over them. And remember that, in most cases, the interviewer is trying to give you the opportunity to put yourself forward in the best possible light, not trying to trip you up.

Negative questions

Don't let negative questions unnerve you; they may be the interviewer's way of making comparisons between the best candidates.

For example:

- 'What are your weaknesses?'
- 'Why is it that you have changed jobs so often?'
- 'You stayed in your last job for ten years. Why so long?'

Don't fall into the trap of defending yourself, as though this were a direct attack. Be constructive and turn the question around to show yourself in a positive light.

Discriminatory questions

These sorts of questions are still asked at interview, particularly of women and minority groups.

Women applying for senior jobs may be confronted with a whole battery of questions about their private lives, which male colleagues might not be asked.

These all need to be handled very carefully. You need to clarify the interviewer's intention and the relevance of the question. Ask yourself and maybe even the interviewer:

- 'Is this question ever put to other candidates?'
- 'How would this affect my performance in the role?'

It could be that the interviewer is just clumsy rather than malicious.

If you feel that you have been discriminated against in your interview, in the UK you can contact the Equality Advisory & Support Service (EASS).

FREEPOST Equality Advisory & Support Service
FPN4431
Telephone: (+44) (0)808 800 0082
www.equalityadvisoryservice.com

In the USA you should contact:

US Equal Employment Opportunity Commission (EEOC)
131 M Street, NE
Washington DC 20507-0100
Telephone: (+1) 800 669 4000
www.eeoc.gov

In Commonwealth countries you should contact:
Commonwealth Secretariat
Marlborough House
Pall Mall
London SW1Y 5HX
UK
Telephone: (+44) (0)20 7747 6500
www.thecommonwealth.org

As well as recognizing the different types of question, it is worth considering the order in which the questions are asked. The use of supplementary and probing questions will often suggest what is in the interviewer's mind; you should notice this and react accordingly.

Good interviewers will be watching your reactions and body language: posture, gestures and facial expressions. You should do the same; some interviewers present an unresponsive, wooden mask. This can be because they are inexperienced or are not comfortable with the role. With practice, you should be able to read and assess intentions and reactions reasonably well. You will undoubtedly also meet some ineffective interviewers.

Interviewers

Simply by putting yourself in the shoes of the interviewer you can begin to see things from their perspective. You can appreciate the investment they've made in the process, the importance of making the right decision or, conversely, the cost of making a wrong decision. Of course, you will have your own objectives and we are assuming you want to get the job, but we suggest that the interview is your final exploration of the role, the expectations and the organization.

Bear in mind, though, that good interviewers are trained, not born. Be prepared for an interviewer who:

● has not read your CV
● gets aggressive, to see how you react under stress
● is constantly distracted
● responds to texts or emails during the interview
● makes remarks about your previous employer or boss
● asks questions but doesn't listen to your answers.

Even the best training can fall on deaf ears and even the best interviewers can have a bad day. If you happen to be on the receiving end of poor interviewing, you can sometimes turn it to your advantage. You may meet interviewers who fall into the following categories.

The disorganized interviewer

Allow them time to settle down and find the papers or notes they need. Establish your preparedness early on and, if necessary, subtly suggest an interview structure.

The unprepared interviewer

Sometimes very experienced interviewers think they can sail in on the day and don't need to prepare. You have to keep calm and be patient. It won't do your cause any good if you try to catch them out or show them up. If interviewers have a position of authority over the post, you may want to consider how you would feel working with them.

The nervous interviewer

You sense that the interviewer would rather be anywhere else than in an interview room and may even be more nervous than you are. This sometimes happens when specialist functional managers are taken out of their familiar work setting and expected to be at ease in a more social setting. They will be grateful if you offer relevant information and loosely control the interview. Be careful not to patronize.

The aggressive interviewer

Don't allow aggressive interviewers to provoke you. Rather than apologizing for the weaknesses, failings or gaps in your CV that they point out to you, give positive explanations and put over what you have prepared.

Being familiar with the process of the interview will enable you to understand the direction it is taking. If you are unclear about a question, try to assess what the reasons are for asking it and answer it accordingly.

The well-informed interviewer

It is now common practice for interviewers to gather information from a variety of sources. You should be prepared for questions on what you have posted on social networking sites, as recruiters may have done their research well.

Be cautious about what you post and the privacy levels you set, as these could trip you up at interview. The last thing you need at interview are probing questions about a recent party you attended.

Summary

We have begun with a general overview of the process of interviews, preparing you for what you should expect.

Interviews come in a variety of forms – so you have to enter the process with an open mind. In recent years, practice in many organizations has become more sophisticated. Interviewers are more extensively trained; they are given a set of developed questions for different roles or a battery of questions that can be used throughout company interviews. This doesn't mean that your experience will always be good, but remember that the process is designed simply to find the right person for the role.

Many of the questions you'll be asked are predictable – so by thinking about your responses to these you should be well prepared and taking the first step to success. Remember that you have had interviews before. Learn from the past to prepare yourself for the future.

Fact-check (answers at the back)

There is more than one possible answer to some of the following questions.

1. What should your first thought be when you are invited to an interview?
    a) I hate interviews. ❏
    b) I hope I don't let myself down. ❏
    c) Great – they think I can do the job. ❏
    d) What will I wear? ❏

2. Interview experience is most like what?
    a) Performance appraisal ❏
    b) Office outings ❏
    c) Team meetings ❏
    d) Internal promotion ❏

3. What does an interviewer aim to find out?
    a) Whether you live up to your CV ❏
    b) Information about your employer ❏
    c) Whether you seem nervous ❏
    d) If you are too good to be true ❏

4. What is the purpose of an interview?
    a) An opportunity to show off ❏
    b) An opportunity to learn about the organization ❏
    c) To be a two-way process ❏
    d) To trip you up ❏

5. What should your interview objective be?
    a) To present yourself well ❏
    b) To explore the benefits package ❏
    c) To meet your prospective colleagues and boss ❏
    d) To be clear about whether or not to accept the role ❏

6. How should you respond to a closed question?
    a) With a simple yes or no ❏
    b) By giving an example ❏
    c) With another question ❏
    d) With a nod and a smile ❏

7. What is the most important part of an interview?
    a) Warm-up questions ❏
    b) Questions about match and suitability ❏
    c) The end of the interview ❏
    d) Your questions ❏

8. What characterizes probing questions:
    a) They require detailed answers ❏
    b) They are unfair ❏
    c) They make you sweat ❏
    d) They indicate the interviewer's interest ❏

9. How should you respond to a discriminatory question?
    a) Get up and walk out ❏
    b) Clarify the interviewer's intention ❏
    c) Ask how it's relevant ❏
    d) Make a formal complaint ❏

10. How should you respond to an interviewer who hasn't read your CV?
    a) Allow them time to do so ❏
    b) Tell them all about it ❏
    c) Keep calm and be patient ❏
    d) Show irritation ❏

CHAPTER 23

Doing your research

It is a natural human reaction to feel nervous and apprehensive going into an unfamiliar situation. Although elements of the interview will be unknown, there are, as we suggested in the previous chapter, many features that interviews have in common. Interviewers will want to know about your previous experience, your personality and what makes you the ideal person for the post, or not. There are, however, aspects that are unique and unpredictable. No two experiences of being interviewed are likely to be the same. It is important, therefore, to gather as much information as you can at the earliest possible opportunity. This is easy to do and has the following benefits:

- You will demonstrate to the interviewer that you have considered the organization's requirements
- You will show your interest in the job
- You will feel more confident knowing that you are well prepared.

We suggest that you research three areas:

1 The interview
2 The job
3 The organization.

By researching, you lessen the risk of feeling that you could have made a better impression or that you haven't done yourself justice. The more you research, the greater knowledge and understanding you will gain. You will be better able to put yourself into the interviewer's shoes and have a sense of what it might be like to work with and for them. You will understand the company's acronyms and operating principles. In addition, you place yourself ahead of the competition.

The interview

If you have been invited for interview, you need to know some basic facts and, if this information isn't supplied, you need to start your investigations to find out:

- how to get there
- who will interview you
- the format of the interview.

How to get there

Finding out how you get to the interview is essential before you start your journey. Once you know the location, you can decide how you will travel. Always aim to arrive early – calculate the journey time and add an hour. Whatever method of transport you choose, delays may happen that are out of your control. Also check what security arrangements there are, as these may add time to your journey. On larger sites, leave yourself plenty of time to get from the reception to the interview building.

If possible, go on a practice journey as it gives you the opportunity to view the site at close quarters without the interview looming.

On the day

If you are delayed, be sure to contact the interviewers and let them know why you will be late and when you expect to arrive. Make sure you have the relevant phone number handy. They will appreciate your call as they may need to make other plans or reschedule.

On arrival

Having arrived early, you will have the opportunity to make last-minute preparations:

- Think through your replies and questions
- Get a feel for the organization

- Complete any further application forms
- Read through the company literature
- Take advantage of other information
- Go on a site tour
- Read your CV again
- Relax.

Who will interview you?

The key information you need here is: name(s), position in the organization and job title.

There may be a number of interviews, particularly for a senior post. The first, in-depth interview is often held on a one-to-one basis with a recruitment consultant, line manager or member of the human resources department. It could take the form of a thorough exploration of your CV or a structured interview.

Candidates shortlisted from the first interview can expect second and third interviews, which are likely to be conducted by one or more senior staff, who may have responsibility for the post or an interest in it. The objectives for these interviews are to explore any aspects still outstanding from the first interview and to assess how well your personality will blend with the team. You may meet the same interviewer more than once – so learn to pace yourself and aim to remember names.

Knowing who is going to interview you will help you prepare your responses. Interviewers' interests may fit into the categories described in the following table.

Organizational role	What they are looking for
Functional head	Qualifications/experience Ability to perform tasks Understanding of the job/technical jargon Transferable skills Match with management style, expectations and culture
Managing director	Ability to meet targets Contribution to growth and profitability Adaptability and aspirations

Organizational role	What they are looking for
Peers	Teamworking, personality and style Shared experiences Work experience
Junior staff	Management style, openness Approachability
Human resources	Your background and career to date Training/development needs Salary and benefits Start date

Organizations employing recruitment consultants often use them to shortlist candidates to ensure that only the most qualified candidates progress. They will be seeking the person who most closely matches the employer's specification, not solely in terms of experience but also in personality and aspirations.

The format of the interview

Interviews can take many forms. The two most common are one-to-one and panel interviews. Some organizations combine different types by shortlisting candidates with a telephone interview, inviting them to a panel and then asking them to return for further one-to-one interviews. Once you have found out the format, you can gear your preparation specifically to suit.

Interview formats include:

- telephone
- one-to-one
- panel
- tests
- presentations
- socials.

Telephone

The informal pre-interview chat is often over the telephone. This may occur when the interviewer is uncertain whether to shortlist you. For you, this call could be very important, making the difference between winning a face-to-face meeting or not. Anticipate this by keeping a checklist by the phone.

One-to-one

This type of interview consists simply of one interviewer talking to one applicant. It is the easiest interview to arrange and conduct and, in consequence, is the type most commonly used.

However, decisions are rarely the result of one person's perceptions. It is common to hold a series of one-to-one interviews, which may be on the same day or extend over months.

Panel

The panel (or 'selection board') may number from two members upwards. It can take many different forms, from a free-for-all, where all interviewers chip in with a variety of questions, to a more formal and structured approach where interviewers will take it in turn to ask questions reflecting their particular interests. At first, this style of interview may feel more threatening, but it tends to be fairer and more equitable.

Panel interviews can be very formal. Responses and further exploratory questions are not always forthcoming because of the limitations of time. It is also more difficult to establish the same feeling of rapport as you can in a one-to-one interview.

The chair of the panel is usually the one who makes the initial introductions and the final remarks. Do not assume that they have the greatest influence in making final decisions.

Do not be unnerved by the panel; treat it as if it is a one-to-one interview, concentrating your attention on the person asking the question at all times. Only include the other members when you are ready to continue with the next question.

- Always look at the person asking the question
- Direct your answer to the questioner
- Glance around to show you are ready for the next question.

 Do not be put off by signals between members of the panel. These probably have little to do with you personally but are more to do with matters such as time.

Tests

Tests are now commonly used to help assess candidates' abilities, aptitudes and personality. They are not an examination of your ability to remember facts but an extra way of gathering information. All applicants will be given the same questions, tasks and parameters. In an assessment centre format these may be carried out in groups.

Test type	Measures
Aptitude	Specific skills for the job: verbal, numerical, spatial, mechanical, clerical
Psychometric	Personality traits and preferences which may be needed to fit into team/project, temperament, disposition
Attainment	Knowledge of procedures, skills: driving, typing, technical terminology
Intelligence	General intellectual potential, problem-solving skills
Physical	Health, eyesight, colour perception, hearing acuity
Group discussions	Communication, judgement, reasoning, problem solving, persuasiveness, listening skills, respect
Presentations	Ability to stand up and speak, arranging information, quick thinking, flexibility
Written exercises	Clarity, legibility, summarizing

If you know there will be some form of test, remember to complete it within the time allowed, read the questions and answer them honestly.

Presentations

It is increasingly common for interviews to require you to give a formal presentation as part of the process. You may get advance warning of this and the particular subject area you are required to present. Be sure to check what equipment will be available to you on the day (projector, laptop, software, flipchart, etc.) and who will constitute your audience. You may want copies of your presentation or a summary to hand out. Be creative and remember that you want your presentation to be memorable.

Occasionally you will receive a topic to present or a project to plan on arrival at the interview and have to prepare there and then. Think through an outline of a presentation – how and in what ways you would address the issues of the day. Then all you need to do if you are faced with this scenario is to adapt it to the specific requirements of the topic.

Your presentation should:

● convince the audience that you are qualified and experienced
● demonstrate successes
● outline your contributions on a strategic and detailed level
● establish good relationships.

Be sure to inject:

● professionalism
● a degree of formality
● controlled enthusiasm
● pace and drive
● humour, as long as it's natural.

Think how to make your presentation unique and interesting. Limit the number of PowerPoint slides you use to five per 20 minutes. Is there something you could take along as a prop that represents you or the organization in a memorable way? One candidate we know took a hat from a Christmas cracker and used it to demonstrate that they considered the interviewing company to be the king of kings in the sector. Corny, perhaps, but she was remembered with a smile and called back for the next interview.

A presentation is an ideal opportunity for you, but only if you can control your nerves and are clear about the messages you want to communicate. It is likely that this presentation will be related in some way to the job in question and most particularly to the main area of responsibility. Presentations can also be used to establish a relationship with the interviewer.

You should also consider whether it is appropriate to take a portfolio with you containing samples of your work. To be helpful, such things must be clearly relevant and easy to handle and look at during an interview.

Socials

Part of your interview day could include meeting the team or taking a tour of the organization. Some organizations arrange social gatherings where you, the other candidates and sometimes partners meet together with your future employers. These may be labelled informal events, but always be on your guard; they are a part of the interview process. Use this as another opportunity to gather information. Be sure to talk to all those representing the organization and limit your consumption of alcohol.

 Investigating what will happen before the interview – who will interview you and the format of the interview – will help you to show your understanding of the role, the organization and current challenges, and also creates a more complete impression of whether the role fits with your career plan.

The job

The essential starting point for success is to know as much as you can about the job for which you have applied. There are several potential sources of information; you should use as many as possible. These include:

● preliminary discussions
● personal contacts – your network
● the Internet.

Preliminary discussions

You will already have received some information about the job, which attracted you enough to make the initial contact. You may now want to know more about:

● the extent of your duties and responsibilities
● the desirable and essential qualities required
● skill levels and academic qualifications needed
● reporting relationships
● opportunities for training and development

- location
- hours of work
- salary and benefits.

Personal contacts

You may decide to collect information about the job by talking to someone involved in the recruitment process. If you remain unsure about any particular aspects of the job or the organization, you can save everyone's time by doing some research. This is your opportunity to check fit and suitability – yours and theirs.

- Does your network extend into the organization?
- Who do you know who works, or has worked, for them?

By talking to insiders, you can get an 'inside' view. Remember that you will be hearing a subjective perception. Their views may be affected by personal circumstances or prejudices. So concentrate on facts rather than opinions.

The Internet

You should be able to find plenty of information via the Internet, depending on the size and type of the organization. The challenge here is to avoid information overload and target your searches to particular areas of interest around the organization and to those relating to the post.

The organization

The interviewer will expect you to have some knowledge of the organization. It is unlikely that it will be either comprehensive or complete. You need to show your interest not only in what you know but in filling in the gaps.

If sufficient information is not already supplied, you should try to find out:

- what the organization does
- product details
- ownership (public, private, group, independent, UK)
- size
- history

- structure (site, area or department)
- management style
- culture
- staff turnover
- outlets/factories/offices
- turnover and profit
- market position
- stability
- reputation
- strengths
- weaknesses
- threats
- markets
- competitors.

The organization itself and, if it is large enough, its public relations or customer services departments, are excellent starting points.

Other potential sources of information include its website, the Internet, directories and databases.

Directories

Key British Enterprises – basic corporate data on Britain's top 50,000 companies. Includes full contact details, names and titles of executives, financial details and industry

Who Owns Whom includes parent companies, subsidiaries and associates

Kompass produces *Regional, Product and Service Directories* on over 40,000 leading companies. Includes contact names of directors, executives and department heads, nature of business, annual turnover
www.kompass.com

More detailed information is available from Companies House.

Companies House
Crown Way
Cardiff CF14 3UZ
www.gov.uk/government/organisations/companies-house

Outside the UK, www.internationalcompanyinformation.com is a good source of data.

Use your networks, arrange to talk to your contacts and, if possible, borrow literature not normally given out to the public. Recruitment consultants are another good source of information; they should be able to help you access the formal information in the form of annual reports, sales literature and in-house magazines. They can also provide you with an insight into informal information: personalities, problems and opportunities. Use everything that is to hand.

It is more than likely that you will use the telephone for some of your enquiries. Be sure to have thought through and have listed in front of you the questions you propose to ask.

For example, you may want more details about:

- the job for which you are being interviewed
- who will interview you – their name and job title
- the format of the interview
- how long you will be there
- the name, address and phone number of the organization
- the name, address and phone number of the interview location
- the date, day and time of the interview
- the availability of parking facilities
- security arrangements
- the name and title of the person arranging the interview
- the job location
- annual reports.

You may also want to ask about salary and benefits. It can save you time if you decide at this stage that you are no longer interested because the salary is too low. Proceed on this basis with caution, though, because salaries are often negotiable within parameters, but the person on the telephone may not be aware of these parameters and the level of flexibility.

These days you may be greeted by a message rather than a person. Consider and write down what you want to say before making the call. The key information you need to leave is:

- your name
- your contact telephone number
- your address
- a brief message, requesting information

- your deadline if you have one
- your availability.

Repeat your name and phone number at the end of your message.
    You may be asked to put all questions into an email for a specific person's attention. Use the guidelines above and frame your email in a way that is not too formal and shows a degree of professionalism. Put yourself in the shoes of the email recipient, be clear which your most pressing questions are and be selective. If you haven't had a response within a week, you might try a reminder email or phone call – you are probably not as high a priority for them as they are for you!

TIP *All preparation is valuable, so invest time and energy into gathering as much information as you can at this stage.*

Summary

In this chapter we have guided you through the research you need to do to prepare for your interview.

To remove uncertainty and apprehension, investigate what will happen at the interview, including who will interview you and the format of the interview. Don't overlook the need to understand how to get to the interview and access the site; and always leave enough time to get there.

We've also encouraged you to research the role and the organization. We are sure that through your application you will have come to understand the role, and as you've been asked to interview you have the right skills and experience, so it's worth revisiting what you said in your application and all the information regarding the role.

If you have contacts within the department or organization, it's worth asking them for advice or further information. Do as much research as you can about the organization – both online and through your networks. Don't base your understanding only on reputation, however: look at current performance and challenges.

Fact-check (answers at the back)

There is more than one possible answer to some of the following questions.

1. Before an interview, what should you do?
   a) Always prepare thoroughly ❏
   b) Never prepare ❏
   c) Only prepare the presentation ❏
   d) Prepare just enough ❏

2. When planning how to get to an interview, what should you do?
   a) Look into transport ❏
   b) Leave enough time to get there ❏
   c) Check security arrangements ❏
   d) Assume there'll be parking ❏

3. Which person is most likely to interview you?
   a) Line manager ❏
   b) HR manager ❏
   c) Recruitment consultant ❏
   d) Any of the above ❏

4. How should you prepare for a telephone interview?
   a) They are informal so no need to prepare ❏
   b) Keep a checklist by the phone ❏
   c) Impossible to prepare for ❏
   d) By making yourself comfortable ❏

5. What can psychometric tests accurately gauge?
   a) Personality ❏
   b) Fit ❏
   c) Ability ❏
   d) How good your memory is ❏

6. When you are asked to do a test, what should you do?
   a) Put yourself in the shoes of the successful candidate ❏
   b) Answer as you think you should ❏
   c) Check that you have been consistent ❏
   d) Answer flippantly ❏

7. Presentations give you an opportunity to what?
   a) Shine ❏
   b) Trip yourself up ❏
   c) Show off the technology ❏
   d) Demonstrate your ability ❏

8. If asked to give a spontaneous presentation, what should you do?
   a) Feel dread ❏
   b) Freeze ❏
   c) See it as an opportunity to show your expertise ❏
   d) Enjoy it ❏

9. How should you research the job?
   a) Go to your network ❏
   b) Read the competencies document ❏
   c) Phone up for more information ❏
   d) Use your intuition ❏

10. Why should you research the organization?
   a) It gives the company view ❏
   b) It gives you a sense of the employer ❏
   c) It is useful whatever the outcome of the interview ❏
   d) It informs your questions ❏

CHAPTER 24

Discovering what differentiates you

Self-knowledge is an essential ingredient of your preparation for the interview.

We have already suggested that you research the interview format, the job and the organization so that you are better informed about the process and will know what to expect. A most important ingredient in this preparation is finding out about yourself, so that you feel comfortable in presenting yourself to the interviewer.

This idea may seem a little strange: after all, if you don't know yourself, who does?

In this chapter we will help you to know yourself better through a process of reflection. We will give you areas to think about and guidance on these.

You will get to know more about:

- yourself as a person
- your skills
- your limitations
- your strengths
- your achievements
- the essence of you.

Complete all the exercises – be brave, and test them out on colleagues, friends and anyone else you trust.

You, the person

When managers are asked to describe themselves, they tend to talk about what they do rather than who they are. They think of themselves in terms of their title and describe themselves as such: Operations Manager, Human Resources Manager, Finance Manager or Project Manager. These are, on many occasions, sufficient descriptors and speak for themselves, but do not expect that this will be enough at an interview. You need to understand and describe what skills make you successful in your role and what strengths make you different.

Being invited to attend an interview suggests that you match the interviewer's specification; you are halfway to success.

However, it is unlikely that you will be the only person who looks good on paper. The interview is your opportunity to stand out and be noticed. You want to convince the interviewer that you can bring enhanced benefits to their organization as well as being able to do the job.

To be successful, you need to make an impression and be different. The interviewer may see many interviewees in the course of a day, so the ones they will remember are the ones who are distinctive, who have something interesting to say or who can make a unique contribution to the organization or department.

The key to presenting yourself is to consider and understand your uniqueness. Ask yourself the following questions:

● What have I got that makes me special?
● What makes me fit?
● What is my key message?

The answers may come easily or you may have to return to these questions at the end of the chapter when you have a clearer understanding of you.

Your skills

The first step in building up a picture of yourself is to appraise your skills.

- What can you offer the organization?
- What are your skills?

These common interview questions, while apparently simple, require thought, preparation and a level of introspection and reflection. Your answer should not simply be a regurgitation of your CV, relating what you have done.

It is more about when and in what contexts you have performed well, and the skills and competencies, contacts, knowledge and attitude you have applied or acquired in the process. Try to answer this question honestly and spontaneously:

- What can I do?

How comfortable would you feel about presenting these ideas to an interviewer? It can feel strange at first to 'blow your own trumpet', but in an interview you are the only one who knows the tune.

The following list of national management standards is basically a set of 'can do' statements. Look down the list of skills in the table and give yourself a score for each statement against the following measures:

1 Very competent
2 Competent
3 Adequate for the task
4 Have not developed the skills

Check afterwards with a colleague to see if they agree with your assessment. You may find you have been overly critical.

People are generally less good at recognizing their own skills than at identifying skills in others. If you find you are struggling with this task, ask for feedback from the people you manage, or those who manage you; alternatively, think back over past appraisals and the feedback you have received.

Assess your skills

	1	2	3	4
Managing self and personal skills				
Manage your own resources	❏	❏	❏	❏
Manage your professional development	❏	❏	❏	❏
Develop your personal network	❏	❏	❏	❏
Providing direction				
Develop and implement operational plans for your area of responsibility	❏	❏	❏	❏
Map the environment in which your organization operates	❏	❏	❏	❏
Develop a strategic business plan for your organization	❏	❏	❏	❏
Put the strategic business plan into action	❏	❏	❏	❏
Provide leadership for your teams, in your area of responsibility and for your organization	❏	❏	❏	❏
Ensure compliance with legal, regulatory, ethical and social requirements	❏	❏	❏	❏
Develop the culture of your organization	❏	❏	❏	❏
Manage risk	❏	❏	❏	❏
Promote equality and diversity in your area of responsibility and in your organization	❏	❏	❏	❏
Facilitating change				
Encourage innovation in your team, in your area of responsibility and in your organization	❏	❏	❏	❏
Lead, plan and implement change	❏	❏	❏	❏
Working with people				
Develop productive working relationships with colleagues and stakeholders	❏	❏	❏	❏
Recruit, select and keep colleagues	❏	❏	❏	❏
Plan the workforce	❏	❏	❏	❏
Allocate and monitor the progress and quality of work in your area of responsibility	❏	❏	❏	❏
Provide learning opportunities for colleagues	❏	❏	❏	❏

Assess your skills

	1	2	3	4
Help team members address problems affecting their performance	❑	❑	❑	❑
Build and manage teams	❑	❑	❑	❑
Reduce and manage conflict in your team	❑	❑	❑	❑
Lead and participate in meetings	❑	❑	❑	❑
Support individuals to develop and maintain their performance	❑	❑	❑	❑
Initiate and follow disciplinary and grievance procedures	❑	❑	❑	❑
Manage redundancies in your area of responsibility	❑	❑	❑	❑
Build and sustain collaborative relationships with other organizations	❑	❑	❑	❑
Using resources				
Manage a budget	❑	❑	❑	❑
Manage finance for your area of responsibility	❑	❑	❑	❑
Obtain additional finance for the organization	❑	❑	❑	❑
Promote the use of technology within your organization	❑	❑	❑	❑
Identify, assess and control health and safety risks	❑	❑	❑	❑
Ensure health and safety requirements are met in your area of responsibility	❑	❑	❑	❑
Ensure an effective organizational approach to health and safety	❑	❑	❑	❑
Manage the physical resources	❑	❑	❑	❑
Manage the environmental impact of your work	❑	❑	❑	❑
Take effective decisions	❑	❑	❑	❑
Communicate information and knowledge	❑	❑	❑	❑
Manage knowledge in your area of responsibility and promote knowledge management in your organization	❑	❑	❑	❑

Assess your skills

	1	2	3	4
Support team and virtual working	❏	❏	❏	❏
Select suppliers through a tendering process	❏	❏	❏	❏
Outsource business processes	❏	❏	❏	❏
Achieving results				
Manage a project or a programme of complementary projects	❏	❏	❏	❏
Manage business processes	❏	❏	❏	❏
Develop and implement marketing plans for your area of responsibility	❏	❏	❏	❏
Develop a customer-focused organization	❏	❏	❏	❏
Monitor and solve customer service problems	❏	❏	❏	❏
Manage the achievement of customer satisfaction	❏	❏	❏	❏
Support customer service improvements	❏	❏	❏	❏
Work with others to improve customer service	❏	❏	❏	❏
Build your organization's understanding of its market and customers	❏	❏	❏	❏
Improve organizational performance	❏	❏	❏	❏
Manage quality systems	❏	❏	❏	❏
Prepare for, participate in and carry out quality audits	❏	❏	❏	❏
Manage the development and marketing of product/service in your area of responsibility	❏	❏	❏	❏

This list may help to define your skills and give you the language to talk about them. The next step is to own them.

Take some time now to tell yourself about your skills, and hear yourself saying them out loud without feeling embarrassed or apologetic. Practise in front of the mirror.

Your limitations

You are very likely to be asked about your weaknesses at the interview. We would prefer to think of them as limitations or areas for improvement and to look for positive ways of presenting them. For example, you know that you can be impatient, but looked at from an alternative perspective it could be seen as an over-eagerness to get things done. This is not hiding from the truth, it is putting an affirmative interpretation on negative characteristics.

Your 'weaknesses' can also be listed to give you an idea of what changes you might want to make.

- What limits you?
- What has held you back in your career?
- In what circumstances have you felt most frustrated and unhappy at work?

Your strengths

Skills are only part of the picture. They will help to show *what* you do. You have individual strengths which will dictate *how* you do things. This is what makes you unique.

The following list outlines the strengths of successful managers. Look at it and see where their talents coincide with yours. Mark yourself on a scale of 1–4:

1 Always
2 Frequently
3 Sometimes
4 Never

Where do your strengths lie?

	1	2	3	4
Quick thinking	❏	❏	❏	❏
Enthusiasm	❏	❏	❏	❏
Presence	❏	❏	❏	❏
Ability to handle conflict and make decisions	❏	❏	❏	❏
Self-confidence	❏	❏	❏	❏
Strength of will	❏	❏	❏	❏
Commitment and determination	❏	❏	❏	❏
Flexibility and willingness to change	❏	❏	❏	❏
Creativity	❏	❏	❏	❏
Willingness to take responsibility	❏	❏	❏	❏
Initiative	❏	❏	❏	❏
Competitiveness	❏	❏	❏	❏
Sensitivity to people and situation	❏	❏	❏	❏
Stamina	❏	❏	❏	❏
Commercial awareness	❏	❏	❏	❏
Judgement	❏	❏	❏	❏
Being personally organized	❏	❏	❏	❏
Ability to take risks	❏	❏	❏	❏
Ability to strike a balance between big picture and detail	❏	❏	❏	❏

You will notice that most of these qualities are not tested by any formal educational system. As a manager you can always learn the *skills* needed for the job. How many of the *strengths* listed can you learn?

Using this list for guidance, try to answer the following questions about your strengths. Be as specific as possible and think about descriptions of how you utilize them.

● What are the strong points of your character and personality?
● In so far as you have succeeded, what has helped you?

Understand your achievements

The most practical way to assess yourself is to make a list of all your achievements, not solely the major ones, but everything that other people should know about. People find this process difficult, so to help you we've given you some ideas. Add any more of your own.

Achievements might include:

- a new idea
- reducing waste
- turning around a bad situation
- avoiding potential problems
- improving customer relationships
- improving results
- costs you managed to cut
- an activity simplified or improved
- a crisis averted
- something you made
- a new skill mastered
- a group you led
- a problem solved
- anything that had a happy ending.

The essence of you

You have considered and listed your vast array of skills, strengths and achievements and examined your limitations. Now is the time to put them together to form a composite picture of you.

Write down a number of sentences beginning with the words 'I am', e.g. 'I am a manager.' Try to think of at least 15 of these.

Be specific

Expand these sentences to show yourself off. Add to the sentences by explaining and giving clear examples. Where possible, angle the examples to match the post for which you will be interviewed.

Produce statements such as:

I am a good manager because I am able to motivate and develop people. In my last job I inherited a team who were bored with the weekly meetings and often strolled in late. I talked to them individually, found out their dissatisfactions and instigated a system of agenda setting that involved them all. As a result the meetings became fun and much more productive.

This is very different from saying: 'I am a good manager because I have an MBA' or, 'I am a good manager because I have worked for "X" for 20 years.'

You can see from this example that the way you describe yourself and the kind of language you use detracts from or adds to the image you portray.

As well as giving concrete illustrations, you also need to think about your language. Be confident and assertive, using phrases like the following to illustrate your point positively:

... which resulted in
... so that
... the benefit was
... the advantage was

Dismiss all your tentative language such as:

I probably could...
I think I can...
I have been told...
Some people think I'm...

Summary statement

You may like to reinforce your other statements by developing a summary career statement about yourself. This has the advantage of creating the right impression in the mind of the interviewer. Produce a powerful statement about the type of person you are and the contribution you can make to the organization. You are then able to create value in the eyes of potential employers and emphasize the benefits you bring.

Statements such as:

I am a successful sales manager with a proven track record of building teams and winning high profile.

I am a determined professional with experience across a wide range of technical products.

These statements should be brief and powerful, highlighting all the benefits of employing you. Be sure to practise saying them out loud; often statements that look good on paper do not translate to the spoken word naturally. After hearing it you may need to adapt it. Also, be sure that you feel comfortable with the statement; if there is any hint of uneasiness, this will show.

Try it out before the interview and validate your perceptions against another reliable source. Use a friend or work colleague who knows you well. Looking at yourself through different people's eyes can demonstrate the different facets of you. Begin by trying to share your findings with a trusted friend or colleague. Ask them what skills they think you have. Ask them in what areas they feel you should be developing. Ask them to comment on your transferable skills.

Self-esteem

Self-esteem is essential to everyone's wellbeing and it is something that can grow or diminish depending on what is happening in our lives.

It can be divided into two parts:

- **Internal self-esteem** comes from your beliefs about yourself, accepting your strengths and limitations rather than striving to be perfect. You see yourself as equal to but different from other people rather than superior or inferior.
- **External self-esteem** comes from interactions with others. You respond to their reactions, opinions and how they relate to you. You let them tell you how good you are.

Many people have an over-developed need for external self-esteem because their internal self-esteem is fragile. As you increase your internal self-esteem, you will lose some of your dependence on external self-esteem.

You may find you spend time rating yourself as better in some areas and worse in others. Internal self-esteem is not dependent on comparisons. It is your own assessment of your self-worth. What you have developed in this chapter is a collection of ideas that reflect your strengths and achievements.

Summary

Modesty or traditional conditioning may have made this chapter challenging, but it's better that the challenge comes in your preparation than at the interview. You need to be able to describe you – what makes you different and fit with the role. Using the organization's language can help, as can the previous chapter's research.

The interviewer wants to know what you offer and the difference you would bring to the role – your skills, strengths and achievements. This is always difficult to communicate on paper, so this chapter was about bringing your CV or application to life. Now is not the time to be a shrinking violet. Let them know confidently and clearly how good you are.

It may help to approach the interview as you would a product launch. At the interview, you are the product; your challenge is to convince the other parties to invest in it. This will help you overcome any nervousness about 'bragging' because you will be one step removed from selling yourself.

Your journey to succeeding at interview is well on its way – you have done your research and prepared responses to questions. The next chapter will be more about how you present yourself.

Fact-check (answers at the back)

There is more than one possible answer to some of the following questions.

1. How should you describe yourself?
   a) Use your job title ❏
   b) Say what you look like ❏
   c) Detail your skills ❏
   d) Feel embarrassed ❏

2. When you describe your skills, what should you talk about?
   a) Your CV ❏
   b) Your successes
   c) What makes you different ❏
   d) How you've made a difference ❏

3. How should you respond to questions about your skills?
   a) Struggle to find the words ❏
   b) Use your organization's competencies ❏
   c) Refer to what you've done ❏
   d) Describe value you've added ❏

4. How would you prepare for questions about who you are?
   a) Talk to your boss ❏
   b) Talk to a colleague ❏
   c) Look back over appraisals ❏
   d) Fail to prepare ❏

5. How should you answer questions on your weaknesses?
   a) By covering them up ❏
   b) By presenting your strengths ❏
   c) With embarrassment ❏
   d) By saying what you learned from them ❏

6. How should you describe your strengths ?
   a) The way you do things ❏
   b) What you do ❏
   c) Your unique contribution ❏
   d) The things that have helped you succeed ❏

7. Which of your achievements would be best to include?
   a) Turning around a situation ❏
   b) Improving results ❏
   c) Acquiring new skills ❏
   d) Surviving interviews ❏

8. What should 'I am' statements be?
   a) Backed up by examples ❏
   b) Clear ❏
   c) Listed alphabetically ❏
   d) Funny ❏

9. What do you demonstrate your strengths in terms of?
   a) Your successes ❏
   b) Your academic achievements ❏
   c) All the jobs you've done ❏
   d) Previous feedback ❏

10. How should you prepare for questions about yourself?
   a) Practise with a colleague ❏
   b) Practise being modest ❏
   c) Practise feeling confident ❏
   d) By using tentative, vague language ❏

CHAPTER 25

Preparing yourself for success

Some people see interviews as threatening situations. They worry about what limits them, about how nervous they get, about what the interviewers will think of them, and about failing to do the job if they were appointed.

For these people, what stands in the way of conveying self-confidence is their overriding fear of failing themselves and their expectations. Their fear of failure overcomes their aspiration to succeed. In some, it can have a paralysing effect and completely ruin the interview.

If this is a description of you, then you need to begin thinking of yourself and your approach to interviews in a more positive light. You started the process thinking about your strengths and limitations; now we will help you to look and act the part too.

Prepare to succeed by:

- thinking positively
- making a good impression
- looking prepared.

Thinking positively

World-class athletes, among others, will confirm the importance of mental attitude to achieving the best performance. To give yourself the best possible chance at interview you will need to think yourself into a fully positive frame of mind. How you set about this will be a personal matter. But concentration on your strengths, and the certainty that you have the internal resources to cope with any difficulties, will go a long way.

Some people find it helpful to relax quietly and picture their success, both at the interview and in the subsequent post. They imagine this in great and vivid detail, visualizing the thoughts and sensations this will bring. Others treat themselves to something new, ensuring that they feel good inside and out.

However you go about this, it is in many ways the most crucial phase of the whole process of preparation. You need an inner conviction that you are important to yourself. If you do not feel a sense of your own wellbeing and self-worth, how can you convince others that you will be an asset to their organization? You have to think positively before you can act positively.

> ### 'Whether you think you can or you can't, you're probably right.'
> Henry Ford

Compare:

Thoughts	'I'm sure they just asked me to make up the numbers. The others are bound to be better.'
Feelings	Hopeless, inadequate, apprehensive
Outcome	Poor impression, no conviction, unsuccessful interview

with:

Thoughts	'They've picked me from all the applicants. I must stand a very good chance.'
Feelings	Calm, confident, positive anticipation
Outcome	Assured impression, mutual fact-finding, beneficial interview

Aim to direct your energy away from worrying about the interview and towards effectively preparing for it. Consider it as an opportunity, where you are both interviewing each other, not as a one-sided test. Most importantly, remember that, of all the people who applied, they have chosen you to interview.

If you are not nervous about attending interviews, then you should have little problem in this respect. But try to monitor whether you may be seen as overconfident and not taking things as seriously as you should. It is common for interviewers to mistakenly confuse confidence with arrogance.

To be just a little anxious, a little apprehensive, is good; it is generally facilitative rather than inhibitive. Only when you become very anxious do you begin to harm your prospects.

Making a good impression

People make up their minds about us in minutes. Never ignore this fact, particularly at an interview when you have a relatively limited time to make an impression.

Your initial impact is vital. You don't get a second chance to make a first impression, so make sure you:

● start well
● pay attention to your appearance
● are aware of your body language
● use your voice skilfully.

Start well

Whenever two people meet for the first time, they automatically start by evaluating each other on the basis of the non-verbal cues they receive. You and your interviewer will be doing just that as soon as you meet, whether in the interview room or on the walk from reception. It is a subconscious 'weighing up' time.

The interviewer will often base their judgement on this initial impression and spend the remainder of the interview looking to reinforce their view. You may be judged by nothing more than how you walk across the room, the strength of your handshake, or when and how you sit.

Evidence is often sought to support an initial impression. You should therefore do all you can to enter confidently, but not brashly, with a pleasant smile.

Do:

✔ Close the door behind you

✔ Walk forward confidently; body straight, head up

✔ Respond to offered handshakes firmly

✔ Wait until you are invited to sit

✔ Remain quiet but alert to the opening moves of the interviewer

✔ Allow them to take the initiative

✔ Be ready to respond appropriately.

Don't:

✗ Shuffle in, head down and hands in pockets

✗ Carry a jumble of paper

✗ Crash into the room pushing out your extended hand

✗ Attempt to dominate an interview, especially in the opening stages.

Dress the part

It is essential that you dress the part. Your appearance reveals a great deal about your self-image, your values and your attitudes towards other people and situations. More favourable qualities are often attributed to smartly dressed people. Those who are perceived to be attractive and well groomed are often treated better than those considered unattractive or inappropriately dressed.

TIP *Beware of the danger of overdressing. A good benchmark is to decide how the holder of the job would be expected to dress, and go just one stage better.*

For interviews, it is wise to find out the dominant style or accepted image of the culture you are trying to enter. If you can visit the organization at lunchtime or the end of the day, go and see what people are wearing. If that is not possible, take a look at the organization's literature and website, which may contain photographs of employees and directors.

If you buy a special interview outfit, accessories or shoes, do ensure that they are comfortable. There can be nothing more distracting than shoes that pinch, a jacket too long in the arms, a material that creases, trousers too long or generally ill-fitting clothes.

Also be conscious of colours. More sober colours are often recommended for interviews: blues, blacks, greys with contrasting shirts and blouses. Your choice of tie, shirt, blouse or scarf is also important; any extremes of colour or pattern will make an impact. Think about the messages your appearance conveys to others.

Pay attention to the finer points of turnout: fingernails, hair, shoes and jewellery. Avoid too much perfume or aftershave. They won't be noticed if they are acceptable – but they will if they are not.

TIP *Avoid drinking alcohol, smoking or eating highly spiced food just before an interview. Eat mints or use a breath freshener before; be cautious.*

Use the right body language

You can communicate far more non-verbally than you may be aware. Although you often concentrate on what you are going to say – and it is important for self-confidence to do so – this must not be at the expense of how you say it.

Research shows that when you are presenting:

● words account for 35 per cent of the message
● tone of voice and body language account for 65 per cent of the message.

Negative thoughts and tension trigger anxious feelings. It is possible to overcome these – think about the directives 'chin up', 'stiff upper lip' and 'swallow your feelings' – using your body to control them. Beware of different messages through your body that can leak out and undermine or contradict what you are saying. If you are thinking positively about yourself and the interview, then your body will give a positive impression too.

Focus your attention on the interviewer to the exclusion of everything else. Ensure that you are comfortable and relaxed in the chair provided.

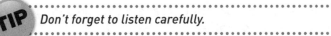

TIP *Don't forget to listen carefully.*

While listening and giving the interviewer your full attention, it is also important that you demonstrate this.

Do:

✔ Sit comfortably, in an upright but relaxed posture

✔ Rest your hands on the arms of the chair or comfortably in your lap

✔ Look at your interviewer with an interested expression

✔ Keep your head raised when you listen

✔ Nod intelligently whenever the interviewer tells you something

✔ Be relaxed.

Listed below are some of the most common blunders that interviewees make. They are things to avoid. In some way, these all suggest a desire to escape, boredom, nerves, or impatience either to speak or to leave.

Don't:

✗ Fidget or bite your nails

✗ Cross your arms or legs, or clasp the chair or your upper arms

✗ Lean backwards, looking away from the interviewer

✗ Gaze fixedly at some point in the room

✗ Become distracted by the carpet or a picture

✗ Point your body towards the door

✗ Kick or tap your foot

✗ Tap a pen

✗ Prop your head on the palm of your hand

✗ Yawn

✗ Stare blankly at the interviewer

✗ Scribble on paper.

Use your voice skilfully

Your voice is crucial to the impression you make. Many people are self-conscious about their voices and accents and, fearing they will let them down, try to mask them. Often all this does is make them unintelligible. Your voice is unique and is part of what makes you who you are. So befriend it and, rather than trying to hide your accent, concentrate on being heard and understood. If you use your voice skilfully, you will sound confident, knowledgeable and enthusiastic.

Always speak in a clear, steady voice. If you hesitate or stumble you will appear nervous and ill prepared. If you are concerned about your voice, take care not to attempt to hide it. You will appear tense and closed up. Speak in your natural voice. Don't try to change it to impress the interviewer. Avoid bad language, slang, or annoying phrases or words such as 'you know' and 'actually', 'with respect' and 'to be honest'. Inject confidence, happiness and enthusiasm into your voice.

TIP A-v-o-i-d m-o-n-o-t-o-n-e.

Listen to your voice and get used to it. Take one of your statements from the previous chapter and record it. Say it as though you're very nervous or unsure. Try it in an angry voice or a suspicious one. Express it as if you feel proud and positive about it and you. Say it with a frown and a smile. Vary the words you emphasize and the way you say them. See how different you can make your voice sound and notice the effect on you of the different ways of saying it.

Do:

✔ Pause and breathe deeply before speaking

✔ Speak slightly more slowly than normal

✔ Speak clearly; open your mouth

✔ Vary the tone to add interest

✔ Relax your shoulders and jaw.

Don't:

✗ Rattle out words 16 to the dozen

✗ Mumble

✗ Cover your mouth as you speak

✗ Stiffen your jaw

✗ Talk to your shoes

✗ Forget to breathe.

Own your responses: when talking about yourself, be sure to use the personal pronoun, 'I'. Identify with your responses, making sure they are specific to you.

Looking prepared

You may want to consider taking a folder with you. It is useful to hold your prompt notes, statements or questions. If not overused, this will give an air of efficiency. It can also help to reduce your nervousness and remind you of the two-way nature of the process.

Look and sound positive. Talk in a positive manner. If you're asked, 'Can you do this job?', the answer must never be, 'I think so'' or, 'I hope so'. It should be, 'Yes, definitely.'

Be calm. Don't be distracted by interruptions. If the telephone rings or an interviewer's colleague enters the room, stay calm. Don't panic if you don't know the answer to a question. If you don't know, admit it. Also, if your mind goes blank, don't worry. Take a deep breath and ask for clarification. You can also repeat the question back to give yourself thinking time, but only do this once or twice, otherwise it can become a pattern and no one will listen to the answer that follows.

 TIP *How you feel is essential to the impression you create. Use this chapter as a practice.*

Summary

You have got an interview and that means that the interviewer believes you could do the job, but there may be others who could do it too – so you have to shine. Your success is all about convincing the interviewer, but you may have to convince yourself first. You need to present yourself in a positive light, building on your skills, knowledge and achievements and, now, you should be feeling more positive about that.

We saw that the impression you make is much more about your presence than simply how you look. It's about everything from the moment you enter the room, greet people and take your seat. You can make a good impression with the tone and pitch of your voice and the energy you put into your responses – so don't allow your body language to let you down.

Don't overlook the need to listen attentively. Looking at the questioner can help, and they could be giving away clues too. Try to relax and not let nerves get the better of you, knowing that you have done your best to prepare.

Fact-check (answers at the back)

There is more than one possible answer to some of the following questions.

1. When approaching the interview, what should you focus on?
   a) Controlling your nerves ❑
   b) Not being able to do the job ❑
   c) What may go wrong ❑
   d) Your success in getting to this stage ❑

2. When preparing for the interview, what should you do?
   a) Think of yourself in the role ❑
   b) Relax ❑
   c) Find it difficult to overcome your negative thoughts ❑
   d) Not bother – you know you'll be all right on the day ❑

3. What's the best way to overcome interview nerves?
   a) Thorough preparation ❑
   b) Spending hours choosing what to wear ❑
   c) Having a couple of drinks for 'Dutch courage' ❑
   d) Talk over the interviewer ❑

4. How should you use your voice during an interview?
   a) Speak faster than normal ❑
   b) Speak more slowly than normal ❑
   c) By relaxing your jaw ❑
   d) By stiffening your jaw ❑

5. To create a good impression, what should you do?
   a) Walk confidently ❑
   b) Allow the interviewer to take the initiative ❑
   c) Ask lots of questions ❑
   d) Wait until you're invited to sit down ❑

6. How should you dress for an interview?
   a) Always in a suit ❑
   b) As you'd be expected to dress for the role ❑
   c) Wearing whatever's clean ❑
   d) It depends on your mood ❑

7. Which of the following should you pay attention to before the interview?
   a) Shoes ❑
   b) Fingernails ❑
   c) Hair ❑
   d) All of the above ❑

8. In the interview room, what should you do?
   a) Get comfortable, whatever the environment ❑
   b) Look at the interviewer who is asking you the question ❑
   c) Suggest a change in the layout of the room ❑
   d) Nod appropriately to show you are listening ❑

9. Which of the following should you avoid?
   a) Tapping your foot ❑
   b) Becoming distracted by activity outside the room ❑
   c) Sitting comfortably ❑
   d) Nodding appropriately ❑

10. In interviews, which of the following should you try to do?
   a) Maintain good eye contact ❑
   b) Stay positive and calm ❑
   c) Look down when responding to questions ❑
   d) Shout your message loud and clear ❑

CHAPTER 26

Responding skilfully

Your preparation for the interview is now well under way. Just like a student before an exam, you should be confident that you have completed your revision, and be eagerly awaiting the big day. Continuing with the imagery, it is now time to look back over past exam papers, examine the questions asked, and plan your answers.

As you would expect, an interview is full of questions. These tend to be the same for each applicant, providing the key points for comparison. We looked at types of questions in Chapter 22; now we will focus on their content and give you guidelines for responding.

It is possible to anticipate and prepare in advance for many of the questions you will be asked. Interview questions have common themes. These are likely to be:

- self-assessment
- work history and experience
- the organization
- the job, ambitions and motivation
- management style.

Thinking about questions

One of the main objectives of the interviewer is to build an impression of the interviewee not solely based on experience and history. Competency-based interviews demand that you present evidence of your past experience and achievements.

When interviewers are more interested in your characteristics and how you see yourself, they are likely to ask questions about:

- reasons for applying for the job
- creativity and problem solving
- adaptability and dealing with ambiguity
- reliability
- ability to delegate
- team player or solo worker
- motivations and aspirations.

Knowing yourself is essential. Completing the exercises in Chapter 24 will have helped you to formulate your answers.

Listed below are some of the questions frequently asked at interviews. Think through your answers and read through the guidelines on responding. It may help to note your thoughts down on paper. They can serve as an aide-memoire for you for the future and something to return to and improve on. You may want to record your answers and listen to them. If you do, practise putting the right enthusiasm and energy into them.

Consider how you portray yourself. You need to be sure that you can leave the interviewer with a positive impression. They need to be confident that you can do the job, fit with peers and contribute to the organization as a whole.

Remember that your application has already impressed the organization and that is why they are interviewing you. The interview is all about bringing what's on paper to life, so everything you do or say should reflect your ability to do the job and deliver the expectations. If you just restate your experience, you'll be missing your best opportunity to sell yourself.

Self-assessment

These questions aim to see how you sell yourself and how well you communicate that to others. They are usually very open questions that leave the direction of the answer up to you.

Tell me about yourself.

Because this is often the opening question in an interview, be very careful that you don't talk too much. Keep your answer brief, covering topics such as early years, development, management style, significant events and people. Think about the type of job and organization; what are they looking for? Choose the bits of you that match best. Be selective; for example, the early highlights and your technical skills may be less relevant to a management role than your proven management skills.

What are your weak points?

Weaknesses can be the other side of strengths. Having prepared yourself, you can make sure that limitations sound like strengths, and give examples. Always admit to one (or, if hard pressed, a second) limitation; if you don't, it suggests you don't know yourself very well.

I can take longer than others to finish a task, unless there is a deadline to meet. My weakness is linked to a strength – being very thorough.

What are your strengths?

Focus these on the post applied for and again give concrete examples. After reading Chapter 24 you will have plenty of successes to relate. Sort through them before you go to your interview and make them relevant.

I can quickly create a harmonious atmosphere with new clients. They feel relaxed and we can talk business straight away.

What can you do for us that someone else can't?

Here you have every right to blow your own trumpet and sell yourself! Talk about your record of getting things done, give examples and be specific. Mention your skills and interests combined with your history of getting results.

This is your opportunity to illustrate your uniqueness and the benefits you can offer the organization. You need to create an image of yourself as someone who stands out as a greater potential asset than any of the other applicants.

Work history

This section of questions focuses on what you can draw from your practical work experiences. It may be that there is little that differentiates you from the other applicants on paper, so the spotlight is on the way you present your employment and its relevance to date.

If you could start your career again, what would you do differently?
After a brief review of options, come back to something very like your work so far. You may want to add something you would have changed earlier in your career rather than starting again. It is fine to be content; explain why you are happy as you are, rather than just saying you would change nothing.

Now I realize how much I enjoy being a manager, I would have put myself forward for a management position sooner.
I knew when I was at school that I wanted to be a chief accountant. I planned my education and job applications to this end.

Why are you leaving/did you leave your present position?
Beware of becoming defensive on this question. Prepare yourself well. If you are leaving your present position because of problems with people, problems in the marketplace or because of withdrawn finances, you need to consider your responses carefully. Look to future opportunities rather than past problems. After all, few decisions are the result of just one factor: they are usually due to a combination of circumstances.

Resist any temptation to criticize or blame other people for your problems. You need to be seen as taking some responsibility for what happens to you.

I believe everyone should manage their careers; I now recognize the limited opportunities for me within my current organization and am actively seeking a change.

In your current/last position, what features do/did you like the most? Which the least?

Be careful and positive. Try to enhance the picture of you that the interviewer already has. Be sure to describe many more features that you liked than disliked. When you mention any you disliked, describe ways in which you overcame them.

I believe in regular communications and I had to work hard to win my colleagues over to a similar belief; we now have systems in place for regular contact that I am proud of.

What were your most significant contributions in your last position?

Have specific examples ready. Link these wherever possible to the achievements you have on your CV and to the post in question. Ensure that these give a balanced impression of you. You may want to describe the contributions you made through managing and developing people, or to areas of organizational development.

Did you think of leaving your present position before? If so, what held you there?

What makes you stay in any particular job and what prompts you to start looking for other opportunities? It may be challenge, colleagues, culture, influence, etc. Ensure you communicate that you know what is important to you at work and that you take control when things don't appear to be going right.

Would you describe a few situations in which your work was criticized?

Be specific. Think about constructive criticism and times when you've asked for feedback. You may then want to relate this to changes you've made to the way you work.

I once lost my temper with a particular member of staff, but it helped me think about the way I give and receive feedback.

How do you react to pressure and deal with deadlines?
Observe that both are facets of your career and give examples
from your experience in which you triumphed. You may also
want to highlight what you have learned to help you deal with
the pressure to ensure it doesn't exhibit itself as stress.

The organization

The interviewer will want to know how well you match their
organization. You are both looking for a good fit: they want
someone who will easily slot in and you want somewhere you
will feel comfortable. All your research should prepare you well
for these questions.

What do you know about our organization?
This question often precedes the interviewer's relating of
a brief summary of the organization. Ideally, you should
be able to discuss products or services, reputation, image,
goals, problems, management style, people, history,
philosophy. Let your response demonstrate that you have
done the research, but don't overwhelm the listener. If you
don't know much about the organization, it is better to say so
than to pretend that you do.

Why do you want to work for us?
Relate this to the organization's needs. Your research may have
shown that the organization is doing things you would like to
be involved with. For example, if the organization is well known
for a particular style of management, your answer should
mention wanting to be a part of that. You should clearly identify
what your contribution would be.

**How long would it take you to make a meaningful contribution to
our organization?**
Be realistic. You may want to ask for further clarification on
what the interviewer means by a meaningful contribution, or
suggest what the most meaningful contribution could be in the
short, medium and long term.

Use what you know about the organization and yourself

The interviewer is interested in how you will fit into the organization. Your research earlier should help you think through how you display your personal and management style. Weave this into all your responses, so that if the organization is dynamic and evolving, with lots of ambiguity, use examples that reflect how you've managed in these environments previously.

But also think about the fit with you – if you enjoy the challenges that change brings but change is slow and there is resistance to it, you could be just what they are looking for but the role or organization may not be what you are seeking.

How long would you stay with us?
Be honest. While obviously interested in a career within their organization, you can outline what would encourage you to stay. This may be challenge, recognition, variety, etc. You may want to highlight your demonstrated loyalty and commitment to your current organization.

I expect to be a senior manager within five years and would be happy to achieve that within this organization.

What important trends do you see in our industry?
Be prepared with two or three. You may consider technology, economic conditions, political climate, responding to market demands or increased global competition. Be sure that you are up to date with your information. Read the relevant journals or visit websites as part of your preparation.

The job

This is the second part of the matching process. If you fit into the organization, do you have the requisite skills and personality to do the job?

What do you find most attractive about this position? What seems least attractive to you?

List three or four attractive features and one single unattractive one. Put a positive suggestion with the less attractive attribute.

I would like to look closely at the budgetary control system, as there seems to be scope for reorganization.

Why should we appoint you?

Be prepared for this as it is a common question. Be clear in your statements of your uniqueness and the ways in which you match their requirements regarding experience, strengths and characteristics.

What do you look for in a job?

Keep your answer oriented to the opportunity in question. You could focus on your desire to perform and be recognized for your contributions, or on your interest in working within that particular organizational environment.

I look for autonomy, which is clearly the way you expect your managers to work.

If you could do any job, what would it be?

It is hoped that your ideal is similar to the job you have applied for. Describe what an ideal job looks like to you in the context of the organization and culture. It should be evident from this why you have applied for the job. If not, then compare these ideals to the job you are applying for.

Management style

What is your management style?

Through your research you should know a little about the organization's styles of management. Find out about general management theory too. Be honest while demonstrating how your style will help you work within and make a contribution to the organization.

Are you a good manager? Can you give me some examples?

Keep your answer achievement and task oriented. Think about examples that demonstrate your success as a manager and the different aspects of this. Always talk of yourself in the present tense and in the first person, 'I am' rather than 'I have been told' or 'others say...'. The latter can sound as though you don't believe it.

Do you consider yourself a leader?

Even though this is a closed question, do not simply respond with a yes or no answer. Describe examples of leadership from your experience of leading a team, within your areas of responsibility and in the context of the organization.

What do you think is the most difficult thing about being a manager?

You could mention planning, implementation and budgets, although motivating, managing others and changing the culture are often cited as the most difficult tasks.

> **TIP** *Be honest! Interviewers are often curious about what you do outside work – your interests and hobbies, or simply how you like to relax. Honesty is always the best policy, however mundane your pastimes may seem to you.*

A word of warning

In responding to the interviewer's questions, there are also some areas to beware of.

Don't:

✗ Let the interview become an interrogation
✗ Use weak evasive phrases: 'I have been told...'
✗ Lie
✗ Be a 'know it all'

✗ Make jokes, especially against the interviewers
✗ Speak ill of third parties
✗ Blame others for what's gone wrong.

Do:

✔ Personalize your answers
✔ Take responsibility for your limitations
✔ Be genuinely interested in what they are saying
✔ Be open to 'difficult' questions.

Summary

In this chapter we have given you real examples of interview questions and answers. We have encouraged you to think about how you can leave the interviewer with a positive impression of you and your experience.

Remember that you are being interviewed because your application has already impressed the organization. The interview is all about bringing that life, so everything you do or say should reflect your ability to do the job and deliver the expectations. Don't just restate your experience and waste the opportunity to sell yourself.

The interviewer is also interested in how you might fit into the organization. Weave what you know about the organization from your research into all your responses. Think how you can best display your personal and management style. But remember that interviews are two-way: think about what you want and the fit with you.

So, have you answered these questions?

- Can you do the job?
- Will you do the job?
- Will you fit in?

Fact-check (answers at the back)

There is more than one possible answer to some of the following questions.

1. Which question types should you expect at interview?
a) Self-assessment and style ❏
b) Work history ❏
c) The role and the organization ❏
d) Personal life ❏

2. What impression should you give at interview?
a) One that reflects your performance ❏
b) One that is positive ❏
c) One that is negative ❏
d) One that overstates your ability ❏

3. When asked, 'Tell me about yourself', what should you do?
a) Tell your life story ❏
b) Focus on the role ❏
c) State what others have said about you ❏
d) Try to change the subject ❏

4. How should you answer the question 'What are your weak points?'
a) By presenting your strengths ❏
b) By saying you don't have any ❏
c) By admitting to all your weaknesses ❏
d) By taking the opportunity to display your self-knowledge ❏

5. How should you answer the question 'Why are you leaving?'
a) By becoming defensive ❏
b) By focusing on problems ❏
c) By discussing future opportunities ❏
d) By using a carefully rehearsed answer ❏

6. How should you describe your most significant contribution?
a) Talk about a specific achievement ❏
b) Relate it to the organization ❏
c) Say very little; you don't want to boast ❏
d) List your achievements ❏

7. What is the purpose of the question, 'How do you react to pressure?'
a) To encourage you to say how you've dealt with pressure ❏
b) To trick you ❏
c) To put you under pressure ❏
d) To lead you to describe learning throughout your career ❏

8. When answering questions about the organization, what should you describe?
a) Products and/or services ❏
b) The sector ❏
c) Challenges ❏
d) Your present organization ❏

9. If asked how long you would stay, how should you respond?
a) Honestly ❏
b) By outlining what would encourage you to stay ❏
c) By changing the subject ❏
d) By answering, 'As long as you'd have me.' ❏

10. How should you describe yourself?
a) In the first person, 'I am' ❏
b) By relating what others say ❏
c) With an air of disbelief ❏
d) As someone who 'knows it all' ❏

CHAPTER 27

Being proactive: asking questions

So far we have concentrated on the interviewee in a reactive role. Now, we will look at the interviewee from a different perspective, identifying opportunities to be proactive, to ask your own questions or to lead the discussion.

The interviewer needs to know that you can think for yourself and take the initiative. Choosing your questions is another important part of your preparation. You might want to prioritize them in order of importance in case you are limited by time. If you have rehearsed these questions, they will sound very natural as you ask them.

Your moves:

- Ask the right questions
- Keep on listening
- Express yourself effectively
- End on a top note.

Ask the right questions

You will usually be given the opportunity to ask your questions towards the end of the interview. This is your chance to fill any gaps in your knowledge about the job and the organization and clarify the next step in the interview process. Even if they do not invite questions, you should make sure that you check whatever you need to know. Few things are worse than leaving an interview thinking, 'If only I had asked... !'

Good interviewers will offer plenty of chances for you to check your understanding about the post and the organization throughout the interview. It is still a good idea to have questions prepared that are based on your initial research and preparation. These may change or evolve as the interview develops.

The questions you ask will depend on how much information you have already collected, and your particular interests in the job. They should reflect your eagerness to work for the organization and show evidence of thorough research. The pattern we suggest relates back to the data you collected in Chapter 23. Your questions may relate to:

- the job
- the organization
- the interview process.

Refer back to Chapter 22 when thinking about the types of question to ask.

TIP *Don't bombard the interviewer. Choose one or two critical questions only. And remember, you are still the interviewee, so watch you do not reverse roles. The interviewer does not want to be interrogated!*

Work within the time left for the interview. If appropriate, check with the interviewer about time and ask no more than can reasonably be answered within that time frame. You can always ask, 'Who else should I be talking to?'

The job

Your questions about the job may fall into the following categories:

- Routine and difficult aspects of the work: day-to-day responsibilities, special projects.
- Full responsibilities of the job: reporting lines (up/down/sideways), shared responsibilities.
- Support and guidance available to you: flexibility of budget, mentoring, coaching opportunities, bonus schemes, welfare.
- Amount of travel involved: relocation plans, other sites to visit.
- How often your performance will be reviewed: company appraisal scheme, performance reviews, are these pay/promotion related?
- Training and development opportunities: in-house schemes, qualifications, conferences.
- Promotion and career paths: company expectations, board appointments, directorships, senior appointments (internal/external).

Maintain the image you have portrayed throughout the interview. If you have focused on the fact that you are a team player, ask questions relating to the team. What are the interviewer's perceptions of its strengths and weaknesses? If you believe your performance will be a key factor in how you will be judged, ask about performance indicators or the organization's expectations over the next six months.

Questions to ask about the job

The following examples may help you formulate some questions of your own:

1 Why has the job become vacant?
2 What will you expect from me in the next six months?
3 What are the key tasks and responsibilities?
4 What is the biggest challenge facing this team at the moment?
5 What are the strengths and limitations within the team?

6 How do you review performance?
7 What development opportunities are there?
8 What would my future career prospects be?
9 Is promotion generally from within?

The organization

There may be some gaps in your knowledge about the organization. Keep your questions to areas that are not sufficiently covered in the information you have previously received during the interview.

Topics for questions about the organization may cover:

● Structure of the organization: hierarchical, flat, matrix, informal structure.
● Success of the organization: turnover, new products/ services, domestic/international markets, financial health.
● Decision making: briefings, consultations, communications.
● Future strategy and long-term plans: mission, strategic plan, philosophy.
● Staffing: contraction, expansion, outsourcing.

These sorts of questions are essential to your decision making. Is this organization really viable in terms of profits and, if not, are funders, holding companies, bankers, etc., prepared to continue backing it for as long as it takes?

People have made bad decisions about jobs based on inaccurate information about the organization rather than based on their suitability and the attractiveness of the job. Continue your investigations after the interview if you are still interested. Research whatever sources are available; contact suppliers, customers, professional bodies, etc.

Questions to ask about the organization

The following examples of questions may help:

1 Could you clarify for me the structure of the organization?
2 How has the market been developing for products/services?
3 How are decisions made?
4 What problems do you envisage for the organization?
5 What plans are there for reorganization, expansion or retrenchment?
6 What are your strategies for growth?
7 How often do you update your business plan?
8 What is the annual staff/financial turnover?
9 How do you plan for succession throughout the company?

The interview process

You need to know what will happen once you have left the interview room. The interviewer should already have told you at the start of the interview, or the information may have been part of the advertisement or your invitation to the interview. If you are still not sure, ask. It is your right to have clarity about the procedure.

Questions to ask about the interview process

The following example questions may help you:

1 When will I hear from you?
2 What is the next step: further interview, medical, tests?
3 How will I be informed: letter, phone call, email?

4 Is there further information you need from me?
5 Is there someone else I should see
   in the organization?

Your prepared questions will serve you well. Be sure to remember:

- Don't ask questions about information you have already been given
- Don't ask questions for the sake of it
- Do listen and ask supplementary questions
- Do demonstrate that you have digested the information previously given.

Keep on listening

Throughout we have referred to the importance of listening to and understanding what the interviewer is saying to you or asking. We believe it is equally important to keep on listening when you are asking the questions. As the interview progresses and your time to ask questions approaches, be careful not to lose concentration. Many of the worst mistakes at interviews arise from candidates who fail to hear or understand the questions. If you're not sure what the interviewer means, ask for clarification; it doesn't mean you're stupid! In fact, just the opposite.

Too often, interviewees are in such a hurry to speak – usually out of nervousness, sometimes out of overconfidence – that they do not fully hear what has been said.

There is also the danger that you hear what you expect to hear rather than what is actually being said. Avoid preconceptions; let the interviewer answer your questions fully rather than prejudge the outcome or response.

Express yourself effectively

You want to present yourself in the best possible light throughout the interview process. This will involve effective answering of the questions asked, but also grasping any other opportunities to make your case. You should:

- Keep to the point
- Be clear
- Know the appropriate jargon
- Speak with confidence
- Keep your answers positive
- Be honest and open with replies
- Give plenty of concrete work-related examples
- Be enthusiastic
- Weigh up the interviewer.

Keep to the point

It is essential that you keep your questions and answers brief. In a short interview, aim to take no longer than two minutes with each. Only address the questions you have been asked and ensure your answers are relevant.

Structure your statements to ensure that your message is clear. You can achieve this in a number of ways. To make the most impact, limit your reply to one subject at a time; the more you try to include in your answer, the less the interviewer will get from it. So take time to think about which subject is most relevant to the job, the organization or the interviewer.

Be clear

Clarity in reasoning and expression is a skill which can be developed. Your aim should be to present your responses in an interesting and intelligible way, so that the interviewers are not left confused or uncertain. Be specific and talk about examples; always ask for precise details.

Know the appropriate jargon

Be careful not to talk in technical, functional or organizational shorthand that may lose the interviewer. We tend to assume the same knowledge base as those to whom we talk. At an interview this can be dangerous.

However, you should be familiar with any jargon connected with the job or the industry so that the interviewer doesn't leave you behind.

Speak with confidence

Be confident in all that you present. If you are not confident it will show. Let your body language reinforce your words. Be natural; let the interviewer see and appreciate the real you.

Be enthusiastic

Enthusiasm is a wonderful quality; it is a combination of energy and determination. Enthusiastic people are those who enjoy what they are doing and convey this to others. They are free from self-consciousness and are more in control of themselves.

Weigh up the interviewer

To succeed, an interview must be a two-way process. The interviewer will be trying (whether consciously or unconsciously) to find out how good the 'chemistry' or the rapport is likely to be. You should do the same from your side; few jobs are worth having if you are unable to get on with your boss. You should be alert for indications of honesty, efficiency, friendliness and the other characteristics you want from your manager.

End on a top note

There is a danger of relaxing too soon when the interview appears to be over and the interviewer is conducting you to the door. Fix in your mind the picture of yourself that you want the interviewer to keep and maintain, if you want to be sure that those last impressions are favourable. You should leave the interview room as you arrived, confidently but not brashly, shaking hands firmly and with a smile.

TIP *Do not assume the interview has ended until the interviewer makes it clear that it has.*

If you are still interested in the job, a short letter to the person you met is invaluable. Handwritten notes are no longer commonplace and will be much appreciated. They show that you have taken some time and trouble rather than quickly sending off an email. You can thank them for the time they took to tell you about the job and the organization. Remind them of the key benefit you would bring to the company and briefly restate your reasons for wanting to work there.

Summary

So far we've encouraged you to prepare so you can respond skilfully. Now we have encouraged you to think about your moves and how you can be spontaneous but in control at the interview.

We've focused on preparing and asking the right questions. Interviewers are always impressed by good questions, which demonstrate that you've thought about the role in some detail. Do beware of going into too much detail, though, as this can come at the next stage.

Also think about the impression you want to create – once you have this fixed in your mind it's much easier to bring it to life.

Always remember:

- Maintain eye contact
- Take your leave smoothly and politely
- Do not add any afterthoughts
- Shake the interviewer's hand
- Thank them for giving you their time
- Send a follow-up letter.

Next we will look at putting your research and preparation together – focussing you on success.

Fact-check (answers at the back)

There is more than one possible answer to some of the following questions.

1. What is the purpose of your questions at interview?
- **a)** To fill gaps in your knowledge ❑
- **b)** To clarify the next steps ❑
- **c)** To fill in time at the end ❑
- **d)** To show that you want the job ❑

2. How many questions should you prepare?
- **a)** One or two ❑
- **b)** At least ten in case you need to play for time ❑
- **c)** Plenty, so that you can choose a few as appropriate ❑
- **d)** None – you expect all points to be answered already ❑

3. What should your questions about the role relate to?
- **a)** Day-to-day responsibilities ❑
- **b)** How your performance will be measured ❑
- **c)** Opportunities for socializing ❑
- **d)** Who you should beware of ❑

4. What should your questions about the organization relate to?
- **a)** Strategic plans ❑
- **b)** Lunch and games facilities ❑
- **c)** The competition ❑
- **d)** Benefits ❑

5. How should you research the organization?
- **a)** Through professional bodies ❑
- **b)** Online ❑
- **c)** Through the annual report ❑
- **d)** Through the information you are sent ❑

6. When exploring what will happen next in the interview process, what should you ask?
- **a)** 'When will I hear from you?' ❑
- **b)** 'What is the next step?' ❑
- **c)** 'Is there any further information you need from me?' ❑
- **d)** 'I've had many offers, so can you let me know today?' ❑

7. If you didn't understand a question, what should you do?
- **a)** Ask for clarification ❑
- **b)** Answer with what you thought was meant ❑
- **c)** Look puzzled ❑
- **d)** Shrug your shoulders ❑

8. When do you express yourself best?
- **a)** When feeling confident ❑
- **b)** When feeling nervous ❑
- **c)** When giving examples ❑
- **d)** When talking a lot. ❑

9. How can you ensure your message is clear?
   a) By limiting your responses to a maximum of two points ❏
   b) By repeating it several times ❏
   c) By its impact ❏
   d) By getting across not only answers to the questions but all the other things you've prepared ❏

10. What kind of impression should you try to leave?
   a) That you are the person for the job ❏
   b) That you are confident ❏
   c) That you are about to be snapped up elsewhere ❏
   d) That you are better than the next candidate. ❏

CHAPTER 28

Putting it all together

We have come to the end and your preparations are nearly complete. By this stage you should be feeling more confident about presenting yourself in the interview. An interview is, after all, your chance to shine.

Throughout we have focused on areas such as what to say, how to say it and what to do. Now we will aim to bring it all together. When you first learn a skill or technique such as driving, using new software or chairing meetings, you are anything but natural. But, with practice, these skills become natural extensions of you. Interviewing skills are no different. By following the steps from the previous six chapters you will have developed your own interviewing style and many of your answers will seem almost instinctive.

Next we will focus on removing all the blocks that prevent you from being yourself. After all, your unique selling point is you. We will consider:

- objectives
- rehearsal
- readiness
- review
- feedback.

Objectives

As we discussed in Chapter 22, interviewers will have set their objectives before the interview and will have planned how these will be achieved. An interviewer's key objective is to find the right person for the job. Other objectives will reflect the stage of the interview; for example, in the final stages there will be greater emphasis on fit and characteristics rather than skills.

As an interviewee, you should also set objectives. Your main objective is to be offered the job. However, there will be secondary objectives ranging from presenting yourself in a positive light and exploring the real culture of the organization, through to deciding whether or not, as a result of the interview, you want the job.

These objectives should help you become more focused in preparing for the interview and clearer in the messages you want to communicate. This will help you make the right impression as the ideal candidate for the job, rather than just another runner.

Rehearsal

Most of us have never been taught to be interviewed. If you are lucky, you may have attended a workshop on the subject or received some feedback on how you presented yourself. It is more likely that the only experience you have had of interviews has been the real thing, for real jobs. You don't have the time to experiment; only poor performers get lots of interview practice. So you need to rehearse:

● your entrance
● your body language
● your voice
● your answers to questions
● the benefits you bring
● asking your questions
● taking feedback.

Don't let the success of your future depend on finding out how you interview on the day. Take time to practice. Practice develops performance in most things; interviews are no exception.

Ask a colleague, your partner, anyone whose opinion you value or trust, to act as the interviewer, then role-play the situation and take feedback. Before you participate in the 'interview' with them, show them your objectives, the job description and a prepared list of the kinds of questions you expect to be asked. Encourage them to ask their own questions too. Then you can see how you handle the unexpected.

TIP *It's a good idea to record your interview practice; you will learn more this way and much of it will be positive learning.*

The better the rehearsal, the better the performance. Actors spend many hours rehearsing so that they are word perfect on the opening night. Remember, this is a performance of sorts and needs thorough preparation.

Your entrance

Have the person in the role of interviewer meet you and invite you to sit down. Don't tell them the image you want to create; check their perception later. Even at rehearsal it is quite likely you will feel nervous. This is fine; you will feel less anxious on the day as a result.

Your body language

We would encourage you to breathe deeply and relax in your own way. Sit upright in a comfortable position and look attentive. You are likely to be attentive if your body is. If you appear uneasy, the 'interviewer' will pick up on this through your body language and may not hear your excellent responses.

Your voice

Can the 'interviewer' hear you clearly? Do you sound convincing and interesting? To which questions do you give the most energetic answers? This can give you an idea of where your key interests lie. Listen to the rhythm in your voice; work at not being monotone. Be sure you have warmed up your voice before the interview starts. On the day you can go through some tongue twisters and vocal stretches as you travel to the interview.

Answers to questions

Experiment with the time you take to answer the questions. Just how long are the silences between the questions and your responses? Make sure to listen right to the end of the question and make your reply clear and specific. Resist the temptation to try to show how in tune you are with the 'interviewer' by jumping in with an answer before you have heard the complete question.

The benefits you bring

It is important to reassure the 'interviewer' throughout the interview that you are the person they seek. Introduce examples and case studies that reinforce your positive statements. Remember to turn any weaknesses into strengths and learning points. Illustrate how you can make a difference and bring something new and exciting to the organization.

Asking your questions

You will have some questions you prepared earlier; use the rehearsal to practise asking unprepared questions too. How clear and thoughtful are they? Be sure to keep them specifically related to that job or organization.

Feedback

After the rehearsal, make sure you have plenty of time to play back and discuss what happened. Listen carefully.

What can you improve? Also accept where you are strong, and feel confident about it. Recognize what you do well and ensure that you do more of it. Keep practising if you can. Draw up a checklist of the things you wish to rehearse and ask your 'interviewer' for comments and suggestions.

Readiness

Here are a few questions you might want to ask yourself just before you go to the interview:

● Am I ready?
● Are my clothes and shoes clean, neat and tidy?
● Is my hair tidy?
● Am I clear what image I want to project?
● Have I decided how to project that image?
● Have I warmed up and relaxed my voice?
● Can I be heard clearly?
● Am I walking/standing/sitting tall?
● Am I relaxed?
● Do I feel confident to answer the questions?
● Have I structured my answers for the best impact?
● Have I prepared a sheet of prompts/questions?

Review

By analysing and reviewing your performance after the 'real' interview, you can see where you might need to improve and so develop the necessary skills. It will help you to identify areas you need to strengthen if you are attending any more interviews. Be honest with yourself and acknowledge where you did well. Don't get into the post-exam habit of focusing on any questions you answered incorrectly and punishing yourself for so doing.

TIP *Review your performance as soon as possible after the interview.*

Remember that one of the most important questions to ask yourself is the one we began with. Answer this honestly: 'Did I present myself in the best possible light?' The following checklist will help you to review your interview performance in more detail.

Did I:	✔
● arrive on time?	
● speak confidently to everyone I met?	
● handle the opening moments well?	
● feel and look relaxed?	
● maintain appropriate eye contact?	
● use the full range of my voice to convey my message?	
● stay cool and calm?	
● answer all the questions well?	
● expand my answers?	
● refer to my strengths?	
● listen carefully to the questions?	
● understand the questions before I replied?	
● work out in advance the points I wanted to make?	
● volunteer information when given the chance?	
● capture and hold the interviewer's attention?	
● impress the interviewer?	
● demonstrate my knowledge of the job and the organization?	
● ask good questions?	
● adapt and adjust my questions?	
● deal well with the closing moments?	
● end on a confident and optimistic note?	

These questions will give you an idea of what you need to focus on. If your answer is 'no' to any of the questions, explore the possible reasons why and ask yourself how you could improve.

Answer the following questions:

● What impression did I create?
● Which questions did I find it difficult to answer?
● Did I say all I wanted to say?
● What will I do differently next time?

The more you know about yourself through this form of review and other forms of feedback, the better equipped you are to present yourself to others.

Interviews are so complex and artificial as a process for all parties that, no matter how thoroughly you prepare, some may not turn out as you hope or expect. Don't dwell on the interviews that don't go well; understand why and learn from them.

TIP *Focus on success and success will come to you.*

Feedback

Don't be afraid to ask for comments from the interviewer. If they are not offered, make a point of asking for them. If there are areas that you suspect, or are told, consistently let you down, seek help or a second opinion. Investigate local sources of help, such as:

● colleges
● business schools/universities
● guidance organizations
● professional institutes, e.g. The Chartered Management Institute in the UK
● DVDs, books and e-books
● careers counsellors
● e-learning programmes.

Don't be afraid to ask! Educational establishments are responsive to their customers and, if you have a need, approach them with it. If nothing currently exists, then why not set something up; organize an event through your local professional institute or with a group of colleagues? Practice is never wasted. Feedback and development are essential to your future success.

Above all, enjoy the experience. The most valuable interviews are frank, open discussions involving facts, ideas and opinions. By following a simple pattern, you can achieve the success you want at interviews.

Summary

You have reached the end and learned what you can do to help yourself shine in interviews.

There are some simple steps to succeeding at interviews:

- Understand the interview process
- Do your research on the interview, the role and the organization
- Discover what differentiates you
- Prepare yourself for success
- Respond skilfully and be prepared for the questions and exercises
- Decide what questions you want to ask
- Put it all together and know that you have done all you can towards your success.

As you are very well prepared, all you need now are our best wishes and a quick reminder: the more you practice, the luckier you get.

Good luck!

Fact-check (answers at the back)

There is more than one possible answer to some of the following questions.

1. What do you need to feel confident about at interview?
a) What you say ❏
b) How you say it ❏
c) That you're better dressed than the interviewer ❏
d) You don't need to feel confident with anything about your performance at interview ❏

2. What are your objectives for the interview?
a) To make it last as long as possible ❏
b) To present yourself in the best possible light ❏
c) To get through the process ❏
d) To keep it as short as possible ❏

3. What should you concentrate on in your rehearsals?
a) Your entrance ❏
b) Your body language ❏
c) What you say ❏
d) Negative feedback. ❏

4. What should your body language be like at interview?
a) Relaxed ❏
b) Tense ❏
c) Show you are paying attention ❏
d) Giving you away ❏

5. How should your voice sound at interview?
a) Convincing ❏
b) Anxious to get all your information across ❏
c) Monotonous ❏
d) Vague ❏

6. When you receive feedback from a practice interview, what should you focus on?
a) What you can improve ❏
b) Where you are strong ❏
c) The fact that they might have got it wrong ❏
d) Things you can't change ❏

7. How do you know you are ready for the interview ?
a) When you've rehearsed ❏
b) When you've planned what you will wear ❏
c) When you think you can 'wing it' ❏
d) When you've arrived. ❏

8. When is the best time to review your performance?
a) Immediately after the interview ❏
b) Never; you are just happy it's over ❏
c) When you receive feedback ❏
d) Once you've got the job ❏

9. What areas of your performance do you need to think about before an interview?
a) The impression you create ❏
b) Answering questions ❏
c) Getting across all you want to say ❏
d) All of the above ❏

10. When is it acceptable to ask for feedback from interviews?
a) Always ❏
b) Sometimes ❏
c) Never ❏
d) If you feel it went well ❏

7 × 7

1 Seven key ideas

- **Know what to expect.** You may have to go through different stages before you come face to face with an interviewer. At each stage of the process, some candidates are sifted and do not proceed to the next stage – make sure this is not you!
- **Do your research.** The old saying 'Fail to prepare, prepare to fail' comes to mind. Your success at interviews depends on how well you understand the role, the organization and the sector.
- **Prepare yourself.** You know you will be facing tough competition, so how you look and feel are important. When you look in the mirror, what is the image you portray? You should look like a person who can perform in the role.
- **Feel confident.** Everyone has different ways of building their confidence. You may feel sure of your skills and what you've achieved to date, but you can enhance your confidence by acknowledging these and remembering the times when you've felt supremely confident.
- **Differentiate yourself.** If you are one of 20 candidates, what will make you stand out? You should understand the challenges of the role and the organization sufficiently to be the ideal candidate.
- **Respond skilfully**. How you respond to questions will distinguish you from the competition. This could include making your responses just the right length and with the right content and creatively highlighting how you will contribute to the organization.

- **Review your performance.** Reflect on how you feel you have performed. If you have the opportunity to get feedback on your performance, take the opportunity and learn from it.

2 Seven great quotes

- 'You never get a second chance to make a first impression.' Oscar Wilde
- 'Nothing can stop the man with the right mental attitude from achieving his goal; nothing on earth can help the man with the wrong mental attitude.' Thomas Jefferson
- 'I've learned that people will forget what you said, people will forget what you did, but people will never forget how you made them feel.' Maya Angelou
- 'Your attitude, not your aptitude, will determine your altitude.' Zig Ziglar
- 'Life isn't about finding yourself. Life's about creating yourself.' George Bernard Shaw
- 'Meditate. Live purely. Be quiet. Do your work with mastery. Like the moon, come out from behind the clouds! Shine.' Buddha
- 'Life shrinks or expands in proportion to one's courage.' Anais Nin

3 Seven influential people

- **Max Eggert** is a psychologist, several of whose books are on the recommended reading lists of international universities. His work has stood the test of time.
- **Professor Steve Peters** is a consultant psychiatrist working in business, education, health, elite and Olympic sport. His specialist interest is in the working of the human mind and how it can reach optimum performance, in all walks of life.

- **Anthony Robbins** is one of the foremost authorities on the psychology of peak performance. He is the guru of personal, professional and organizational turnaround and he has been called one of the greatest influencers of his generation.
- **Dale Carnegie**, known as 'the arch-priest of the art of making friends', pioneered the development of personal business skills, self-confidence and motivational techniques.
- **Martin John Yate** is a best-selling author of books on careers and being interviewed.
- Find your own inspiration – who, in your network, has been successful at interview?
- Be your own inspiration!

4 Seven great resources

- Max Eggert, *Perfect Interview: All you Need to Get it Right First Time* (Random House, 2007) – a classic book on being interviewed
- www.interviewgold.com – a website offering fresh ideas on being interviewed
- www.myinterviewsimulator.com – a website with tough questions and answers
- www.nationalcareersservice.direct.gov.uk – a service available nationwide in the UK for jobseekers
- www.learndirect.com/help/job-help/virtual-job-interview – an interactive site where you are asked questions by virtual employers and scored on your response
- www.youtube.com – many examples of being interviewed
- Richard N. Bolles, *What Color Is Your Parachute? 2015; A Practical Manual for Job-Hunters and Career-changers* (Ten Speed Press, published annually) – the world's most popular job-search book

5 Seven things to avoid

- Lack of preparation – make time to prepare thoroughly for the interview.
- Insufficient research into the organization – your research will help you understand their culture, language and the challenges for them and you in the role.
- Not understanding why you want the role – it's the simplest question but often trips people up. Make your responses authentic.
- Not answering the questions – listen to each question carefully and answer it thoroughly, addressing the question itself and not just responding with your prepared answers.
- Not selling yourself – this is your opportunity to blow your own trumpet.
- Only asking questions about salary and benefits – instead, ask questions that put you in the role, such as 'What would be your advice to me on induction?'
- Rushing – leave enough time to prepare and get there.

6 Seven key actions

- Think about yourself in the role.
- Be clear what success looks like in this role.
- Plan time to research the role and the organization further by talking to someone who knows the organization.
- Put yourself in the interviewer's shoes. What impression do you want to leave them with and how can you achieve this?
- Prepare your questions and practise your answers and say them out loud.
- Think about the impact you make at every stage of the interview process, and particularly think about your first impressions.
- Remember to ask the interviewer for feedback. They should be happy to do this and it also gives them a chance to ask you further questions, should they wish to.

7 Seven trends for tomorrow

- There will be different stages to the selection process and methods of selection. More of these will be conducted virtually.
- Your interviewers will gather information on you from a variety of sources. When you put your name into a search engine, what do you find?
- Your success at interview will be as much about cultural fit as capability.
- Questions will get fewer and tougher.
- You will be more likely to have to demonstrate your achievements through examples, such as a portfolio or a presentation.
- Employers are increasing their expectations when it comes to standards of literacy.
- People who show that they can communicate and interact effectively will command an advantage.

Answers

Part 1: CVs

Chapter 1: 1b; 2d; 3b; 4b; 5d; 6c; 7a; 8b; 9b; 10a.

Chapter 2: 1a; 2c; 3c; 4b; 5c; 6b; 7a; 8b; 9a; 10a.

Chapter 3: 1d; 2c; 3b; 4b; 5d; 6b; 7b; 8a; 9b; 10a.

Chapter 4: 1d; 2a; 3b; 4c; 5b; 6a; 7a; 8b; 9b; 10d.

Chapter 5: 1d; 2a; 3d; 4d; 5b; 6c; 7a; 8d; 9a; 10d.

Chapter 6: 1b; 2b; 3c; 4d; 5d; 6c; 7d; 8c; 9a; 10d.

Chapter 7: 1b; 2a; 3d; 4b; 5b; 6c; 7d; 8c; 9c; 10a.

Part 2: Job Hunting

Chapter 8: 1c; 2a; 3d; 4b; 5c; 6c; 7d; 8c; 9b; 10d.

Chapter 9: 1c; 2d; 3b; 4a; 5d; 6a; 7d; 8c; 9c; 10b.

Chapter 10: 1d; 2c; 3b; 4a; 5b; 6a; 7c; 8a; 9b; 10c.

Chapter 11: 1a; 2b; 3d; 4a; 5b; 6c; 7c (or a); 8a; 9d; 10d.

Chapter 12: 1b; 2a; 3d; 4c; 5c; 6c; 7a (or d); 8b; 9c; 10b.

Chapter 13: 1d; 2c; 3d; 4b; 5d; 6b; 7c; 8b; 9b; 10a.

Chapter 14: 1c; 2c and d; 3b; 4a; 5a; 6c; 7c; 8b; 9b; 10c.

Part 3: Cover Letters

Chapter 15: 1c; 2c; 3c; 4b; 5d; 6a; 7d; 8b; 9b; 10c.

Chapter 16: 1b; 2a; 3c; 4a; 5d; 6a; 7b; 8c; 9c; 10b.

Chapter 17: 1d; 2b; 3a; 4d; 5c; 6b; 7c; 8c; 9a and c; 10b.

Chapter 18: 1b; 2a; 3d; 4b; 5c; 6c; 7a; 8b; 9d; 10d.

Chapter 19: 1b; 2d; 3a; 4c; 5d; 6c; 7a and c; 8b; 9d; 10d.

Chapter 20: 1b; 2d; 3a; 4b; 5c; 6d; 7b; 8d; 9a; 10d.

Chapter 21: 1b and d; 2d; 3a; 4c; 5b; 6d; 7c; 8b; 9a; 10d.

Part 4: Job Interviews

Chapter 22: 1c; 2a, d; 3a; 4b, c; 5a, c, d; 6b, c; 7d; 8a, d; 9d; 10a.

Chapter 23: 1a; 2b; 3a; 4a; 5a, b; 6a, b, c; 7a, c, d; 8b, c; 9a, b, c; 10d.

Chapter 24: 1a, c; 2b, c, d; 3b, c, d; 4a, b, c; 5, b, d; 6a, c, d; 7a, b, c; 8a, b; 9a, b, d; 10a, c.

Chapter 25: 1a, d; 2a; 3a; 4b, c; 5a, b, d; 6b; 7d; 8d; 9a, b; 10a, b.

Chapter 26: 1a, b, c; 2 a, b; 3 b, c; 4a, d; 5 c, d; 6a, b, d; 7a, d; 8 a, b, c; 9 a, b; 10a, b.

Chapter 27: 1a, b; 2c; 3a, b; 4a, c; 5a, b, c; 6a, b, c; 7a; 8a, c; 9c; 10a, b.

Chapter 28: 1a, b; 2b; 3a, b, c; 4a, c; 5a; 6a, b; 7a, b; 8a, c; 9d; 10a, b.

Notes